DANI

FRANCIS
of ASSISI
and the
FUTURE
of FAITH

EXPLORING FRANCISCAN
SPIRITUALITY AND THEOLOGY
IN THE MODERN WORLD

CW00701035

Francis of Assisi and the Future of Faith
Exploring Franciscan Spirituality and
Theology in the Modern World

Daniel P. Horan, OFM

Cover image: iStockPhoto.com
Cover and book design: Tau Publishing Design Department

For information regarding permission, write to:
Tau Publishing, LLC
Attention: Permissions Dept.
4727 North 12th Street
Phoenix, AZ 85014

ISBN 978-1-61956-041-3

First Edition August 2012
10 9 8 7 6 5 4 3 2 1

Published and printed in the United States of America by Tau Publishing, LLC
For additional inspirational books visit us at TauPublishing.com

TauPublishing.com
Words of Inspiration

To
Julianne Wallace,
Lisa Biedenbach,
and
Franciscan-Hearted People Everywhere

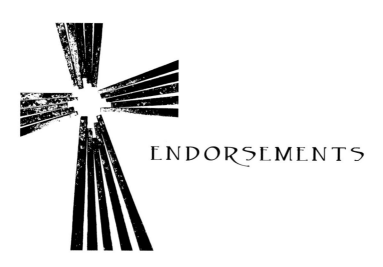

ENDORSEMENTS

"When I was a kid, in many gardens there were birdbaths decorated with a small statue of St. Francis surrounded by birds. I recall a somewhat crusty Franciscan friar, having noticed one of these for sale in a gardening store, remarking, "It's time to get St. Francis out of the birdbath." That friar, were he still alive, would love this book. In Dan Horan's new book, we are introduced not to a decorative saint who got on well with birds but a man who shook the foundations of medieval Europe and who – along with other key figures of the early Franciscan movement – still challenges us today."

— Jim Forest, author, *All Is Grace: A Biography of Dorothy Day*

"In 1972 a Jesuit, Mario von Galli, authored a book entitled *Living our Future: Francis of Assisi and the Church of Tomorrow*. In it he argued that the insights of Francis (long dormant in a Europe beset with political and religious wars) had finally flowered into full view and vitality in the Church through the Second Vatican Council. Now, as we celebrate the 50th anniversary of that great Council, Friar-Author Dan Horan opens the doors of the Church which for his generation is "today," not "tomorrow!" Fr. Horan is particularly adept at translating the importance of a Franciscan approach for today's "digital natives." His voice is sure to capture the attention of contemporaries and create a bridge for older readers who know themselves to be strangers to this new way of learning and knowing. He also brings fresh reading to ancient sources and arguments and forces his readers to take stock of the originality of a bold 21st century exegesis. One of the treasures contained in Part III of the volume is a carefully constructed collection of the sermons and short addresses of Pope Benedict XVI on Franciscan themes. The work Fr. Horan did to assemble them is a special gift for those seeking to understand this pontiff's frequent turn to Francis and Bonaventure and to understand how they speak to the task of the new evangelization."

— Margaret Carney, OSF, STD, President, St. Bonaventure University

"Most writers tend to write their essential book that they keep re-writing, clarifying, and modifying for the whole of their writing lives. I believe this is Fr. Daniel Horan's seminal book; I know it will be a "vade mecum" for my own Franciscan living. In a style that is both scholarly and highly readable, he brilliantly uncovers and elucidates the "foolish" wisdom of Franciscans as it is lived and voiced first of all in St. Francis and then as it is perpetuated and developed in significant Franciscan thinkers and saints from the Middle Ages to the present Millennial generation. The voices explored not only continue St. Francis' voice but they enrich it and make it relevant to their own times by voicing their individual and collective lived experiences as Franciscans. The depth and range of this book makes it an indispensable source for how the Franciscan spiritual and intellectual tradition has been lived and voiced in the past and a blueprint for how it can be lived at the beginning of the 21ˢᵗ Century."

— Murray Bodo, OFM, author, *Francis: The Journey and the Dream*

"'I am pleased that you teach sacred theology to the brothers,' St. Francis of Assisi wrote to St. Anthony of Padua more than eight hundred years ago. Readers of *Francis of Assisi and the Future of Faith* will be pleased that Franciscan Father Daniel Horan, too, is a teacher of theology. Far too often theology is sterile, and the intellectual tradition fails to heed Francis's caution to Anthony when giving him permission to teach theology to the other friars: 'Do not extinguish the spirit of prayer and devotion during study of this kind.' With a great spirit of prayer and devotion, Horan helps us discover how Francis of Assisi is anything but the patron of those who are spiritual but not religious, spiritual but not theological. Rather, Horan gives us sound spirituality and theology grounded in the perennially relevant and popular Franciscan tradition. Past speaks to the present and guides us into the future. Francis and Anthony both would be pleased."

— Mary Stommes, editor, Give Us This Day: Daily Prayer for Today's Catholic

"*Francis of Assisi and the Future of Faith* is the perfect book for anyone who wishes to follow in St. Francis' footsteps and embark on the "foolish" business of following the Gospel. As a member of the Millennial generation, Dan Horan speaks to the current generation of young adults and to those who strive to understand these tech savvy and spiritually wandering pilgrims. Dan asserts, "If Francis of Assisi were alive today, one might very well find him on Facebook!" Using the writing of St. Francis as his guide, Dan Horan explores a Franciscan approach to technology, ministry, stewardship, death, evangelization, and spirituality in today's society. Dan offers a renewed appreciation for this spiritual master whose teachings remain relevant almost 800 years after his death. With the vision of St. Francis, Dan Horan challenges people of all ages to embrace a spirit of poverty in a culture where consumerism reigns, forgive our enemies in a world that advocates revenge, speak a message of peace when gun violence terrorizes our cities and streets, and preach the gospel at all times… online and in real time. This is truly Franciscan spirituality for our times at its finest!"

— Beth Knobbe, author, *Party of One: Living Single with Faith, Purpose, and Passion*

TABLE of CONTENTS

PART I: THE FRANCISCAN TRADITION IN THE MODERN WORLD

ACKNOWLEDGEMENTS

The interesting thing about a collection of essays such as the one contained in this book is that there is no singular marathon period of writing that usually accompanies other types of projects. Therefore, there are many people to thank over the course of several years during which each of these essays was conceived, researched, written, and published, many of whom I will inevitably forget to recall and I apologize for that oversight from the outset.

There are several editors of different journals with whom I have worked over the years in which earlier versions of many of these essays were first published. I especially wish to acknowledge Daria Mitchell, OSF; Edward O'Donnell, OCD; Patrick McCloskey, OFM; Noel Muscat, OFM; Jon Stanley; and the late David Fleming, SJ. The opening chapter, "From Generation to Generation: A Franciscan Millennial and the Memory of 9/11," was originally published in the book *Franciscan Voices on 9/11* (St. Anthony Messenger Press, 2011). I am grateful to the editor of that volume, John Feister, and the publisher, Franciscan Media, for permission to reprint that piece here in a slightly expanded form.

I have been blessed to have a number of teachers, mentors, and friends from whom I have learned a great deal and by whose example I have been inspired to continue studying the Franciscan intellectual tradition over the years. I am honored to count Joshua Benson; Susan Abraham; Ilia Delio,

OSF; Regis Armstrong, OFM Cap.; Dominic Monti, OFM; Michael Blastic, OFM; and so many others, among those who have at various points in my academic life taught me, guided me, challenged me, and continue to personally inspire me in exploring many of the themes presented in this book.

This book was finally edited and revised while I had the great privilege to serve as a newly ordained deacon at St. Francis of Assisi Parish in Triangle, Virginia. I am grateful for the opportunity to minister to and with some outstanding women and men who take seriously their faith and live in such a way as to reveal the compassionate face of God to all they meet. Special thanks goes to my Franciscan brother Kevin Downey, OFM, the pastor of St. Francis, whose support in both my parochial and academic ministries has been exemplary. If only all people could encourage one another to use their gifts for the service of others in the humorous, loving, and reassuring way Kevin has. I wish also to acknowledge my confrere Frank Critch, OFM, who was likewise assigned to St. Francis with me during that year and who, like Kevin, was nothing but supportive of both my parish work and academic ministry. I am blessed to have such fraternal brothers in community.

The staff at *Tau Publishing*, particularly Jeffrey Campbell, deserves a note of gratitude. Rarely have I experienced the alacrity from a publisher that Jeff exhibited from the first moment we discussed the possibility of this project. In an age when the publishing industry is fraught with concerns about its future, Jeff and his team have sought to imagine and bring to life a new model of publishing that is sustainable, personal, and very Franciscan in its own right. I wish to offer a special note of thanks to Mary Esther Stewart, my editor for this book, for her keen editorial eye, and for making the editorial process as painless as possible. I am pleased to work with such a publishing house and hope this is but my first of many projects with them.

Finally, I am always grateful for the support, inspiration, and challenge of my family – Kevin and Ann Marie Horan, my parents, and Sean, Matthew and Ryan, my brothers – and friends. This book is dedicated to two of my friends, Julianne Wallace and Lisa Biedenbach, as well as to all Franciscan-hearted people like them. While technically not a professed member of a Franciscan Order, Julianne has come to appreciate, embrace, and reflect the Franciscan charism in her life and ministry over many years. As a campus minister at St. Bonaventure University, the director of liturgy and music for the Franciscan Institute, and a regular collaborator with Franciscan entities in liturgical planning, Julianne has found her place in the Franciscan world and has revealed her love of the eight-hundred-year-old tradition of Francis and Clare of Assisi in manifold ways. Lisa has been instrumental in the acquisition and publication of many influential and important books in the Franciscan tradition. She continues to be a source of encouragement to so many authors and editors in the Catholic publishing industry. Lisa and I are also both proud alums of St. Bonaventure University, the renowned Franciscan college in Western New York. I am continually grateful for her friendship and support. This book is humbly offered to all people with Franciscan hearts who desire to explore their faith and this tradition in the modern world.

Daniel P. Horan, OFM
June 2012

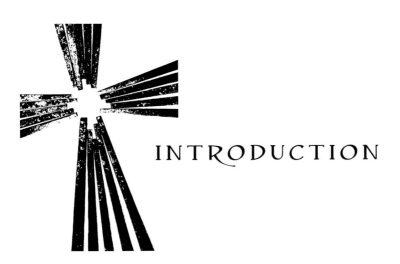

INTRODUCTION

The Franciscan spiritual tradition is one of the richest, most diverse, and attractive sources for prayerful inspiration and guidance in all of Christianity. It is no surprise that Francis of Assisi remains one of the most revered and venerated saints in history, despite the fact that he lived more than eight-hundred-years ago in a time and place very foreign to the globalized, pluralistic, and complex context in which we find ourselves today. After Jesus of Nazareth and his mother, Mary, there is perhaps no figure in the Christian narrative that inspires women and men of so many faiths and many who profess no religious tradition at all.

Seen as an icon of humanity's right relationship with creation, Francis of Assisi was named the "Patron Saint of Ecology" by Pope John Paul II on Easter Sunday in 1980. Seen as a beacon of honest and respectful interreligious dialogue, his example of embracing the Muslim Sultan in Damietta, Egypt, during the Fifth Crusade has been recalled in our more contemporary times of Christian-Muslim tensions as a prophetic example of hopeful encounter, dialogue, and friendship.[1] Seen as a prophet of peacemaking, the prayer attributed to his memory continues to challenge

---

[1] Two recent books that examine this encounter between Francis of Assisi and Sultan Malek al-Kamil and explore the relevance of that model of dialogue for our time are, George Dardess and Marvin Krier, *In The Spirit of St. Francis and the Sultan: Catholics and Muslims Working for the Common Good* (Maryknoll, NY: Orbis Books, 2011); and Paul Moses, *The Saint and the Sultan: The Crusades, Islam and Francis of Assisi's Mission of Peace* (New York: Doubleday, 2009).

all Christians and people of good will to become the instruments of God's mercy, forgiveness, justice, and love in the world. Seen as a man of simplicity and humility, no one can discuss the meaning of evangelical poverty without some mention of the *poverello*, the little poor man from Assisi.

Francis was and is many things to many people. His life and legacy bespeak a multiplicity and diversity that is only seen more starkly in the vast variety of those millions who admire the saint all over the world. That diversity stands near the heart of the Franciscan spiritual tradition as a core characteristic of the worldview that began with one medieval Italian who recognized the Spirit's call to live his baptismal vocation more authentically in following in the footprints of Christ should come as no shock to those who pause and consider the multivalent meanings the name "Francis of Assisi" and the subsequent term "Franciscan" present to us. For Francis of Assisi is as complex and human a figure as we can imagine and his legacy is as multifaceted and surprising as we might ever guess.

But this is just the tip of the spiritual iceberg. The Franciscan tradition, despite bearing the name of its beloved patron and founder, is *much more* than just the insight, wisdom, and challenge left to us by the medieval friar. Even in his own lifetime, initially inspired by the Spirit's work in the *Poverello's* life, other women and men helped shape what this tradition has come to represent and helped compose the spiritual resources, writings, and traditions that are rivaled by no other Christian religious order or community. For example, one might think about the contemporaneous influence that St. Clare of Assisi or St. Anthony of Padua exerted over the early Franciscan movement.

We remember that just a generation after the death of Francis, spiritual and theological luminaries the likes of St. Bonaventure and Blessed Angela of Foligno arrived on the scene and reflected more systematically and, at times, mystically on the example of Francis on the Christian journey to follow in the footprints of Christ. Bonaventure's work, likely unknown by most Christians, provides us with an impressive collection of writings that elucidate the Christian faith in ways that seek to be faithful to Francis's way of living in the world, while at the same time revealing the compassionate and overabundant love of God. Angela's writing, a rare collection of mystical insight from the inspired perspective of a medieval lay woman, presents us with a creative and powerful look at what a deeply intimate relationship with one's Creator looks like according to the pattern of life modeled for us by Francis of Assisi.

One only has to look at the surfeit of Franciscan wisdom that is passed on to us from the period of a century after Francis's death – a timeframe which includes spiritual, theological, and philosophical geniuses like Blessed John Duns Scotus, the anonymous authors of influential Franciscan texts, and others – to become overwhelmed at the potential for contemporary appropriation and spiritual guidance.

While so many women and men see in Francis of Assisi an intuitively inspiring and genuinely holy example of Christian discipleship and authentic human relationship, most of those who admire him know very little about the manifold sources of spiritual wisdom that are also included under the aegis of "Franciscan Spirituality." Even if one is aware of some of the more popular depictions of and associations made with Francis of Assisi – lover of creation, model of interreligious dialogue, peacemaker, exemplar of evangelical poverty, and the like – very few are familiar with the impressive diversity of the tradition and the many ways in which the tradition continues to speak a prophetic message to us today. The aim of this book is to highlight both of these facets of the Franciscan spiritual tradition.

The essays published here might at first strike the reader as disparate, but rather than being unrelated, each chapter tackles one of two themes that has gone largely overlooked throughout the years when it comes to explorations of the Franciscan spiritual tradition: (a) the contemporary relevance of the Franciscan spiritual tradition for Christians and all people of good will, and (b) the diversity of the influences and sources within the tradition. This book is organized into three sections, each of which focuses on one of these two overarching themes of diversity and relevance.

The first section, "Franciscan Tradition in the Modern World," examines the question of how the Franciscan spiritual tradition continues to be relevant in our contemporary setting. Opening with a reflection on a Franciscan view of the memory of the terrorist attacks of September 11, 2001, the chapters organized in this section explore themes such as what a Franciscan approach to ministry might look like, how this tradition might speak to today's young adults, and how the shifts in technology and communication affect our spiritual lives (and what the Franciscan tradition has to say by way of guidance and response). Additionally, this section includes two chapters that consider new ways to read frequently overlooked Franciscan sources – a text by Bonaventure and a letter from Francis to Clare and her sisters – in our own day and in such a manner as to help us see ourselves, God, and the world anew.

The second section, "Franciscan Spirituality, Theology, and Intellectual Tradition," takes a look at several themes, resources, and figures in the tradition that are not often considered, even by those who identify themselves as Franciscans of one sort or another. While the great majority of people who know of St. Francis associate him with a love for creation (or, as I have often heard it put: "love for animals"), very little of the content of that love for creation is examined in the popular recounting of Francis's model for right relationship with the rest of creation. The first chapter in this section shines a light on the ostensibly radical worldview that Francis espoused and that his followers in the tradition developed further concerning what it means to talk about humanity's relationship with creation. The next essay explores what is and what is not "Franciscan" about supralapsarian Christology or the orthodox belief that the Incarnation of the Word would have taken place even if humanity had not sinned. On one hand, it is true that such an outlook is part of the Franciscan spiritual tradition, but, on the other hand, it is not an exclusively Franciscan insight. Next is a chapter on the Franciscan view of death, which is unique and offers a hopeful take on this dimension of our existence that many find so frightening. The last two chapters in this section present insights from a notoriously avoided contributor to the Franciscan spiritual tradition – John Duns Scotus. Known as the "Subtle Doctor," Scotus is best recalled for his brilliantly dense, incredibly nuanced, and deeply logical philosophy. However, Scotus – a Franciscan friar who died in 1308 – was an amazingly spiritual man of faith. The first of these two essays offers a glimpse into the creative work of Scotus and his predecessor, Robert Grosseteste, on the questions of how and why creation came into existence. The answers might surprise you! The second essay is a reflection on three ways in which Scotus's thought offers us a particularly new and refreshed perspective on our Christian faith.

The final section includes a chapter on Pope Benedict XVI's addresses on the Franciscan tradition and a conclusion. Benedict XVI, as the young Joseph Ratzinger, was deeply influenced by the theology of Bonaventure. His second doctoral dissertation, a requirement to teach in the German education system, was written on Bonaventure's theology of history and the future pontiff's life work continued to bear the imprint of the "Seraphic Doctor's" theological and spiritual outlook. As pope, Benedict XVI dedicated several catechetical talks during his regular public audiences to the Franciscan spiritual tradition. He does this mainly by speaking about particular figures in the tradition, but he doesn't simply focus on Francis, Clare, and Anthony of Padua. He also includes many of the figures that do not get as much attention like Bonaventure, Scotus, Angela of Foligno, Elizabeth of Hungary, Veronica Giuliani, and Lawrence of Brindisi. This chapter explores how a recent pope understands the Franciscan spiritual tradition and sees its contributing figures and their insight as relevant for our time.

As a young Franciscan friar, I continue to find myself in awe of the seemingly endless sources of inspiration within the Franciscan tradition. In fact, I have been so captivated by the wisdom, humanity, generosity, and hope that shines forth in the hardly ubiquitous movement we generically call "Franciscan," that I entered the Order of Friars Minor as a young college graduate and have dedicated my ministerial life so far to the academic study and pastoral application of this tradition. My hope is that the diversity of the tradition reflected in the variety of these essays and the ongoing relevance of the Franciscan spiritual insight might also inspire and shape your worldview and encourage you to walk in the footprints of Christ as Francis, Clare, and the many women and men who followed them centuries later have striven to walk, living the Gospel in every age.

PART I

THE FRANCISCAN TRADITION IN THE MODERN WORLD

FROM GENERATION
TO GENERATION:

A Franciscan Millennial
and the Memory of 9/11

In 2001 I was a freshman at a Franciscan college. A decade later, I found myself teaching, among other things, a class of freshmen at a Franciscan college. It can be difficult to anticipate where the Spirit will lead and what might happen in a period as short as a decade. When I was a student at St. Bonaventure University in Western New York I could never have imagined that I would, in what would seem like a few short years, be a Franciscan friar and professor at a similar institution of higher education.

While technically the young women and men I taught this past academic year at Siena College near Albany, New York, are part of the same generation as I am – fellow Millennials or those born from about 1982 through 2002 – their experience of the events of the morning of September 11, 2001 and mine differ quite perceptibly. For one thing, I was an "adult," on my own for the first time and free to form my own opinions and analyze the information provided by the world around me in my own ways. My freshmen students were about eight-years-old, or in third grade, that Tuesday morning a decade ago. Their experience of the day was marked, as they have admitted to me, by some personal recollection not unlike the memory of those young Baby Boomers whose school day was once interrupted with the news of President Kennedy's assassination, but their memory has largely been shaped by the narrative history that confronted them growing up in a world quite unlike my own.

I can still recall a world that did not know of an institution called "Department of Homeland Security," the invasive and at-times offensive "security measures" at airport screening lines (an experience I had for the first time, despite my frequent air travel, shortly before boarding the plane on which I am currently writing this essay) or the fear of the ubiquitous "terrorist attacks" that seem to be imminently on the fearful horizon of so many minds of the young and old alike. This is not the memory of the younger members of my generational cohort. This is the reality, the quotidian experience they have only ever known. Much of this reality, whether we like to admit it or not, stems from the events that began on that Lower Manhattan morning in September ten years ago. That so much of the memory of today's young adults has been informed and shaded by that singular event of violence and fear complicates the way in which one might approach the remembrance, the commemoration, and the mourning of this historical milestone.

Ten years later the specter of that day haunts the collective memory of the Millennials, while the shadow of fear and a spirit of retributive violence continues to be cast upon the lives of the populace. As we pause to remember, commemorate, and mourn, what can the Franciscan tradition offer those who look for spiritual direction and resources for theological reflection? What does it mean to speak with a Franciscan voice in the wake of 9/11?

The Franciscan intellectual and spiritual tradition offers us much by way of an approach to the remembrance of that fateful and tragic day. To speak with a Franciscan voice today is, as it has always been, a challenge for both the speaker and the hearer. To follow the Gospel of our Lord Jesus Christ, which always and everywhere stands at the core of the Franciscan life, is no easy task. Following the Gospel is really what is at the heart of anything that might be called a Franciscan "voice" or "response" to the memory of 9/11. The reason that following the Gospel is so challenging, that engaging the world from a Franciscan perspective is so difficult, is that in a world that organizes its thoughts and responses according to the logic of violence and the possible, the Good News of Jesus Christ is communicated in the poetics of the Kingdom of God, which is an expression of the impossible experience of love, forgiveness, and peace.

So much public discourse is centered on the collective and individual memories of 9/11 that is shaped by a capitulation to a spirit of vengeance and worldly "justice," which is shouted and celebrated according to the grammar of violence under the guise of worldly wisdom, common sense, and logic.[1] And so speaking in the language of the Gospel becomes threatening, unpatriotic, and unnerving, grating on the ears of those who listen for the words of the possible, only to be confronted with the Truth that is said to set us free, but which also led to the crucifixion of the incarnate Word of God. Preaching love, forgiveness, and peace is a dangerous and risky business for those who have forgotten (literally do not have a *memory* of) what it means to bear the name of the Prince of Peace. But this is the business of the Franciscan voice nonetheless.

This essay is a brief exploration of this task, the task of the Franciscan voice today. Mine is a perspective that comes from and seeks to return to my generation, those young women and men who might otherwise be called "the 9/11 Generation" in place of the Millennials, but whose memory has been shaped by forces – intentionally meaningful, but oftentimes antithetical to the Gospel – both collectively and individually not their own.

I am in a unique position as a member of a generation that has been so significantly shaped after the events of 9/11. I have one foot in the world of my generational peers, while I also have a foot planted in the world of my religious profession, the Franciscan tradition. As I look back over the last ten years, I offer a reflection on what it means to approach this memory with a Franciscan voice. It is, perhaps, not the *only* voice of the Franciscan tradition, for I would never claim to speak universally for all Franciscans, but mine is indeed *a* Franciscan voice contextualized by my place in the world and informed by the signs of my time. It is important, I will argue, for us to not lose sight of the fact that what we are dealing with is indeed *a memory*, a trace that is imbedded in the thoughts, words, and actions of individuals and society. It is *a memory* then that must be confronted. But how?

With the voice of the Gospel, which speaks in the language of a poetics of the Kingdom of God, a grammar of love, forgiveness, and peace, the message is ultimately one of unwavering Christian nonviolence and it will certainly be met by the world with hostility. But this is the Truth of the

---

[1] For more on this theme see Daniel Horan, "The Grammar of the Kingdom in a World of Violence: The (Im)possible Poetics of John D. Caputo," in *Violence, Transformation and the Sacred: They Shall Be Called Children of God*, eds. Margaret Pfeil and Tobias Winwright (Maryknoll, NY: Orbis Books, 2012): 71-84.

Gospel, the voice of the Franciscan tradition and the Good News that we are called to continue passing on from generation to generation.

The Challenge of Selective Memory

As we approached the tenth anniversary of 9/11, and at each subsequent anniversary, we are called to remember, commemorate, and mourn. Each of these practices or actions is an engagement with memory. The first (remember) is to "call to mind," to "bring forward" a concept or image or experience. This "thing-to-call-to-mind" can be positive or negative, but it remains in the past or in the realm of memory. The second (commemorate) is a collective or communal engagement, to remember with others usually in a public way. The third (mourn) is to bring to mind in order to let go or reconcile. But what is this memory that we are asked (expected?) to engage?

In one sense it is a very personal or subjective reality. So much of my memory is cast, edited, recast, forgotten, and so on by "me." Yet, there remain public or shared factors that inform much of a memory I claim as my own. This is done through the narration or story telling of society in forms like news media, political rhetoric, and religious images. The constant repetition of "the story of 9/11" in the news, in political-campaign speeches, from sermon pulpits, and around the patriotic hearth of American domestic households seems to convey a sense of objective truth that "this story" is "*the* story." However, this is not the case.

For reasons both laudable and regrettable, the way in which the story of the events of 9/11 and those in days, months, and years that followed have constructed a *memoria*, which in Latin is the object of our recollection and the subject of our story. So much of the shaping of this memory has been done by language that is constricted by the discourse of American patriotism, nationalism, and vengeance. It is a memory of attack and violence that has been shaped to justify the retributive action of the United States across the globe. Two wars, thousands of deaths, trillions of dollars, and lost civil liberties later, one must only allude to 9/11 in order to justify violence, discrimination, and abuse. As such, the memory of 9/11 becomes not a token of solemn reflection fit for remembrance, commemoration, or mourning, but a political and military pawn in the game of global power.

Recently I was eating lunch with some other Franciscan friars and two employees who work for the friars in Albany. Having just returned from an academic conference in another part of the country, I shared my frustration about the loss of once-protected civil liberties exemplified in the highly invasive and restrictive procedures of airport security. One of the employees said that she would rather feel violated (as I had that week) and restricted in what items one could carry and be open to further limitations in order to "be safe." When I and some others at the table explained that studies often show that such actions are simply theatrical and reactionary, that these invasions of emblematic American rights for the ostensible protection of the very same rights were in fact not making anybody safer, but were just creating a "sense of security," she admitted that either way she would support the surrender of her rights. Her memory has been so shaped by the popular language of the possible and the collective narratives of violence that she, and so many like her, could not see the inherent contradiction present in the sacrificing of one's rights in order to "protect" these very same rights, which in reality no one possesses because of their willing surrender.

This memory is highly selective. The images and emotions evoked by the way people discuss 9/11 perpetuates the belief that "justice" means vengeance and "peace" is only attainable by means of a *war* on *terror*. That this sort of rhetoric, which draws on religious symbolism, blatantly contradicts the core of Christian belief, which so many of those who willingly capitulate to this narrative claim as their own, is often never considered. If the memory of 9/11 wasn't limited to the language of the possible; a concern with the economy of offensive and defensive military action; or the need for a population to surrender its right to privacy, space, free speech; and so on, then more people might see that what we pass off as "the memory of 9/11" is really just a tiny sliver of the fuller story and its use has not been to authentically remember, commemorate, or mourn a tragedy, but perpetuate injustice and violence in our world.

The thirteenth-century Franciscan saint, theologian, and doctor of the church, St. Bonaventure, explains that memory is not only shaped by our own experience, thoughts, and the influences of the community or those outside of us, but can be informed and shaped "from above" by those things that cannot be perceived through our senses.[2] In other words, our memory can also be affected by the divine light of God, illuminated and made clear

---

[2] For more see Bonaventure, *Itinerarium Mentis in Deum*, III, 2, eds. Philotheus Boehner and Zachary Hayes, Bonaventure Texts in Translation Series, vol. 2 (St. Bonaventure: Franciscan Institute Publications, 2002), 83.

through the Spirit. What the selective memory of 9/11 has done, I suggest, is preclude the memory of the tragedy from receiving the light of God and instead remains in the shadow of worldly wisdom. St. Paul reminds us of how Christians are to approach the wisdom of the world.

> Has not God made foolish the wisdom of the world? For since, in the wisdom of God, the world did not know God through wisdom, God decided through the foolishness of our proclamation, to save those who believe. For Jews demanded signs and Greeks desire wisdom, but we proclaim Christ crucified, a stumbling block to Jews and foolishness to Gentiles, but to those who are the called, both Jews and Greeks, Christ the power of God and the wisdom of God. For God's foolishness is wiser than human wisdom, and God's weakness is stronger than human strength (1 Corinthians 1:20-25).

A Christian response to worldly wisdom, to the factors of popular, civil, and political influence on memory, is to question what might at first seem wise and appropriate in order to allow God to illuminate the true wisdom.

St. Paul and St. Bonaventure challenge the conventional notion of the memory of 9/11 by reminding us to examine what has shaped and informed it. Is this how God sees what happened on 9/11? Is this how Jesus Christ would respond after such an event?

In order to speak with a Franciscan voice, to remember, commemorate, and mourn as one who lives the Gospel would, we must be willing to step back and challenge the individual and collective memory of that fateful day years ago. We must be willing to ask about what factors have come together to produce the story that is passed along as the memory of 9/11, challenging the conventional or popular wisdom as Jesus Himself had. "You have heard that it was said, 'You shall love your neighbor and hate your enemy.' But I say to you, love your enemies and pray for those who persecute you" (Matthew 5:43-44). While to many a Franciscan voice will sound foolish, it is nevertheless rooted in the wisdom of God.

Finding Your Franciscan Voice

Francis of Assisi was a real fool, which is one way he liked to be known. Francis referred to himself as "ignorant and stupid."[3] He was

---

[3] Francis of Assisi, "A Letter to the Entire Order" 39, in Regis J. Armstrong, J.A. Wayne

remembered as such in the early biographies like Thomas of Celano and Julian of Speyer's respective versions of *The Life of Saint Francis*,[4] as well as in the collected stories of the early brothers such as *The Legend of the Three Companions* where we read, "Francis excused himself claiming he was simple and stupid."[5] St. Bonaventure, while preaching to the Franciscan community in 1267 on the Feast of St. Francis, reminded the brothers of Francis's professed foolishness and humility, admonishing those who followed in the footprints of the poor man from Assisi to adopt a similar disposition in the world.

As if to take St. Paul's reflection to heart, Francis identified human foolishness, what appeared to be stupid in the eyes of the world, to be acceptable and perhaps unavoidable if one was to really follow Christ. Love of enemies, forgiveness of sins, embracing the poor, and shirking the lure of personal gain all appear counterintuitive to those who are concerned with things described in the language of the possible. Yet, Francis was not so interested in what at first appeared logical and sensible; he instead made it his business to follow the Gospel, which is expressed in the poetic language of the Kingdom of God where the first will be last, where the sinful will be forgiven, and where the dead will be raised.

Francis's radical embrace of the Gospel, desiring nothing more than to follow in the footprints of Jesus Christ, is found starkly in what is likely his most famous piece of writing, *The Canticle of the Creatures*. Many people tend to look at that poetic and prayerful reflection as Francis's homage to God's creation of the natural order, which it most certainly is. However, few stop to consider when, why, and how Francis mentions human beings in his canticle. Only fourteen-verses-long, *The Canticle of the Creatures* names various elements and non-human dimensions of creation for the first nine verses. In each brief stanza we read about how each element of creation naturally praises God in and through its very existence and by doing whatever it is it does (fire through giving light and heat, earth through producing fruit and sustaining us, and so on). When Francis gets around to mentioning human beings, the pattern continues but instead of glorifying God by simply *being*, human beings are said to glorify God – to

---

Hellmann, and William Short, eds., *Francis of Assisi: Early Documents*, 3 vols. (New York: New City Press, 1999-2001), 1:119. Further citations of this source will be noted as *FAED* followed by the volume and the page number.

[4] See *FAED* I.

[5] "Legend of the Three Companions" 64 in *FAED* II: 106.

live up to who they were created to be – by loving, forgiving and enduring in peace.

> Praised be You, my Lord, through those who give pardon for Your love, and bear infirmity and tribulation. Blessed are those who endure in peace for by You, Most High, shall they be crowned.[6]

Human beings are called to love, to forgive, and to work for peace just as the purpose of fire is to provide heat and light and the wind is to be serene and provide the weather. To worldly wisdom, this might seem absurd. Isn't the purpose of being a human to earn lots of money or be successful in the business realm? Shouldn't people strive to care for their families? What do love, forgiveness, and peace have to do with being human? Francis answers in the way of Christ: it has *everything* to do with being human.

In light of Francis's willing appropriation of St. Paul's description of the foolishness of God, which of course is wiser than human wisdom, and the *Poverello's* insistence on the Gospel Truth that what it means to be human centers on love, forgiveness, and peace, we can begin to grasp a sense of what a Franciscan voice might sound like today. It is willing to be perceived as foolish or stupid, for the Franciscan voice will speak a message of the impossible like that of forgiving our enemies instead of launching attacks of revenge. It will be focused on the absolute and inherent dignity of every person because, as the medieval Franciscan theologian Blessed John Duns Scotus reminds us, we are individually loved into a contingent existence. God wills each particular creature into being when this or that person or thing could otherwise not have been created. Who we are – our unrepeatable individuality, our intrinsic dignity, our identity as known by God – is identical with our existence and no matter what we do or don't do, that value cannot be taken away from us.

A Franciscan voice will insist on loving one another as God has loved us to an extravagant and foolish degree because it is how, as Francis explains in his *Canticle*, we give glory back to God. Having been created in the image and likeness of God, unlike trees or flowers or fire or the moon, we are most fully human when we love, forgive, and work toward peace. To be violent, vengeful, or selfish is to be un-human!

---

[6] Francis of Assisi, "The Canticle of the Creatures" 10-11, in *FAED* I: 114.

A Franciscan Voice and the Memory of 9/11

The wisdom of the world suggests that the assassination of Osama bin Laden on May 1, 2011 is something about which to celebrate. And so many people did. Many people, particularly young people, *Millennials*, entered the streets to rejoice and proclaim victory in the death of another. Certainly bin Laden's actions and the actions of his followers were simply evil, but does that mean that we have a right to kill even one more person or celebrate such a person's death?

One week after the announcement of the killing of bin Laden by United States President Barack Obama, at which time he said that bin Laden had finally been brought to "justice," *New York Times* columnist Maureen Dowd wrote a piece titled, "Killing Evil Doesn't Make Us Evil." Dowd's column sought to defend the actions of those United States citizens who had celebrated in the streets and otherwise rejoiced in the death of bin Laden. She began her column, "I don't want closure. There is no closure after tragedy. I want memory, and justice, and revenge."[7] Like the popular imagination, drawn on the language of worldly wisdom found in the President's address citing this act of murder as "justice," Dowd admits that she is not at all interested in recognizing the humanity in another person whom she labeled "evil," suggesting that bin Laden was something akin to evil itself or evil incarnate. The truth is that in a world where justice is viewed as "an eye for an eye," perhaps the killing of another person simply follows suit. But this is in no way a Christian response, let alone a *Franciscan* one.

Dowd goes on to explain in her column that "the really insane assumption behind some of the second-guessing is that killing Osama somehow makes us like Osama, as if all killing is the same. Only fools or knaves would argue that we could fight Al Qaeda's violence non-violently... Morally and operationally, this was counterterrorism at its finest. We have nothing to apologize for." What Dowd doesn't realize is that a Christian response to the killing of Osama bin Laden is to recognize that *all* killing is the same. Some will argue that self-defense and military actions justify occasional murder, but that is an argument that cannot be supported by the Gospels nor by the first three-hundred-years of Christian history until Christianity became so closely tied to the Roman State after the Emperor

---

[7] Maureen Dowd, "Killing Evil Doesn't Make Us Evil," *The New York Times* (May 8, 2011): WK8.

Constantine. It is no wonder that the so-called "Just War Theory" only began to be developed around the time of Augustine, late in the Fourth Century, decades after Rome and Christianity became symbiotic and State violence had to be reconciled with the new faith.

Dowd is correct to say that "only fools or knaves" would argue for nonviolence. This is precisely the point that St. Paul and St. Francis have made. We Christians, we Franciscans are indeed fools and knaves, proclaiming the Gospel amid a world of violence, bearing the name of the Prince of Peace. Unfortunately, Dowd is incorrect about her assertion that this was "counterterrorism at its best" and that "we have nothing to apologize for." We, as a society, a country, and a community of believers, have much for which to apologize. Acknowledging the fact that we don't readily act more foolish like St. Francis of Assisi did and instead act in ways complicit with making our world a more violent place might be a good place to begin.

To speak with a Franciscan voice is to speak the Truth to power that either *all* life is sacred or *no* life is sacred. It means opposing all forms of violence, retribution, and worldly "justice." Jesus Christ rejected this notion of "justice" when he said: "You have heard it was said, 'An eye for an eye and a tooth for a tooth.' But I say to you, do not resist an evildoer. But if anyone strikes you on the right cheek, turn the other also" (Matthew 5:38-39). And so should we. This is no easy task, it requires effort and consciousness about how we have shaped and reshaped our memory.

What is it that we allow to inform our understanding of the events of 9/11? Of suffering in our lives? Of violence in our world? If we let the worldly wisdom that St. Paul cautions us to resist take precedence over the divine wisdom of the Gospel, then we will only aid in perpetuating violence in our world. But if we remain committed to following in the footprints of Jesus Christ as Francis of Assisi was, then what we see, what we hear, and how we speak will be different.

It is fair to say that much of what might have shaped and informed Maureen Dowd's memory of 9/11 over the last ten or more years, the memory that she claims to want so badly in the opening of her column, is likely the same as what has shaped and informed the memory of my freshman students. It is a memory molded in the image and likeness of fear and violence, a narrative scripted according to the desires and agendas of those in power – some with very good and others with perhaps less-good intentions. Yet, as Dowd suggests, this type of memory does not really permit a sense of "closure," that which Dowd claims is unattainable. I believe that she is correct on this point. I believe she is correct in claiming that the closure she and so many seek is unattainable given the memory and the narrative with which she and others are left. The reason is that this particular memory, this version of the story that is called to mind, is fueled by fear, violence, and revenge, which is an endless cycle of sin. There is no closure in such a cycle.

But if our memory is informed by the poetics of the Kingdom of God, the proclamation of Jesus Christ that calls for an end of this sort of violent logic, some form of closure may be on the horizon. This is the way in which we need to strive to form our memory of 9/11. Instead of succumbing to fear, violence, and vengeance, we must follow Francis of Assisi and embrace love, forgiveness and peace. Only in this way might we be able to authentically remember, commemorate and mourn in the true spirit of Christ. We will remember what it means to identify the value of *all* human life and see in each unnatural death – especially murder – a tragedy and something sorrowful. We will commemorate the events without rallying for vengeance or retribution, for that which we call to mind is indeed something that has affected the entire community and out of our pain we might find the strength to support one another. We will mourn the loss of loved ones and strangers, knowing as Christ has shown us, that death does not have the last word and more violence will not resolve the suffering we experience or replace the absence we feel.

Returning to my freshman students, those little children whose lives changed before they knew what would be different a decade ago, for their sake, for our sake, and for the sake of the generations to come, we must stand up and confidently speak with a Franciscan voice of love, forgiveness, and peace. In doing so, I believe that we might live more authentically what it is we profess in our Baptismal promises, namely to follow the Gospel. To speak with a Franciscan voice, which is to be foolish for peace in the world that seeks violence, is to model a new way of living in the world. It is a way of living that needs to be embraced and so modeled for each generation to come. This new way of living is what Jesus demonstrates for us time and again in his words and deeds; it is the Kingdom of God: *Thy Kingdom Come, Thy Will Be Done.*

A FRANCISCAN WAY OF MINISTRY

"No one showed me what I had to do, but the Most High Himself revealed to me that I should live according to the pattern of the Holy Gospel." *St. Francis of Assisi*[1]

During his final days, Saint Francis of Assisi began to reflect on how he had lived his life and spent God's time. As death approached, Francis dictated his *Testament* to some of the friars who were caring for him so that his recollections of the birth of his new religious order and of his hopes for the future could be preserved. In this text he recalls the story of his conversion to follow Christ and shares what it means to be a Franciscan: to live the Gospel. The Testament is only the last of a series of writings by Francis that reveals his vision of ministry. Today, nearly eight centuries after his death, Francis continues to inspire people from all parts of the world and every faith tradition. Beyond his valuable insight often called "Franciscan spirituality," stands a vision of ministry in the Church. It is a manner of living in the world, being in relationship with God, and serving our sisters and brothers.

The year 2009 marked the eight-hundredth anniversary of the founding of the Franciscan Order. As we celebrated this milestone (and now carry it into the future), it seemed good to consider the example of Francis and

---

[1] Francis of Assisi, "The Testament" 14, in *FAED* 1:125.

reflect on his vision of Gospel life that serves as a source of inspiration and guidance. In this chapter, I will highlight five themes that emerge from the writings of Francis to form a ministerial ethos that is particularly Franciscan. One does not need to be a Franciscan friar, Poor Clare sister, or a Secular Franciscan to adopt a Franciscan approach to ministry. Rather, any pastoral minister or person engaged in charitable work can benefit from reflecting on the insights of one of the greatest saints and reformers in Christian history.

1. Everything Done in Humble Service

When Francis started to work in God's name, having renounced his worldly possessions and aspirations, he began to do penance and followed the Gospel as he felt led to by God.[2] It was not long after Francis began living this new way of life that others came seeking to imitate his efforts and follow his manner of life in what Franciscan scholar Thaddée Matura calls the "Franciscan project."[3] This project, while initially devoid of an articulated course of development and not the intentional goal of Francis himself,[4] quickly grew within Francis's lifetime to include thousands of friars and hundreds of sisters. What attracted such a number to follow in the footsteps of this medieval man through the renunciation of property, the adherence to a life of obedience, and the voluntary adoption of chastity?

One element of the Franciscan project that emerged from the work of those who were with Francis was the radical adherence to subordinate positions in society. Those early followers of Francis saw the humility of a man who left behind the life of a wealthy merchant to live among lepers and outcasts. In his *Earlier Rule*, Francis instructed those who were to come after him where within the social strata they should strive to live. He says, "Let no one be called *'prior,'* but let everyone in general be called a lesser brother. Let one wash the feet of the other." Francis continued by enjoining his brothers to be "lesser ones" who should always "be subject to

---

[2] Francis of Assisi, "The Testament" 1, in *FAED* 1:124.

[3] Thaddée Matura, "Francis of Assisi and His Posterity Today," in *Gospel Living: Francis of Assisi Yesterday and Today*, ed. Elise Saggau (St. Bonaventure, NY: Franciscan Institute Publications, 1994), 263-267.

[4] Matura makes the comparison of Francis to Jesus while explaining the similar trajectories of the Franciscan Orders and the Church. While Francis is held as the founder and model for the three Franciscan Orders (much like Jesus is for the Church), he is not credited with intentionally *founding* a new movement in the proper sense. See Matura, "Francis of Assisi and His Posterity Today," 264.

all."[5]

This spirit of humility acts as the foundation for all subsequent characteristics that compose a Franciscan approach to ministry. Francis was less concerned about *what* someone did in the world than about *how* someone did it. Here we see the saint's admiration for the humility of Christ emerge as part of the centerpiece of his spirituality; to be a Franciscan is to live the Gospel by following in the footprints of Jesus Christ. Michael Blastic summarized this well when he wrote, "As Jesus turned toward those around him, so Francis and Clare in contemplation and compassion incarnate the praxis of Jesus as they follow him in their world by turning to those around them."[6] From the Incarnation and birth to death on the Cross, Jesus' life served as Francis's model for humble service.

Perhaps the most succinct articulation of Francis's image of humble service is found in *Admonition XIX*. Here Francis says,

> Blessed is the servant who does not consider himself any better when he is praised and exalted by people than when he is considered worthless, simple, and looked down upon, for what a person is before God, that he is and no more. Woe to that religious who has been placed in a high position by others and [who] does not want to come down by his own will. Blessed is that servant who is not placed in a high position by his own will and always desired to be under the feet of others.[7]

Humility is a virtue of ministry, being of service to and among people, that Francis often reiterated in his writings. In addition to being a reoccurring theme in his *Admonitions*, humility becomes concretized as a constitutive characteristic of the Franciscan way of life when it appears three times in his *Later Rule*. In chapter III, we read, "I counsel, admonish and exhort my brothers in the Lord Jesus Christ not to quarrel or argue or judge others when they go about in the world; but let them be meek, peaceful, modest, gentle and *humble*, speaking courteously to everyone, as is becoming."[8] Two chapters later in the same document, Francis exhorts his followers to, at all

---

[5] Francis of Assisi, "Earlier Rule" VI:3-4; VII:2, in *FAED* 1:68.
[6] Michael Blastic, "Contemplation and Compassion: A Franciscan Ministerial Spirituality," in *Spirit and Life* Vol. 7, eds. Anthony Carrozzo, Vincent Cushing and Kenneth Himes (St. Bonaventure, NY: Franciscan Institute Publications, 1997), 172.
[7] Francis of Assisi, "TheAdmonitions" XIX: 1-4, in *FAED* 1:135.
[8] Francis of Assisi, "The Later Rule" III:10-11, in *FAED* 1:102. Emphasis added.

times, work humbly as a servant of God and a disciple of poverty.[9] Toward the end of the Rule, Francis again reminds his followers that even amid persecution, hardship, and infirmity, they are to have humility and patience while loving those who persecute them.[10] Francis echoed the theme of humility at every opportunity because it was in this way that Christ served his brothers and sisters, and it was in this way that Francis desired to serve.

Matura makes a keen observation about the importance humility held for Francis's way of life and the subsequent movement that emerged from his example. Matura believes that Francis was well aware of the temptation, perhaps within himself, for pastoral ministers to consider themselves better or above those whom they served.[11] It is possible that his concern about friars judging others and seeking special privileges was rooted in his own experience as the son of a wealthy merchant, a well-off young man who was disgusted by lepers and people of lower social status. Regardless of Francis's initial motivation, we are the inheritors of a vision that inspires ministers to always put others before themselves.[12] In a world that is fraught with the promotion of self-centeredness and material accumulation, where even good-minded ministers are tempted to seek personal reward, a Franciscan approach to ministry rooted in humility remains a prophetic stance.

2. Relationship Takes Priority

Francis's way of being-in-the-world centered on following the example of Jesus Christ. Blastic insightfully connects the humility of God that Francis recognized in the Incarnation and sought to emulate with God's outward movement toward humanity.[13] Once rooted in humility, God Incarnate – Jesus Christ – entered into relationships with the people around him. All four Gospels recount the multitude of encounters Jesus had with many: the marginalized, outcast, wealthy, powerful, average, violent, peaceful, and so on. Because he lived in such a perfect state of humble existence among his

---

[9] "The Later Rule" V:4, in *FAED* 1:103.

[10] "The Later Rule" X:7-10, in *FAED* 1:105.

[11] Thaddée Matura, *Francis of Assisi: The Message in His Writings*, trans. Paul Barrett (St. Bonaventure, NY: Franciscan Institute Publications, 1997), 167.

[12] The Franciscan saint and doctor of the Church, St. Bonaventure, later wrote about the importance of humility as an aspect of the evangelical life, beginning his treatise *Disputed Questions on Evangelical Perfection* with the subject of humility. See Bonaventure, *Disputed Questions on Evangelical Perfection*, Works of St. Bonaventure vol. XIII, trans. Thomas Reist and Robert Karris (St. Bonaventure, NY: The Franciscan Institute, 2008).

[13] Blastic, "Contemplation and Compassion," 153.

sisters and brothers, Jesus was able to meet those he encountered as they were and treat them with the inherent dignity rightly deserved by virtue of their humanity. For Francis, this became a major component of his way of life and remains a characteristic of Franciscan ministry today.

While most of the preserved writings of Francis are letters, prayers, admonitions or ways of life addressed to large audiences, we have one letter that was written to a particular minister. The identity of this brother remains anonymous, which at first causes frustration in an age full of people impatient for instant gratification; however, the anonymity of the recipient allows us to stand in his place as the receiver of wisdom from Francis concerning ministry. The letter provides a touching look into the heart of Francis. Francis is concerned about the attitude and disposition of his brother friar and instructs him:

> I wish to know in this way if you love the Lord and me, His servant and yours: that there is not any brother in the world who has sinned – however much he could have sinned – who, after he has looked into your eyes, would ever depart without your mercy, if he is looking for mercy.[14]

Mercy trumps retributive justice. Relationship remains the primary hermeneutic for interpreting every encounter with another. While in retrospect this sort of observation may at first appear obvious, it is only because our familiarity – if only subtly and indirectly – with Franciscan ministry informs our way of seeing. However, this had not always been the case. Franciscan historian Joseph Chinnici describes the early Franciscan movement as a radically new form of "penitential humanism."[15] Chinnici understands this term as the unifying tendency of the Franciscan movement to connect people amid "social discord and violence." This approach to ministry is one that places relationship and community above one's personal faith journey and conversion. In fact, one's own conversion, if indicative of a Franciscan hue, should lead toward humanity and away from only one's self.[16] It is for precisely this reason that Francis insisted that the friars were

---

[14] Francis of Assisi, "A Letter to a Minister" 9, in *FAED* 97.

[15] Joseph Chinnici, "Penitential Humanism: Rereading the Sources to Develop a Franciscan Urban Spirituality," in *Franciscans in Urban Ministry*, ed. Roberta McKelvie (St. Bonaventure, NY: The Franciscan Institute, 2002), 119.

[16] Chinnici, "Penitential Humanism," 119-122.

to remain mendicants and not monks, to live as if the whole world were a cloister and not be limited to the four walls of private religious life.

A Franciscan approach to ministry is not simply a praxis of good method and skillful implementation of model practices; rather it is an ethical project that seeks to unite those who are separated by the violence of social, political, and ecclesial dissent.[17] To further stress the importance of relationship as the operative approach to ministry, Francis often used familial terms in his writing. In his *Earlier Rule*, Francis says, "Let each one love and care for his brother as a mother loves and cares for her son."[18] The familial understanding of relationship in the spirituality of Francis even extended beyond human relationships to include all of God's creation as found in his most famous work, *The Canticle of the Creatures*, where he addresses all elements as brother or sister. In an age of heightened ecological awareness the notion of relationship with the earth and the rest of creation can positively influence our approach to ministry. We are called to minister to all with a deepened sense of our interdependence and relatedness as children of God and brothers and sisters of all God's creation.

3. Avoid Attachment

There is great wisdom in a mendicant model of life. In a life content with divestment of personal property and nonattachment, pastoral ministers become less preoccupied with maintaining *their* status, *their* control, and *their* property. If a particular ministry does not "belong" to a particular minister, then one's attitude is that of a steward or curator who oversees something of value not his or her own. This is in direct contrast to the common oligarchical approach that so often limits the growth or creativity of a ministry, which remains confined within the boundaries of one person or a small group's charism or vision. Francis was quite convinced that appropriation of anything, including one's work as a minister, would ultimately lead to other problems. His *Earlier Rule* is filled with admonitions and warnings about the danger of attachment. For example in chapter VII he exhorts, "Wherever the brothers may be, either in hermitages or other places, let them be careful not to make any place their own or contend with anyone for it."[19] He goes on to warn, "Guard

---

17 See Chinnici, "Penitential Humanism," 123.
18 Francis of Assisi, "The Earlier Rule" IX:11, in *FAED* 1:71.
19 "The Earlier Rule," VII:13, in *FAED* 1:69.

yourselves against the anxieties of this world and the cares of this life,"[20] and summarizes his concern for attachment, saying:

> Let all the brothers strive to follow the humility and poverty of our Lord Jesus Christ and let them remember that we should have nothing else in the whole world except, as the Apostle says: having food and clothing, we are content with these.[21]

While today most ministers, including professed Franciscan women and men, would find it difficult to live in this world strictly observing the instruction above, the key to Francis's insight is found in the word "strive." Here we understand this as a more perfect vision of an imperfect manner of living in this world. It is the model for which a pastoral minister should enter into one's work, *striving* in humility and poverty to not appropriate work as their own.

4. Thy Will Be Done

Naturally, the divestment of property and ownership of even one's ministry leads to the question, "then to whom does it belong?" For Francis the answer is simple: all good things come from and belong to God. It is in the perfect prayer of Christians that we find the source and purpose of our ministerial endeavors, "*thy* will be done." When our efforts in ministry become more about our will, our ambition, or our desires, then we have left the realm of ministry and entered some level of self-centeredness. Closely linked to Francis's view of attachment, his understanding that all ministry is the work of God, for God renews in those who aim to follow a Franciscan approach to ministry an affirmation of their vocation to service. It redirects the gaze of the minister from the individual back toward God as the source of inspiration and the origin of his or her ministerial vocation.

Francis often wrote about God's will in connection with his own ministry and the broader work of the Order of Friars Minor. In his *A Letter to the Entire Order*, Francis reminds his brothers of their vocation and its connection to God's will. He writes:

> Give praise to Him because he is good; exalt Him by your deeds; for this reason He has sent you into the whole world:

---

[20] "The Earlier Rule," VIII:2, in *FAED* 1:69.
[21] "The Earlier Rule," IX:1, in *FAED* 1:70.

that you may bear witness to His voice in word and deed and bring everyone to know that there is no one who is all-powerful except Him.[22]

Matura highlights this notion in the thought of Francis when he says, "Anything good that we have or do, no matter how personal it is, comes to us from God, and we are only administrators of that good, as it were."[23] In addition to the right attribution of our gifts and vocation to God, this aspect of a Franciscan approach to ministry frees the minister of the weighty burdens of self-sufficiency and responsibility. Unfettered by the lack of self-pressure frequently found in the lives of ministers, we are free to view ourselves as God's instruments, working in partnership with Christ and others. In this way we leave the world of "lone rangers" and enter the community of Christians working toward the Kingdom.

5. Pray Without Ceasing

A Franciscan approach to ministry must always be rooted in a life of *lived* prayer. Those who adopt a Franciscan approach to ministry are not just people who pray, but people whose whole life serves as a prayer by their words and actions. Lived prayer is the openness to ongoing conversion that allows God to enter one's life and transform it from the preoccupations of worldly concerns and triviality to an expression of authentic Gospel living – following Christ's footsteps and working as God's instrument of peace today.

In a very brief letter to St. Anthony of Padua, Francis wrote in response to his request for permission to teach theology. This was a new initiative, for up to this time the Franciscans had largely avoided academic ministry. Francis was known to be very cautious of higher education because of the tendency for the educated to think better of themselves, look down on others, and generally move away from the characteristics of ministry we have examined above. However, Francis knew of Anthony's gifts and the many requests the other friars had made to him for his instruction on theology. Francis told Anthony, "I am pleased that you teach sacred theology to the brothers providing that, as is contained in the Rule, you 'do not extinguish the Spirit of prayer and devotion' during study of this

---

[22] Francis of Assisi, "A Letter to the Entire Order" 8-9, in *FAED* 1:117.
[23] Matura, *Francis of Assisi*, 132.

kind."[24] Even a ministry as foundational as the training of other friars for pastoral ministry was viewed as secondary to prayer and devotion.

Francis writes in his *Earlier Rule* that those who come after him are to love the Lord God, who has given everyone everything, with their whole heart, soul, mind, strength, understanding, powers, effort, affection, feeling, desire, and wish.[25] Additionally, this is not an occasional experience or segmented time apart from the rest of life, but the *modus operandi* of ministry. Later in the same text, Francis writes:

> Wherever we are, in every place, at every hour, at every time of the day, every day and continually, let all of us truly and humbly believe, hold in our heart and love, honor, adore, serve, praise and bless, glorify and exalt, magnify and give thanks to the Most High and Supreme Eternal God Trinity and Unity.[26]

This is another echo of the Franciscan understanding that one's entire life should be given back to God as prayer. Such a life naturally nourishes a vocation to service and ministry. When the focus of one's actions are directed back to God with humility, relationship as the priority, unencumbered by attachment and recognizing everything as God's work, then life is transformed into prayer. Ministry then is not the original effort or fabrication of one person, but the natural outpouring of God's gifts shared with others that is rooted in a life of lived prayer.

Franciscan Ministry Today

More than eight-hundred years after the first Franciscan began to do ministry in the small town of Assisi, we find ourselves continuing the mission of God's work in our world inspired by the example of Francis. Regardless of one's particular manifestation of God's work, all pastoral ministers can find a renewed sense of purpose and life through reflecting on a Franciscan approach to ministry. Humility keeps us approachable and in a position of loving service. The prioritization of relationship reminds us of the connection we have to our sisters, brothers, and creation. Avoiding attachment helps to refocus our energy toward correct ends, without being distracted by worldly concerns. Recalling that God is the source of all

---

[24] Francis of Assisi, "A Letter to Brother Anthony of Padua" 2, in *FAED* 1:107.
[25] "The Earlier Rule," XXIII:8, in *FAED* 1:84.
[26] "The Earlier Rule," XXIII:11, in *FAED* 1:85.

our gifts and vocation puts our work into perspective, while bolstering our sense of purpose as part of God's work. Finally, we are called to do more than just "say our prayers," but live a life that is prayer. It is through prayer that we are nourished and renewed in our ability to be effective ministers of God's love in our world.

CHAPTER THREE

FRANCISCAN SPIRITUALITY FOR "DIGITAL NATIVES"

"What a person is before God, that one is and no more"
St. Francis of Assisi[1]

"The supremacy of technology tends to prevent people from recognizing anything that cannot be explained in terms of matter alone"
Pope Benedict XVI[2]

There are two types of people in this world: Digital Natives and Digital Immigrants. At least this is the view forwarded by John Palfrey and Urs Gasser in their book *Born Digital: Understanding the First Generation of Digital Natives*.[3] Palfrey and Gasser suggest that in today's society one can better understand the differences between the Millennial generation – those women and men born in or after 1982 – and all those who were born before them by characterizing them in terms of their respective relationship to technology. These authors explore the manifold ways technology has influenced, impeded, and reshaped adolescent identity formation in recent years. Their research, one of the more recent studies on the role technology

---

[1] Francis of Assisi, "The Admonitions" XIX: 2, in *FAED* 1:135.
[2] Pope Benedict XVI, *Caritas in Veritate* §77 (Vatican City: Libreria Editrice Vaticana, 2009).
[3] John Palfrey and Urs Gasser, *Born Digital: Understanding the First Generation of Digital Natives* (New York: Basic Books, 2008).

plays in the lives of Millennials, provides a helpful glimpse into the world of young adults who have only ever known a technologically advanced and digital world.

One of the challenges that quickly emerges from a close examination of the characteristics and behavioral traits of the Millennials is figuring out how this generation relates to God and others in terms of spirituality. There have been a number of recent studies that explore the relationship of the Millennial generation to the world around them,[4] but few have seriously considered the way in which this technologically advanced and saturated world has affected the spirituality of the Millennial generation or examined possible resources for today's young adults. Those few who have considered the spirituality of the Millennials do not often take into consideration the role technology plays in their lives. Additionally, the concept of being born into an environment unlike that of their predecessors, which is where the term Digital Native comes from, does not enter into the discussion of the Millennial spiritual landscape. Digital Immigrants, those most likely to be the parents, educators and spiritual mentors for the Digital Natives, would do well to consider the nexus of technology and spirituality in searching for helpful resources to better aid today's young adults in their faith journeys.

I suggest that Millennials might benefit from looking back in the history of Christianity to another young adult, Francis of Assisi, who, when faced with a changing world, culture and church in his own time, committed himself to living the Gospel in a new and inspiring way. The influence of Francis continues to be seen in our contemporary and globalized world. In a recent survey young adults were asked which people in all of Church history were the most inspiring to them. After a first-place tie between Mother Teresa and Pope John Paul II, St. Francis of Assisi emerged in next place.[5] Even amid the dynamic and shifting world that is the twenty-first

---

[4] In addition to Palfrey and Gasser's *Born Digital*, a few examples include: Don Tapscott, *Grown Up Digital: How the Net Generation is Changing Your World* (New York: McGraw-Hill, 2009); W. Lance Bennett, ed., *Civic Life Online: Learning How Digital Media Can Engage Youth* (Cambridge: MIT Press, 2008); Tara McPherson, ed., *Digital Youth, Innovation, and the Unexpected* (Cambridge: MIT Press, 2008); David Buckingham, ed., *Youth, Identity, and Digital Media* (Cambridge: MIT Press, 2008); Eric Greenberg and Karl Weber, *Generation We: How Millennial Youth Are Taking Over America and Changing Our World Forever* (Emeryville, CA: Pachatusan, 2009); and the now classic Neil Howe and Wiliam Strauss, *Millennials Rising: The Next Great Generation* (New York: Vintage Books, 2000).

[5] William D'Antonio, James Davidson, Dean Hoge and Mary Gautier, *American Catholics Today: New Realities of Their Faith and Their Church* (Lanham, MD: Rowman & Littlefield, 2007), 151.

century a poor man from a small thirteenth-century Italian town continues to attract followers. Francis has been an inspiration for Christians and non-Christians alike in every new age. How might he and his way of life continue to speak to citizens of today's world in a digital age?

This chapter is organized in three parts. The first section is a look at who these Digital Natives are and what some of their characteristics look like. The second section is a look at how today's young adults are challenged by technology in living a Christian spiritual life. The last section is an exploration of what Franciscan spirituality might offer as a resource for Millennials in the digital age. While the impetus for these reflections is rooted in the pressing need to respond to a new generation's desire for credible and relevant resources for the spiritual life, it is my hope that all women and men – Digital Natives and Digital Immigrants alike – might find a renewed sense of God's work in their lives and world.

Millennials: The Digital Natives

In recent years Millennials have captured the attention of researchers, sociologists and generational demographers. Since 2000 several studies have been published on the Millennial generation ranging from how employers can better engage and understand their next-generation employees to how Millennials form their identities in new and public ways. The work of John Palfrey, Urs Gasser, and Don Tapscott has been particularly enlightening in helping to make sense of how today's young adults go about the world, saturated as it is with technology, with relative ease and comfort. What has taken previous generations (Baby Boomers, Gen-Xers, etc.) laborious effort to learn and practice, Millennials have negotiated from the earliest days of childhood. Much like we can describe those who belong to Generation-X and the Millennial generation as neither pre-nor post-Vatican II because they never knew a Church prior to the Second Vatican Council, so too we can understand Millennials as Digital Natives because they are born into a world that has always consisted of computers, cellular phones, and the Internet. In other words, as there was no transition from Latin to the vernacular for those born after Vatican II, so too there is no transition from the language of an analog world to a digital one. The digital world is their home; it is where they were born and raised.

Palfrey and Gasser summarize this world in which Digital Natives live and interact as a new dimension of reality. This dimension is not something completely distinct from the world as we have known it, but it is unlike that which has come before.

> Unlike most Digital Immigrants, Digital Natives live much of their lives online, without distinguishing between the online and the offline. Instead of thinking of their digital identity and their real-space identity as separate things, they just have an identity (with representations in two, or three, or more different spaces). They are joined by a set of common practices, including the amount of time they spend using digital technologies, their tendency to multitask, their tendency to express themselves and relate to one another in ways mediated by digital technologies, and their pattern of using the technologies to access and use information and create new knowledge and art forms. For these young people, new digital technologies – computers, cell phones, Sidekicks – are primary mediators of human-to-human connections.[6]

Furthermore, with electronic books, virtual worlds, GPS navigation systems, and so forth, there is hardly anything exempt from its duplicate electronic or virtual counterpart. To say that Millennials take technology for granted is an understatement. Millennials live and have, for the most part, only ever known a technologically advanced and digital world.

There is no doubt that Digital Natives think, learn and communicate differently than those who have come before them, but do they pray differently? One way this population has been categorized in recent years is as a cohort of "seekers." Robert Wuthnow has observed that, "young adults are no longer born into faith communities that embrace them fully and command allegiance over a lifetime."[7] Without the security or stability once guaranteed by familial association with particular religions or faith claims, today's young adults are largely left to chart their own spiritual path. This is further complicated by the abundance of material that is accessible via the Internet or other forms of social communications media that are so ubiquitous today. How are the Digital Natives to find their way on the spiritual pilgrimage?

---

[6] Palfrey and Gasser, *Born Digital*, 4.

[7] Robert Wuthnow, *After the Baby Boomers: How Twenty- and Thirty-Somethings Are Shaping the Future of American Religion* (Princeton: Princeton University Press, 2007), 124.

Drawing on the theology of Karl Rahner, Mike Hayes, in his book *Googling God*, observes: "Indeed, young adults of all kinds are on a search for answers. In a sense they are, in Rahner's own words, 'infinite questioners' of life."[8] The seeking that Wuthnow describes is made manifest in the search for answers the Hayes observes in his study. Like all people, regardless of age or generation, Millennials are in the life-long experience of uncovering meaning and discovering truth. In other words, a quest to understand what Rahner calls the "transcendental experience" of the human condition is shared by all people of all generations. This is the experience that is beyond the ordinary, "categorical" experiences of life, yet it is already always present to us by virtue of our being loved into creation by God. Millennials, in light of their status as Digital Natives, might be less apt to tap into this dimension of their existence. Hayes explains:

> Young adult angst often comes from this ceaseless questioning/longing because they live in a world of immediate gratification, the world of Google. Answers can be arrived at by the touch of a button or the click of a mouse. The result is a world that young adults live in where they expect answers that are simple, clear-cut, and require little thought.[9]

As Digital Natives, Millennials spend a significant portion of their lives in a new form of categorical living. One in which "reality" as such is at one and the same time connected and alienated from the created world. The challenge for these Digital Natives is that the quest they are on, the pilgrimage of seeking and questioning, is not easily concluded or resolved online with a quick trip to Google or Wikipedia. For a generation that has spent its entire life straddling two worlds, created and digital, it can be difficult to know how to grapple with the inherent desire to seek the absolute mystery that is God. Where can the Digital Natives go when they cannot click their way to a spiritual answer online?

The Challenge of Spirituality for Digital Natives

In his most recent encyclical letter, Pope Benedict XVI dedicates the last

[8] Mike Hayes, *Googling God: The Religious Landscape of People in Their 20s and 30s* (New York: Paulist Press, 2007), 140.
[9] Hayes, *Googling God*, 141.

section to what he calls, "The Development of Peoples and Technology."[10] The pope both highly praises the technological advancements of humankind, and also warns the world of the danger associated with forgetting that technology is but one of many human tools and not simply an end in itself. He writes, "Technology – it is worth emphasizing – is a profoundly human reality, linked to the autonomy and freedom of [men and women]. In technology we express and confirm the hegemony of the spirit over matter… it touches the heart of the vocation of human labor."[11] Technology is a gift that in large part reflects our co-creative possibility as human beings created in the image and likeness of God (Genesis 1:27). However, he goes on, "technology is never merely technology" and "technological development can give rise to the idea that technology is self-sufficient when too much attention is given to the "how" questions, and not enough to many "why" questions underlying human activity."[12]

The "why" questions are precisely the concerns for which Digital Natives are seeking answers. While Pope Benedict does not believe that technology is intrinsically problematic, he does keenly note that obsession with or over-dependence on technology distracts us from some of the most fundamental questions of human existence. This is the particular challenge that Digital Natives face in an acute way. Technology saturates the world of Digital Natives to a point where it can be hard to discern what is real from what is artificial. As Wuthnow has observed, these young adults are seeking the spiritual, but they will not likely find it online.

Although the answers to the "why" questions of human existence and relationship will not be found in a Google search, technology does play an important role in the way today's young adults are shaped and developed into individuals. In his book, *Technology and Spirituality*, Stephen Spyker writes: "I believe that creation is ongoing, that God isn't finished with us yet. I believe this both on a personal level – God isn't finished with *me* yet, therefore that fact that I'm not perfect doesn't give me a free pass – and on a corporate level – God isn't finished with *us* yet, so we, as a society and as a species, can become more congruent with God's design."[13] Spyker is introducing the possibility that God may be working through technology

---

[10] Pope Benedict XIV, *Caritas in Veritate* §68 and following.

[11] Pope Benedict XIV, *Caritas in Veritate* §69.

[12] Pope Benedict XVI, *Caritas in Veritate* §69-§70.

[13] Stephen Spyker, *Technology and Spirituality: How the Information Revolution Affects Our Spiritual Lives* (Woodstock, VT: SkyLight Paths Publishing, 2007), 69.

to continue shaping humanity. He reminds us that although all of the answers in our spiritual journey are not found in technological advances, we are nevertheless shaped and formed by such developments. For Digital Natives and those who will come after them, the evolution of humanity as spiritual creatures in relationship to the Creator will continue to be shaped by technology. Franciscan spirituality might provide a resource for today's Christians as they grow and adapt to the world in which they find themselves.

Franciscan Spirituality and Digital Natives

Although the challenges were different from those of today, Francis of Assisi – a young adult of only 24-years-old when he began to live a new religious life – grew up in an era of unrest and change. While the thirteenth-century saint did not have to navigate the technological neighborhood that is home to the Millennial generation, he did have to negotiate meaning and faith in a time saturated with violence, class struggle, and the emergence of new worldviews.

Francis of Assisi struggled his entire life to understand what God was calling him to do. At the end of his life he said, "And after the Lord gave me brothers, no one showed me what I had to do, but the Most High Himself revealed to me that I should live according to the pattern of the Holy Gospel."[14] Looking back on his experience of lifelong conversion and discernment, Francis recognized that he was not in control of his circumstances. He found himself wrestling with what it meant to live in a way pleasing to God, while at the service of others. It is at this nexus of evangelical life and humble service that Francis encountered his authentic self.

In this way Millennials can identify with the medieval saint. Today, perhaps even more than in thirteenth-century Italy, young adults face the unsettling question, "How should I live?" The cultural environment of contemporary America provides the conditions to lure away or distract Millennials from confronting and embracing who they really are and who God really is, leaving them to settle for the allurements of our consumer-driven society. In an effort to answer questions of vocation and purpose, contemporary young adults are dealt and sold empty products by popular culture, ultimately left unhappy and more confused than when they began.

---

[14] Francis of Assisi, "The Testament," in *FAED* 1:125.

The consequence of settling for inauthenticity is gravitation toward a behavioral model that Jean Twenge calls "Generation Me."[15] This is what happens when a Millennial (or any person in our time) turns to the culture to fill the gap once occupied by faith experience. In other words, behavior rooted in consumerism, competition, and self-centeredness arises from embracing a superficial system of identity formation. When Millennials look for identity and meaning in the marketplace, they will never really find themselves.

Francis, who knew the pain of once living an empty life, models the way toward answering the question "what should I do?" His answer is to listen to God. Thanks to the gifts of technology, medicine and other sciences, we have been led to believe, given enough time and resources, that humanity can find the answer to any problem unaided. This is what Hayes is referring to when he speaks about the Digital Natives' need for instant gratification and answers provided by technology. Now we are left with a cultural milieu that can be described as absent of God, and a population that has forgotten *the* source of its very being. It is no wonder this generation struggles with discovering what they should do and who they are.

Throughout the latter part of his life, Francis went around to various communities of his brother friars and preached a series of sermon-like admonitions. Within the corpus of his collected work, we have preserved twenty-eight of these admonitions, each of which addresses a topic of Christian living. While these writings do not receive the popular attention of his other work, like his famous *The Canticle of the Creatures*, these brief teachings articulate the theological and social view Francis passed on to his followers.[16] I believe three of these admonitions speak a particularly relevant word to today's young adults, the Digital Natives.

Admonition VII, titled "Let Good Action Follow Knowledge,"[17] is a polemic that warns the early Franciscans of the danger education and social status pose to building relationships with God and others. Francis was a firm believer that to live simply was the key to authentic Gospel life. Having seen how education, wealth, and high social status created barriers

---

[15] See Jean Twenge, *Generation Me* (New York: Free Press, 2006).

[16] It should be noted here that the collection of Francis's 28 admonitions is the only document found in all five manuscript-collections that date back to the thirteenth century. This attests to the great import these writings had to the early Franciscan community. See *FAED* 1:128.

[17] Francis of Assisi, "The Admonitions," VII, in *FAED* 1:132.

between people and a sense of self-sufficiency that disregarded God, Francis wished to end divisions that impaired Christian love. Even those who used their education, wealth, or status to help others must be cautious not to substitute themselves for God.

In a post-enlightenment era marked by advancement in all technological and scientific fields, Francis warns Millennials not to forget the source of these gifts. With great gifts comes great responsibility. As Millennials confront questions of future decisions and direction, Francis's advice speaks of belongedness that reminds this generation of their source and end. The humility and gratitude that arise from acknowledging God as the source of all good gifts should lead us to freely share those gifts with others. Hoarding our talents, resources, and power for our own good or glory is an injustice. Francis calls us to use our gifts wisely, serving God and others through good works.

Admonition XII, titled "Knowing the Spirit of the Lord,"[18] is the natural progression from Admonition VII. After recognizing our giftedness as rooted in God's loving generosity and, therefore, moved to share our gifts with others through good works, Francis suggests that we should recognize the direct work of God in our lives. This has a twofold implication. First, when we do not recognize God's work through us, Francis says that our "flesh" – our human weakness – gets in the way. If we don't see God's good, then we are probably interfering with its actualization. It is also implied that God is always present to us, whether we like it or not.

For Millennials, the first part of this admonition's meaning has great import for those challenged by uncertainty or confusion concerning the future. While struggling to discern how to live and what to do, prayerful reflection on where and how God is working in their lives can lead Millennials to see a clearer path ahead. The second part of this admonition speaks directly to the despair and implicit nihilism often present in today's culture. It can be difficult to see God's love in our world when faced with violence, illness, and poverty, but God's gracious presence is made manifest in our good works. In someway, it is up to each of us to help bring the presence of God to our world.

Admonition XIII, titled "Patience,"[19] is Francis's proverb on patience in times of trial or distress. Francis draws a connection between the notion

---

[18] Francis of Assisi, "The Admonitions," XII, in *FAED* 1:133.
[19] Francis of Assisi, "The Admonitions," XIII, in *FAED* 1:133.

of peacemaker from the Sermon on the Mount (Mt 5:9) and the need for trust in God. Francis interprets the peacemaker as one who is patient, even in the face of the most extreme pain and suffering. There is also a strong connection between patience and humility. When tempted to protest situations that render us embarrassed or unappreciated, patience is the humble person's response, acting as God would and not as we would. Only through patience, encountering others where we find them and not where we would like them to be, can we make peace.

Millennials looking for meaning and purpose in life are wise to heed Francis's admonition on patience. It can be frustrating to navigate life in a world shattered by violence, hatred and human brokenness, but patience is a virtue intrinsically tied to both inward and outward peacemaking. Inward peacemaking is a needed action for the troubled soul, lost and confused by the challenges of our modern world. Millennials, having been raised in a fast-paced society, are desperately in need of inward peacemaking. Outward peacemaking is the *modus operandi* of healthy relationships. Recognizing our own needs and weaknesses allows us to act patiently with others and make peace in our world. Faced with the questions of purpose and meaning, Millennials who strive to live patiently with themselves and others make God's peace present to a world desperately in need of it.

Suzanne Mayer has written that Millennials look to a figure like Francis of Assisi and take to heart his example of Christian living because he represents a model of authenticity and truth.[20] Today's young adults, precisely as Digital Natives, are in need of solid models of Christian living that help point the way toward uncovering and engaging the "why" questions of spirituality. It is my hope that the reflections presented here might offer a preliminary introduction to the many ways Franciscan spirituality can serve the Millennial generation – the first of the Digital Natives – in their quest to better know God and themselves.

---

[20] Suzanne Mayer, "Merton and the Millennials," *Spiritual Life* 50 (Winter 2004): 238.

ST. FRANCIS AS SPIRITUAL ROLE MODEL FOR TODAY'S YOUNG ADULTS

They were both young adults when they gave religious life a try, if only 800 years apart.

Alexander La Point was 23-years-old, about the same age Francis of Assisi was when he first made the decision to change his life in 1206. Eight centuries later, during the anniversary year of the papal approval of St. Francis's way of life in 1209, La Point follows in the saint's footsteps by entering religious life with the Franciscan friars in 2009.

La Point, like St. Francis before him, had not always thought about religious life. Before going off to college, the Plattsburgh, NY, native says he did not go to church or take his faith very seriously. In 2003 he went to study mathematics and creative arts at Siena College, a small liberal arts college outside of Albany, NY, founded in 1937 by the Franciscans of Holy Name Province.

"During my time at Siena, the Franciscan tradition was made evident through the concept 'preach the Gospel, if necessary use words," La Point recalled. "It was in seeing the way the Friars behaved, engaging them in conversation, learning about Franciscan spirituality on my own, and eventually hearing the Friars preach and conduct church services, that I discovered the importance and beauty of the Franciscan tradition at Siena."

The lived example of St. Francis that La Point first encountered in college inspired him to consider what role God was playing in his life. "In my case the Franciscan tradition encouraged me to return to my faith, engage in conversation about the poor and underserved, eventually take part in a year of volunteer service and then begin formation as a friar," La Point said.

La Point, a Millennial, is not alone. The Millennial generation, those young women and men born after 1982, is the latest group to reach adulthood. The earliest members of this cohort began graduating from high school around the year 2000 (hence the term Millennial) and have since gained notoriety and attention as the first of them graduate from college, enter the workforce and start their own families.

Today's young adults see something inspiring in the life and spirituality of Francis of Assisi. In a survey conducted in Washington, DC, young adults were asked which people in all of Church history are the most inspiring to them. After a first-place tie between Mother Teresa and Pope John Paul II, St. Francis of Assisi emerged in next place.[1]

There is much about the life of St. Francis and the Franciscan tradition that inspires Millennials. We will look at three characteristics of the Franciscan tradition that seem to align well with what researchers and Millennials themselves are saying today's young adults are looking for.

Community, Solidarity, and Fraternity

One element that captures the emerging attitudes of the Millennial generation is the strong desire to be part of a community. In a way unique to this group of young adults, the Millennials have grown up in a time of increasing global-consciousness, easily accessible travel and nearly instant communication. With the advent of the Internet and other technologies, Millennials, from an early age, have been connected to others unceasingly. However, the hyper-connectedness of technology leaves many young adults with much to be desired.

Tara Dillon, 32, was the director of the "20s/30s Boston" young adult group at St. Anthony Shrine and Ministry Center, an urban Franciscan church located in the heart of the Downtown Crossing section of Boston. Dillon describes the group, which meets one or two times a month and is composed of about sixty men and women from a variety of professional and socio-economic backgrounds, as an opportunity for young Catholics

---

[1] D'Antonio et al., *American Catholics Today: New Realities of Their Faith and Their Church*, 151.

in their 20s and 30s to meet one another and learn more about their faith.

"The meetings have tended to focus on the social dimension of the gathering, but have been moving more and more towards 'enrichment,'" Dillon said. She sees the young adults of Boston "yearning for religious education."

But that is not all these young adults are looking for. Dillon sees members of the Millennial generation and those younger members of Generation X "looking for family" in the Church. "Many young adults are transplants from other cities and states; they are looking for a community atmosphere to share their faith," she added.

While Millennials have nearly unlimited opportunities to 'connect' with friends, family, and others through communication technology and media, they remain distanced from personal interaction with others by those same means. This phenomenon has influenced the way young adults view their encounters with others – especially with God and the Church – and might be the source of their desire to seek more authentic relationships.

The Franciscan tradition has long focused on the communal dimension of Christian life. The personal history St. Francis models and the subsequent Franciscan spiritual tradition emphasizes three modes of relating to others, creation, and God. This uniquely Franciscan way of viewing relationship includes a focus on community, a commitment to solidarity, and a life lived in fraternity.

Millennials hunger to be connected to something larger than themselves, a trait that has been highlighted by many generational researchers and one that serves as a connecting point for young adults seeking a spirituality that is not just about "me and God."

Additionally, the commitment to solidarity – standing with and advocating for the poor and marginalized – speaks to the hearts of young people. Millennials can see in Francis's conversion to live among the poor lepers a reflection of their own desire to work toward a world where each person's human dignity might be protected and celebrated in the human community.

Melissa Cidade, director of Pastoral Assistance Surveys and Services at the Center for Applied Research in the Apostolate (CARA) of Georgetown University, explains that the Franciscan emphasis on the global poor resonates with today's young adults. According to her research, Millennials are the generation most likely to "strongly agree" that the United States should spend more money to deliver medical care to victims of AIDS in other countries, that an equitable society can be achieved only if special attention is given to the needs of the poor, and that people in rich countries have an obligation to help those around the globe, not just people in their own communities. "Franciscans not only have a special charismatic responsibility to the poor, they also have a global presence which speaks to Millennials," Cidade added.

The climax of the Franciscan view of relationship is fraternity. Francis called all aspects of creation his brother or sister, transcending just human relationships to include all of God's loving work. In an era marked by ecological crises and global warming, the call to relate to all of creation in a deeper way is indeed appealing to a generation that has grown up witnessing the decline of the earth's health.

Profit or Prophet?

Eric Greenberg and Karl Weber, in their book *Generation We: How Millennial Youth Are Taking over America and Changing Our World Forever*, decided on the name "Generation We" to describe Millennials because they see this cohort as a "caring generation, one that appears ready to put the greater good ahead of individual rewards."[2] Even though contemporary society, marked by increased consumerism and economic greed, presents an image that at times normalizes self-centeredness and competition, there has been a noticeable enthusiasm for volunteer work and meaningful service among young adults.

Like many young adults today, La Point felt drawn to volunteer service after college. He knew that he wanted an experience that would continue what he had first come to know at Siena College. After exploring the possibilities, La Point committed to a year of service with FrancisCorps, a Franciscan lay volunteer service founded by the Conventual Franciscans of the Immaculate Conception Province in Syracuse, NY.

La Point said that, while there are a variety of volunteer organizations available to young adults to choose from, "the Franciscan spirituality that exists in a program like FrancisCorps makes the program more accessible to a young adult." He sees his experience as a Franciscan volunteer as both formative and challenging. "This spirituality is going to offer more [than other volunteer opportunities] in the way of community, guidance, and

---

[2] Greenberg and Weber, *Generation We*, 13.

faith."

Francis of Assisi, in his *Letter to the Entire Order*, concluded a reflection on the Eucharist and wrote, "Hold back nothing of yourselves for yourselves, that He who gives Himself totally to you may receive you totally."[3] We read here of the deep connection Francis makes between Christ's real presence and our need to empty ourselves in self-gift to God and others.

Francis's own life provides a helpful model for this way of living and conversion. We often forget that Francis was only in his early 20s when he began his way of life and started to receive the first brothers in community. He was a young adult who was at first captivated by the nascent materialistic culture he was so familiar with during the rise of the merchant class in Assisi. The son of a wealthy cloth broker, Francis aspired to riches and fame as his family's financial means increased.

Francis's first biographer, Thomas of Celano, wrote that after his conversion, "he who had once enjoyed scarlet robes now traveled about half-clothed."[4] Francis, who was once oriented toward business for fame and profit, was now living the life of service as a prophet.

Millennials, through exploring the writings and prayers of Francis, are challenged to ask themselves whether they are motivated to make profit or to live as a prophet. This is seen in the way young adults give of their time and service as long-term volunteers in programs like Franciscan Volunteer Ministries at St. Francis Inn in Philadelphia or FrancisCorps in Syracuse. The prophetic call to hold back nothing of oneself in today's economic environment provides a message of hope and value that market capitalism simply cannot deliver.

Looking for Welcome and Acceptance

The way Millennials practice their faith can look very different from those generations of Catholics that have gone before them. For many of the Millennial generation's elders, this characteristic has elicited both concern for today's young adults and skepticism about their commitment to their faith. One popular slogan frequently used to describe today's young adults is: they are "spiritual," but not "religious."

Cidade believes that statements like this do not accurately reflect the faith experience of Millennials. "I think the issue here is not that Millennials

---

[3] Francis of Assisi, "Letter to the Entire Order," 29, in *FAED* 1:118.

[4] Thomas of Celano, The Life of Saint Francis, VII:, in *FAED* 1:194.

are 'spiritual' or 'religious,' but rather that their spirituality 'looks different' than previous generations," she said.

CARA research suggests that Millennials report the highest participation in certain Lenten practices including abstaining from meat, receiving ashes on Ash Wednesday, 'giving up something other than meat,' and making extra positive efforts during Lent such as giving money to charity. However, Cidade points out that "one third (33 percent) report attending Mass 'rarely or never.'" Millennials are also "most likely to agree 'strongly' that one can be a good Catholic without going to Mass every Sunday."

These seemingly contradictory trends can confuse Church leaders and others. Cidade suggests that what the data tells us is that "Millennials are trying to figure out what is 'core' and what is 'peripheral' to their faith." What has often been the standard mark of a 'good Catholic,' that is attending Mass, no longer offers a satisfactory test of committed faith. That is not to suggest that Millennials want to 'do away with' Mass or find it of no value, but it should not be the only indicator of this generation's religiosity. Because of this shift, Millennials are looking for faith communities that welcome them in their journey of religious discovery and exploration, and accept them as they are at the moment.

One of the most memorable experiences in the life of Francis of Assisi was when he and a friar companion traveled past the crusaders in Egypt to meet with the Muslim Sultan Malek-al-Kamil during the height of the fifth crusade. St. Francis's encounter with the Sultan was marked not by wartime negotiations or efforts to establish a truce, but by a commitment to the Gospel instruction to "love your enemies and do good to those who hate you" (Luke 6:27).

His message was one of peace, not of violence or proselytizing. Other Christian missionaries had crossed the boundaries of battle, not to meet the Muslims where they were, but to 'convert' them. Those missionaries were all killed, but Francis and his companion were welcomed as friends.

The experience of encountering the Sultan changed Francis and led him to add a chapter to the Franciscan Rule that described the way in which the brothers were to engage with people of other faith traditions or those who had no belief at all. He wrote, "one way is not to engage in arguments or disputes, but to be subject to every human creature for God's sake and to acknowledge that they are Christians."[5] Francis expressed a

---

[5] Francis of Assisi, "The Earlier Rule" XVI:6, in *FAED* 1:74.

lived commitment to follow the example of Christ in welcoming all and meeting people where they are and not where he wanted them to be.

This dimension of the Franciscan tradition speaks to the heart of Millennials. Dillon knows that it is acceptance and welcome that draws many young adults to St. Anthony Shrine in Boston. "So many people come here, but don't understand the [friars'] habits, or Francis and Clare," she said. "They just see the welcome, hospitality and personalities of the friars and feel comfortable with them."

Like St. Francis with the Sultan, today's Franciscans live out a tradition that strives to accept people as they are and welcome them into a community of faith. This has left a positive impression on many Millennials. Dillon recalled one comment a young adult shared with her after speaking with a friar. She said, "that the priest at St. Anthony's seemed like he really cared and he didn't even know me."

La Point's experience echoes that of the Millennials in Boston. He sees the effect of the Franciscan tradition as an invitation to pass along "Franciscan hospitality" while working for others. "During the pivotal moment of development in a young adult's life, Siena College's Franciscan tradition can soften the heart of a student to be empathetic to the plight of those less privileged," he shared.

It is after being welcomed into the community that many young adults begin to practice their faith more regularly and share that experience of welcome and acceptance with others.

The Future and Franciscan Millennials

As Millennials seek guidance and inspiration in their spiritual journeys, the model of Francis of Assisi and the ensuing Franciscan spiritual tradition offer a rich resource. In many ways the Franciscan tradition is infectious, which perhaps explains its popularity and longevity over eight centuries.

Dillon, in addition to being the program director of "20s/30s Boston," is also a religion teacher and chair of the theology department at Archbishop Williams High School in Braintree, MA. She, like those polled in the Washington, DC, study, has two heroes: Pope John Paul II and Francis of Assisi. "All of my students know that. I have quotes all over my classroom from both of them," Dillon said. "Whenever I talk about Francis, the students always say 'he's one of your heroes."

When asked what about St. Francis makes him a hero, she said, "I try to live his example 'to preach the Gospel at all times and if necessary use words.'" Dillon sees Gospel living as important but also adds that Francis's example of simple living, although a challenge, is something she strives to follow and model for her high school students. As Millennials experience, embrace, and pass on the Franciscan tradition to those who follow them – like Dillon to her high school students – the spirituality of the saint from Assisi continues to live on, inspiring others for another eight centuries.

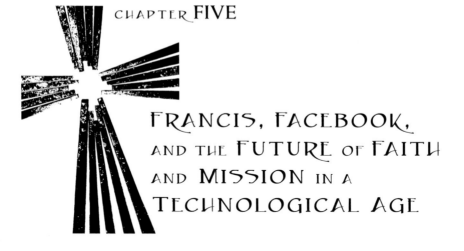

FRANCIS, FACEBOOK, AND THE FUTURE OF FAITH AND MISSION IN A TECHNOLOGICAL AGE

On September 4, 2011, the *New York Times* ran an article that bore the title, "Facebook Page for Jesus, With Highly Active Fans."[1] The story focused on the hobby of a North-Carolina doctor who was the son of a southern preacher. Having begun using Facebook in 2009 to promote his diet book and online diet business, Aaron Tabor, who is 41-years-old, decided to create a Facebook page titled "Jesus Daily" (a title that is now trademarked) through which Tabor "draws on the words of Jesus and posts them four or five times a day." What captured the attention of the *Times* was that in recent months "more people have 'Liked,' commented, and shared content on the Jesus Daily than on any other Facebook page, including Justin Bieber's page."[2]

On one hand, it is not all that surprising that a webpage dedicated to Jesus Christ could boast of more than eight million "fans," given that Christianity is, for the time being at least, still the largest religion on the planet. Yet, on the other hand, we are left wondering what the short and long-term implications of new social media might be for religion in the twenty-first century. In the same article the *Times* makes a similar observation.

---

[1] Jennifer Preston, "Facebook Page for Jesus, with Highly Active Fans," *New York Times* (September 4, 2011).

[2] Data provided by AllFacebook.com as cited in Preston, "Facebook Page for Jesus."

> Facebook and other social media tools have changed the way
> people communicate, work, find each other and fall in love.
> While it's too early to say that social media have transformed the
> way people practice religion, the number of people discussing
> faith on Facebook has significantly increased in the last year,
> according to company officials.[3]

It seems that nearly everyone can agree that almost every aspect of our lives
has been impacted in one form or another by technology in this time that I
will refer to as the digital age. It also seems safe to say that technology has
inexorably impacted the way we think about and practice our faith. While
there is much to be said about how technology is impacting various world
religions, and even Christianity in its broadest sense, I am interested today
in exploring some of the ways the Franciscan tradition might engage or be
attentive to the shifting social, emotional, and spiritual contexts of this age.

Among the many ways such a consideration might proceed, I propose
taking a look at three areas of Franciscan spirituality and mission in light
of our technologically hegemonic era, attempting along the way to hold
together both the centuries-old tradition of the Franciscan movement
inaugurated with Francis and Clare of Assisi in the early thirteenth century
and the immediate reality of our contemporary experience, respecting both
the positive and negative dimensions present within such a matrix. The
three areas include (a) our evangelical and missionary vocation, (b) our
tradition's constitutive renunciation of power, and (c) the centrality of the
Incarnation and blessing of embodiment in our spirituality. Coincidentally,
these three thematic foci also represent three very different engagements
between the Franciscan tradition and contemporary culture. The first is
what I would call a positive exhortation, the second is a cautionary tale,
and the third is a challenge to the Christian and broader communities
concerning technology from a Franciscan perspective. This chapter will,
therefore, not be an explicit endorsement, nor will it be a condemnation
of new social media, the latest technology, or anything of the sort. On
the contrary, like so much of the Catholic Christian tradition, I believe
the wisdom of the Franciscan movement offers us a nuanced "both/and"
approach to authentically living out our spirituality and following our
mission in a digital age.

---

[3] Preston, "Facebook Page for Jesus."

The Franciscan Evangelical and Missionary Vocation

"And after the Lord gave me some brothers, no one showed me what I had to do, but the Most High Himself revealed to me that I should live according to the pattern of the Holy Gospel," says Francis of Assisi in his *Testament*, written near the end of his life while looking back over his experience of living in this world.[4] At the heart of the Franciscan way of being in the world stands this simple summary statement: *Franciscan* life is *Gospel* life. So central is this evangelical quality of living in the world that the *Rule*, or official way of life, of the Order of Friars Minor begins with this same description, stating rather succinctly that "the Rule and Life of the Lesser Brothers is this: to observe the Holy Gospel of Our Lord Jesus Christ by living in obedience, without anything of one's own, and in chastity."[5] The Franciscan First Order, or friars minor, is not unique among the manifold branches of the Franciscan family in this regard, for each part of the broader community – religious and secular, male and female – includes this Gospel or evangelical imperative as the starting point for its way of living in the world. The second part is an elucidation of this general evangelical vocation, more clearly expressing how the given branch of the Franciscan family is to live the Gospel. For the friars this means professing the three evangelical counsels or vows.

In looking at the foundation of the Franciscan movement, we have to remember that Francis of Assisi had no intention of creating a religious community. His spiritual experience was very much a matter of individual conversion, a change of life that reflected what was happening to him personally. Franciscan scholar Regis Armstrong has often remarked that what Francis was seeking in his particular way of living in the world stemmed from his baptismal vocation, the call that all Christians receive by virtue of entering into the Body of Christ through the Sacraments of initiation.[6] Francis was interested, first and foremost, in how to live rightly in this life, which meant striving to follow more authentically Jesus's instruction in the Gospel. What quickly happened, however, was that others witnessed this change in the life and attitude of this young man from Assisi. They, too, "wanted in" and began approaching Francis for advice and to inquire about the possibility of joining him to pursue a similar course of Gospel life. It

---

[4] Francis of Assisi, "The Testament," 14, in *FAED* 1:125.
[5] Francis of Assisi, "The Later Rule" I:1, in *FAED* 1:100.
[6] Regis Armstrong and Ingrid Peterson, *The Franciscan Tradition*, Spirituality in History Series (Collegeville, MN: The Liturgical Press, 2010), xi.

was then, confronted with an unexpected "change in plans," that Francis appears to have first realized the need to organize some sort of description of the way of life of this new band of penitents.

Everything that is used to describe this particular way of living in the world that would come to be known as Franciscan is predicated on, or refers back to, *observing the Holy Gospel.* Franciscan scholar Michael Blastic explains that, in the original Latin, the word *observare* bears the sense of contemplation or gazing upon, and not to observe as one might conceive the verb in a juridical sense (e.g., "observe the letter of the law").[7] A Franciscan's life, therefore, is to be marked by continual contemplation, reflection, and emulation of the Gospel. The way of life is not about particular tasks, responsibilities, duties or rules (although they certainly exist and rightly so), but about the style of living in whatever context one finds him or herself.

Very early on in the newly emerging Franciscan movement there was a desire on the part of some of the brothers to move beyond the geographical confines of their community near Assisi, Italy, to other parts of the known world. This, in a sense, mirrored Francis's own lived example of transcending the interpersonal and cultural confines of his society and class. One of the most startling aspects of Francis's early conversion story was his sudden willingness to embrace the outcast and marginalized, often times depicted as lepers. Such was also the case later in life when Francis and a companion crossed the threshold of the Muslim world to peaceably engage the Sultan in prayerful, constructive, and fraternal dialogue at a time when the Western Christian world was at war with the Muslims. Whether it was a more explicit rendering of the Gospel imperative to "go out to all the nations" (Matthew 28) that Francis sought to live out or simply a result of the freedom that comes with openness to total-life transformation that arises from a commitment to live a radically evangelical life, Francis and his brothers often traversed the borders of lands, religions, cultures in order to establish and support relationships in new territories.

This is what we might call the missionary vocation of the Franciscan way of life. Emerging from a commitment to follow in "the teaching and footprints of Jesus Christ," this is a disposition that orients the believer

---

[7] Michael Blastic, *A Study of the Rule of 1223: History, Exegesis and Reflection* (New York: Holy Name Province, 2008), 16.

outward and toward others as opposed to inward and focused on the self.[8] Like Jesus in the Gospels, Francis saw an inherent value in not acquiring the security and comfort afforded by the appropriation of property, resources, and status. Made emblematic in his renunciation of his father's wealth and social position, Francis rejected the structures and system that defined relationship in his day, which elevated certain families to nobility and wealth, while subjugating others to marginalized and powerless statuses of poverty and social dislocation.

The Franciscan historian Dominic Monti has described this beginning of the movement of Francis and the early brothers as the concrete expression of their desire to "dwell physically apart from 'the world,' in a remote, abandoned place on the edge of settled Assisi," a geographic location that externally illustrated what the friars sought to live spiritually as those committed to a life of solidarity among the disenfranchised of their day.[9] Monti continues:

> Instead of accepting the society driven by the quest for power and wealth in which they had been born and bred, the brothers deliberately chose to "follow the humility and poverty of our Lord, Jesus Christ. This was the only way they felt they could escape the vicious circle in which their contemporaries were caught and which prevented them from opening their hearts to God and each other.[10]

Thus began the paradigmatic expression of ministry and lifestyle that would become characteristic of the Franciscan tradition. The friars were always and everywhere committed to standing at the margins of society in order to enter into relationship with those for whom ordinary means of social interaction was prevented, forbidden, or abridged.

The friars saw in the call to live the *vita evangelica* a mandate that compelled them to missionary activity. It is important to recall that, despite the very real concerns and ill effects of the history of colonialization in our world, the term mission finds its origin in the ordered and intentional "sending forth" of a person or community for a particular political, religious,

---

[8] See Francis of Assisi, "The Earlier Rule" I:1, in *FAED* 1:63-64
[9] Dominic Monti, *Francis and His Brothers: A Popular History of the Franciscan Friars* (Cincinnati: St. Anthony Messenger Press, 2008), 19.
[10] Monti, *Francis and His Brothers*, 20.

or social goal. The Gospel, as it were, was that which sent the Friars Minor forth into the world to serve the Church, which is the Body of Christ, in a particular way.

The *modus operandi* of the brothers was always that of solidarity. Elsewhere I have written about some of the constitutive characteristics of what we might call "Franciscan ministry," among which is counted "humble service."[11]

> This spirit of humility acts as the foundation for all subsequent characteristics that compose a Franciscan approach to ministry. Francis was less concerned about *what* someone did in the world than about *how* someone did it. Here we see the saint's admiration for the humility of Christ emerge as part of the centerpiece of his spirituality; to be a Franciscan is to live the Gospel by following in the footprints of Jesus Christ. Michael Blastic summarized this well when he wrote, "As Jesus turned toward those around him, so Francis and Clare in contemplation and compassion incarnate the praxis of Jesus as they follow him in their world by turning to those around them." From the Incarnation and birth to death on the Cross, Jesus's life served as Francis's model for humble service.[12]

This prioritization of humility in ministry and living in the world allowed Francis and his brothers to interact with all sorts of people just as Christ had. The Franciscans were not inhibited by the social stigmas of class and status, but engaged the poor and voiceless as well as the wealthy and powerful alike.

This also allowed them to move beyond the perceived borders and limitations of the ecclesiastical or ministerial norms of the day. It is no wonder that the Franciscans quickly became some of the most popular preachers and confessors of their day. Their willingness to incorporate contemporary or popular culture into the explication of the Christian faith, combined as it were with their stance of humility (which meant that no one was threatened by their undisclosed agendas or ambitions), led to a popularity and accessibility rarely seen before in Christian ministry.

---

[11] Daniel Horan, "A Franciscan Approach to Ministry," *Review for Religious* 68 (2009): 132-143. Also see chapter two of this book.

[12] Horan, "A Franciscan Approach to Ministry," 133-134.

In many of the same ways Franciscans of our own day continue to be popular preachers, retreat leaders, educators, and pastors. For better or worse, many of our parishes and ministerial centers are viewed as "destination churches," for which many people are willing to travel some distances to participate in the life of the faith community. This is, in several ways, a contemporary parochial and pastoral iteration of what was experienced by those first friars early on. It is not at all unusual for Franciscans to be associated with innovative and novel ministries. Whether it takes the form of interreligious dialogue (one thinks of the longstanding Franciscan presence in the Holy Land), direct service to the poor and marginalized (one thinks of some of the first HIV/AIDS ministries in the 1980s), missionary work abroad (lest we forget the Franciscan presence among the Columbian exploration campaigns and elsewhere), and the like. It only seems fitting that, as the friars have for centuries embraced the challenge and joy of serving the Church and world in new frontiers, the Franciscans might be inspired to be on the frontline of the latest territory in need of pastoral care and evangelical engagement: the Internet.

In some ways the Internet, and all the new social media it has spawned, is the great equalizer of our history. Although nothing in this life is entirely egalitarian, the World Wide Web has revolutionized the manner in which information is accessed, communication is carried out and business is transacted. Where once most people were subject to more arcane structures of social interaction, limitations on access to news information, restrictions on communication and relegation to the realm of the voiceless in a society where the powerful few were heard, now anyone with access to a computer and an Internet connection can conceivably engage in public and constructive discourse previously unimaginable. I think that it is was said best by the advertising industry's standard publication, *Ad Week*, in a recent article about new social media and high fashion: "Digital is democratizing; it's about accessibility. The brand image for high-end fashion is all about inaccessibility: keep the masses out so that the people who can afford to buy their way in feel they're exceptional."[13] The categories of the *maiores* and *minores* of the Internet, if such adjudication is even possible in such a milieu, have radically changed. The general setting of the technological context seems easily compatible with the ministerial disposition of the Franciscan tradition. There is something to be said for the systemic

---

[13] John Ortved, "Is Digital Killing the Luxury Brand?" *Ad Week* 52 (September 12, 2011): 56.

structures of injustice that continue to exist in the analog world, issues that still require addressing. The landscape of pastoral ministry has shifted in such a way that we cannot simply ignore the emergent structures of cultural and interpersonal engagement made available through the ubiquity of technology, particularly as it is manifested in new social media.

Beyond the potential for increased equity brought about by technology in the form of the Internet with all its subsidiary realities, we must also recognize the importance that the identification of a new territory presents to the Christian world. Both Pope Benedict XVI and the United States bishops have spoken about the need to "evangelize the Internet," by bringing the Gospel in explicit and implicit ways to this "new world."

In his address on the occasion of the 44th World Communications Day, Pope Benedict XVI spoke of what he calls "the important and sensitive pastoral area of digital communications," through which people can "discover new possibilities for carrying out their ministry *to* and *for* the Word of God."[14] Benedict XVI continues, emphasizing the ministerial imperative present in this new and challenging landscape:

Responding adequately to this challenge amid today's cultural shifts, to which young people are especially sensitive, necessarily involves using new communications technologies. The world of digital communication, with its almost limitless expressive capacity, makes us appreciate all the more Saint Paul's exclamation: "Woe to me if I do not preach the Gospel" (1 Cor 9:16). The increased availability of the new technologies demands greater responsibility on the part of those called to proclaim the Word, but it also requires them to become more focused, efficient and compelling in their efforts. Priests [and other ministers] stand at the threshold of a new era: as new technologies create deeper forms of relationship across greater distances, they are called to respond pastorally by putting the media ever more effectively at the service of the Word.[15]

The Pope is acutely aware of the role that technology plays in our contemporary world. No longer, he suggests, is the Church's engagement in new social media and other forms of digital communication an optional enterprise, but it has become a constitutive element of ministry to God's people in our age. From Benedict XVI's perspective, the Church's call to

---

[14]   Pope Benedict XVI, "The Priest and Pastoral Ministry in a Digital World: New Media at the Service of the Word," Vatican English trans. (Sunday 16 May 2010). [Available at http://www.vatican.va]

[15]   Pope Benedict XVI, "The Priest and Pastoral Ministry in a Digital World."

engage technology also bears a missionary character. "God's loving care for all people in Christ," the Pope writes, "must be expressed in the digital world not simply as an artifact from the past, or a learned theory, but as something concrete, present and engaging. Our pastoral presence in that world must thus serve to show our contemporaries, especially the many people who experience uncertainty and confusion, that God is near; that in Christ we all belong to one another."[16]

Through the use of technology, Christians are called to reach out to the world within this new environment to bring the Word of God into the digital public square. As the Pope says elsewhere, this is not an invitation for Christians to proselytize, but to respect the beliefs of so many throughout the world who are also present online, observing the sincere desire for enduring truth and the absolute among "people of every culture," "those who do not believe" and "the disheartened," as perhaps a first step of evangelization.[17]

Similarly, the United States Conference of Catholic Bishops (USCCB), in a number of formats and venues, has also addressed the necessary place technology now has in Christian outreach, ministry, and preaching today. In what I would characterize as one of the best addresses given by a Catholic bishop in recent history, Bishop Ronald Herzog of the Dioceses of Alexandria spoke to the American bishops during their annual fall meeting in 2010. He highlighted both the democratizing quality of new social media and the sense in which the Internet and other technology is a new territory, or what Pope Benedict XVI has termed a new and "digital continent."

Herzog began his remarks with a stern and direct admonition for his brother bishops: "I am here today to suggest that you should not allow yourselves to be fooled by its appearance. Social media is proving itself to be a force with which to be reckoned. If not, the church may be facing as great a challenge as that of the Protestant Reformation."[18] He quickly assures his fellow bishops that his comment is in no way hyperbolic, but a serious call for consideration. Herzog reflects on the challenge that the democratizing reality of the Internet poses for ministers in the Church.

---

[16] Pope Benedict XVI, "The Priest and Pastoral Ministry in a Digital World."
[17] Pope Benedict XVI, "The Priest and Pastoral Ministry in a Digital World."
[18] Ronald Herzog, "Social Media: Friend or Foe, Google or Hornswoggle?" an unpublished address delivered at the Fall 2010 USCCB annual meeting (November 15, 2010).

> One of the greatest challenges of this culture to the Catholic Church is its egalitarianism. Anyone can create a blog; everyone's opinion is valid. And if a question or contradiction is posted, the digital natives expect a response and something resembling a conversation. We can choose not to enter into that cultural mindset, but we do so at great peril to the Church's credibility and approachability in the minds of the natives, those who are growing up in this new culture. This is a new form of pastoral ministry. It may not be the platform we were seeking, but it is an opportunity of such magnitude that we should consider carefully the consequences of disregarding it.[19]

Herzog wisely draws attention to the shifting power dynamics ushered in by the technology of the digital age. No longer is power limited to the elite, the clergy, the wealthy and those who have maintained a hegemony of authority. Now a new generation is arising within a context that recognizes a newfound egalitarian platform from which all have a voice and the otherwise marginalized might dwell. The Church, Herzog implies, must reconceive its identity as something apart from other institutions and realities in order to transcend the boundaries built over centuries of exclusivity and membership, thereby entering into conversation and engagement with folks from all walks of life.

Additionally, Herzog, drawing on the comments of Pope Benedict XVI, notes that a new *location* has been discovered in the emergence of the Internet and social media. Herzog explains that "Pope Benedict XVI calls the world of social media a Digital Continent, with natives, immigrants, and even missionaries. He encourages Catholics, especially our priests, to approach this culture of 140 characters and virtual friendships as a great opportunity for evangelization. We are asked to respect the culture of these Twitterers and Facebookers, and to engage on their terms to bring Christ into their 'Brave new world.'"[20]

As already highlighted, the charismatic impulse for Franciscans to live among the marginalized and otherwise voiceless and to move beyond the ordinary boundaries of social, cultural, and religious demarcation suggest that what Pope Benedict XVI and Bishop Ronald Herzog are prophetically announcing is an intuitively recognizable opportunity for the Franciscan

---

[19] Herzog, "Social Media: Friend or Foe, Google or Hornswoggle?"
[20] Herzog, "Social Media: Friend or Foe, Google or Hornswoggle?"

family. What is already always at play in the heart of a tradition that began with a handful of the faithful following Francis's model for evangelical life aligns well with the need of the world and Church today. What might seem like a novel form of engagement, preaching, and ministry is, it would seem, a natural expression of what it means to live out the Franciscan way of life, the *vita evangelica*, in our contemporary world. Although such statements are often dismissed as too speculative or flippant, there appears to be some truth in the tradition that suggests if Francis of Assisi were alive today, one might very well find him on Facebook. Yet, because he is not, the responsibility is passed to us – his spiritual sons and daughters in faith – to preach by our deeds and proclaim the Word to the world, both in real time and online.[21]

Peaceable Franciscans and the Renouncement of Power

If the evangelical and missionary vocation of the Franciscan tradition compels contemporary Franciscan men and women to engage the culture of the digital era in ways that honor the egalitarian quality and missionary character of this new world, as I believe it does, then it represents something of a "green light" for technological ministry today. While there are clearly positive and necessary dimensions to this new ministerial landscape, there are also cautions that we must consider in light of the same Franciscan tradition. In other words, along with a "green light" one finds a "yellow light," urging careful consideration of the complex reality of the technological age, a reminder that discernment must always be taken seriously in any form of ministry and community. I believe that this "yellow light" appears in the Franciscan model of peaceable living arising from the renouncement of power.

In Francis's time the renouncement of power for which he is best known takes the form of rejecting the economic or monetary system of his day. Surely this remains an important element of the Franciscan disposition toward the world today. Franciscan men and women are, at least in part, supposed to live prophetically as people committed to speaking out against the systemically sinful nature of capitalism and unbridled consumption that continues to wreak havoc in our nation and world. Yet, there are additional ways in which Franciscans can continue to live out the

---

[21] This is, of course, an allusion to Francis's instruction to "Let all the brothers, however, preach by their deeds," found in Francis of Assisi, "The Earlier Rule" XVII:3, in *FAED* 1:74.

renouncement of power first modeled in the lived example of Francis. As it concerns technology and social media, it stems from the *how* a Franciscan is supposed to go about living in the digital world as opposed to the *why*, which was presented in the last section.

Among the manifold features of technology that might be classified as inherently good or even neutral presences in our world, there remains a shadow side to the widely popular and accessible tools of the Internet and social media. Identity manipulation, harassment, uncharitable discussion, libelous commenting, the option for anonymity and the like all coalesce to create a specter of disunity and fear online. While the Internet and social-media platforms provide the otherwise voiceless with an opportunity to speak and engage the world, these same realities provide the condition for the possibility of contentious disputes, hateful speech, and mean-spirited engagement with people of different cultures and those who hold different beliefs. This sort of digital environment mirrors the "real time" power games of cliques or insular and exclusive groups.

Who has the voice and who gets the attention are the primary foci of some Internet interlocutors. Whereas the ability to disagree disrespectfully with others is often not an option in "real time" due to the limitations of geography and other aspects of the analog world, the digital world can provide a vehicle for those with malevolent agendas and insidious interests. Many, including Pope Benedict XVI, have lamented the lack of civility in certain fora online.[22] Responding to concerns related to the all-too-often vitriolic discourse on so-called "Catholic blogs," the Pope called for men and women to adopt a "'Christian style presence' online that is responsible, honest and discreet."[23] This sense of a disrespectful environment present online is exacerbated by the option to hide behind pseudonyms, all the while circumventing the social (and even juridical) means of accountability upon which we have come to rely in the conventions of debate and discussion in the public square offline.

Francis of Assisi's way of living in the world – following in the footprints of Jesus Christ – is a model that offers an implicit, yet powerful, critique of a digital culture that can at times reflect the worst rather than the best of humanity. Time and again in Francis's writings we read of the Saint's

---

[22] See Nicole Winfield, "Pope Benedict XVI Weighs in on Social Media," *The Associated Press* (January 24, 2011).

[23] Winfield, "Pope Benedict XVI Weighs in on Social Media."

insistence that those who desire to live the Gospel and follow in his way of life are to be peacemakers in the world. Among the frequent references to peaceable relationship as a goal in Francis's writing is this rather direct admonition in Chapter Three of the *Later Rule*: "I counsel, admonish and exhort my brothers in the Lord Jesus Christ not to quarrel or argue or judge others when they go about in the world; but let them be meek, peaceful, modest, gentle, and humble, speaking courteously to everyone, as is becoming."[24] So central is this theme that Francis makes a concerted effort to incorporate peacemaking into the way of life of the brothers.

Elsewhere in the *Later Rule* Francis again highlights the way in which the brothers are to go about the world, drawing from the experience of the friars encountering each other to illustrate his point. Francis writes, "Wherever the brothers may be and meet one another, let them show that they are members of the same family."[25] It is this fraternal, familial notion of relationship that guides the way the Franciscans are to encounter each other and others in the world. One also finds the theme of peacemaking in Francis's undated series of conferences commonly referred to as the Admonitions. "Admonition XV" presents a succinct reiteration of this Franciscan theme: "Those people are truly peacemakers who, regardless of what they suffer in this world, preserve peace of spirit and body out of love of our Lord Jesus Christ."[26]

Yet, Francis's most powerful and explicit reference to peacemaking as a constitutive element of Gospel living comes in his famous *The Canticle of the Creatures*. In that masterful and renowned poem, Francis names different elements of the created order, always prefacing the respective part of creation with the familiar title "brother," "sister" or even "mother." It isn't until he gets close to the end of the text that he mentions human beings at all. Up until that point, Francis had named the ways in which the elements of creation praise God in and through what it is they are created to be, for example, Brother Sun through light and Brother Wind through weather. What is it that human beings are created to do? How is it that they are to praise God? Francis explains, "Praised be You, my Lord, through those who *give pardon for Your love*, and bear infirmity and tribulation. Blessed are those who *endure in peace* for by You, Most High,

---

[24] "The Later Rule" III:10-11, in *FAED* 1:102.
[25] "The Later Rule " VI:7, in *FAED* 1:103.
[26] Francis of Assisi, "The Admonitions" XV: 2, in *FAED* 1:134.

shall they be crowned."[27] Human beings live out their vocation as part of God's inherently good creation through exercising forgiveness and peace.

The French scholar Jacques Dalarun, in his magisterial study on the life and writings of Francis of Assisi and his refusal of power, summarizes what he sees as the initial trajectory and guiding principles of Francis's early movement, that which we have inherited today.

> In its beginnings, the Order that is called "Franciscan," or more accurately, "The order of Friars Minor," was a fraternity of mostly lay individuals who decided to do penance. The founder, in his concern to live "according to the form of the Holy Gospel," chose to establish in a rule of religious life the condition shared by the most powerless classes in the society of his time: destitution, precariousness, itinerancy, manual labor. He showed a loathing for all forms of power and went far beyond the scorn of the world found in the monastic and ascetic tradition. With Francis, there is less of a merely visible break with the world; at the heart of his life there is instead more intransigence toward any compromise with the world and its powers.[28]

There is in Dalarun's observation a key truth that must never be overlooked when examining the mission and spirituality of the Franciscan movement in the world in any given age. Francis never sought to retreat from or enter into a cloister apart from the world. Instead, the Franciscans were always to be deeply involved in the life and activity of the world, meeting all sorts of people where they were and living among and for them. This refusal to flee the quotidian world was a radical departure from most of the religious-community traditions of the day. So, too, was Francis's particular way of living in that world. The refusal to "play by the rules" of the world permitted Francis and those who would come after him to enter into relationship with people of all backgrounds, including the voiceless and marginalized of his day. His example offered a sense of hope and direction that sought to reflect the goodness of God revealed in Christ and presented in the Gospel.

---

[27] Francis of Assisi, "The Canticle of the Creatures," 10-22, in *FAED* 1:114.
[28] Jacques Dalarun, *Francis of Assisi and Power*, trans. Anne Bartol (St. Bonaventure, NY: Franciscan Institute Publications, 2007), 17.

For us in today's technological milieu, there is yet another iteration of Francis's wisdom, admonition, and example to embrace. As "lesser" brothers and sisters, we, too, are challenged to live up to our vocation as part of God's good creation. We are to be peacemakers in the world, which now includes the frequently contentious milieu of the Internet and across social-media platforms. We are not only called to dwell among the people of God online and bring our faith onto the "Digital Continent," but we are to do so in peace, while refusing to embrace the lure of power found in the competitive and ubiquitous land of technology. It is in this way that our engagement with technology can truly translate the wisdom of the Franciscan tradition, particularly in terms of mission and spirituality, into a modern language for a world desperately in need of hearing and receiving the Good News. We are commissioned, by virtue of our Baptism and our Franciscan heritage, to be ambassadors of peace and reconcilers of community in our own age and in our own ways. We are to refuse the temptation to quarrel and attack, to hide behind screen names created for anonymity and to diminish, in any way, the dignity of any human being.

It is a caution, but it is also a mandate: Franciscans are to go into the digital world bringing the Good News of Christ and the peace of reconcilers.

The Blessing of Embodiment

One of the most persistent challenges to authentic Christianity over the course of two millennia has been the appearance and reappearance of a way of thinking most popularly referred to as Manicheism, an unorthodox view of the human person and creation that advances a very dualistic worldview. Manicheism is named for the third-century figure that advanced a spirituality rooted in Neoplatonic-like influences that subordinated the created world, especially the reality of human physicality, to the world of ideas and the spiritual. A common, albeit imperfect, way to summarize a general Manichean disposition would be to say that the human soul is all that really matters, while the human body is merely an imperfect and temporal product of a bad demigod. This type of thinking, namely that which elevates the mind or soul over against the body or creation, has proven to be immensely popular throughout history. At various points over the centuries some form of this way of thinking generally appears to emerge. I believe that one of the most significant dangers of an uncritical appropriation of the products of our digital age, including the use of the

Internet and social-media platforms, is that we risk subordinating our physical embodiment to an over-emphasizes of the mental or spiritual dimensions of our reality.

At this point we have looked at two areas of the Franciscan tradition relevant to our contemporary situation: (a) the evangelical and missionary vocation as well as (b) the Franciscan call to be peacemakers who renounce the power structures of the world. They have been described as "green" and "yellow lights," respectively, for the first strikes me as a genuine and powerful call to engage technology, while the second offers us a way to approach this new landscape with caution. This last area focuses on a challenge that the Franciscan tradition presents to us as we move forward to pursue the first point (the "green light") with the sensitivity encouraged by the second point (the "yellow light"). We will spend just a short amount of time examining this challenge, if only because for some it might prove an understandably tenuous concern. Nevertheless, when looking over the Franciscan tradition for resources, direction, and guidance in our present age, this is something that captures the attention of those aware of the need for discernment in living the *vita evangelica* today.

Unlike several of the contemporaneous religious movements of the day, Francis's community of Lesser Brothers did not espouse this Manichean tendency to look down on the created world and the human body. Instead, as exhibited in Francis's most famous text, *The Canticle of the Creatures*, Francis intuitively recognizes the sacredness of all creation. The material world is not something to be disparaged or rejected, but embraced as part of the family of God's created cosmos. Francis's *modus operandi* was to view creation as intrinsically good and from which no escape is needed.

In the first program of life for the Franciscans, popularly called *The Earlier Rule*, Francis inserted a rather lengthy prayer that comes to us as chapter twenty-three. In this prayer, Francis opens his "prayer and thanksgiving" with a threefold hymn of thanks: first, for God in God's self; second, for all of creation; and third, for the Incarnation, through which Christ has redeemed and glorified us. The section on creation is important for, although it is brief, it reacts in a direct way against the Manichean strains of thinking in his time. "You have created everything spiritual *and corporeal* and, after making us in Your own image and likeness, You placed us in paradise."[29] While many religious movements were preaching against

---

[29] "The Earlier Rule " XXIII:1, in *FAED* 1:82.

the possibility that God would have created the corporeal world, Francis boldly reasserts this basic tenet of the faith.

Furthermore, Francis placed a tremendous emphasis on the significance of the Incarnation for creation in general and humanity in particular. This is a paradigmatic theme that those who will follow in Francis's footprints in centuries to come will develop further, great thinkers the like of St. Bonaventure and Blessed John Duns Scotus. Perhaps one of the most revealing passages from the early Franciscan sources about Francis's understanding of the centrality of the Incarnation is found in a collection of stories and remembrances of the early friars who knew Francis.

> For blessed Francis held the Nativity of the Lord in greater reverence than any other of the Lord's solemnities. For although the Lord may have accomplished our salvation in his other solemnities, nevertheless, once He was born to us, as blessed Francis would say, it was certain that we would be saved. On that day he wanted every Christian to rejoice in the Lord and, for love of Him who gave Himself to us, wished everyone to be cheerfully generous not only to the poor but also to the animals and birds.[30]

Francis knew that the Incarnation was the highest example of the reality that God created the entire cosmos – things *seen* and unseen – very good. In fact, so good was creation that God desired from all eternity to enter into Creation in a very particular and direct way. Franciscan theologians like John Duns Scotus express precisely this latent thought in Francis's own spiritual writing and worldview in a more substantially theological presentation.

While oftentimes the Passion, Death, and Resurrection of the Lord more readily captures the attention and imagination of Christians – such as what we witnessed in the blockbuster phenomenon of Mel Gibson's grotesque film, *The Passion of the Christ* (2004) – Francis challenges us to recall that the very condition for the possibility of the Resurrection, and therefore Salvation, occurs in the act of God becoming one like us through the Incarnation, through the Word becoming Flesh. There is a popular temptation to forget the *real* humanity of Jesus Christ and think of Him as simply "God in human clothing" (something that was indeed a

---

[30] *The Assisi Compilation*, 14, in *FAED* 2:130.

heresy condemned in the earliest centuries of the church), but instead the truth is that God took on our very weakness and suffered our lowliness as the Christological hymn in St. Paul's Letter to the Philippians proclaims: "He emptied himself, taking the form of a slave, being born in human likeness. And being found in human form, he humbled himself and became obedient to the point of death – even death on a cross" (Phil 2:7-8, NRSV). We must strive as best we can to remember the inherent goodness of our embodiment, its gifted state in the plan of God's creation.

This brings us to the topic at hand. While it seems like a concern reserved for the Stephen Spielberg movies about artificial intelligence or science fiction, the truth is that an overly dependent relationship on technology can promote a sense of disembodiment. Although such a stark experience of "losing one's self" in the digital world is hardly a everyday reality for most people, the condition of forgetfulness about what it means to be a fully integrated person is exacerbated by the omnipresence and multi-platform ubiquity of digital technology.

We see examples of this all the time and lament its unfortunate presence. From an initial glance around any given public space, office building, restaurant or even home, fewer people connect to each other in a "real-time" or physical way. Instead, it's a matter of routinely (to the point of obsessively) checking the BlackBerries, iPhones and Droids; it's going to the Internet, sending an email, or collectively watching the TV instead of engaging in dialogue and human communication; it's staying more and more in our heads instead of integrating our minds with our hearts and souls. Franciscan theologian Ilia Delio offers this reflection along similar lines: "The prevalence of anonymity marks our culture today; hence the desire for some people to be identified either by dress, tattoos, or sculptured hair. We are wired together on the Internet, on our Droids, iPhones, and video screens, but face to face we are like marble statues."[31] I often wonder if this is not exactly what contributes to the so-called "obesity epidemic" with North American youth today. So fixated have we become on our thoughts, trapped at times in our heads, that we neglect the corporeal dimension of our existence. That we are embodied is not accidental to who we are – to think so is to reinvent the Manichean problem of ages past and present. That we are embodied is how we were created by God.

---

[31] Ilia Delio, *Compassion: Living in the Spirit of St. Francis* (Cincinnati: St. Anthony Messenger Press, 2011), xiii.

There is perhaps more that can be said about this challenge to us in the digital age, but I think that simply naming the issue provides us with the opportunity to reflect individually and collectively on the ways in which we excel or fail to live as fully functioning and integrated human persons. What Francis and his followers provide us with is a challenge to the entirely passive embrace of technology. These things are not inherently bad, quite the contrary. Pope Benedict XVI, among others, has commented on the truly awesome reflection of human creativity in the emergence and development of technology. It is but one of the many iterations of our co-creative vocation as those created in God's image and likeness. But we must not let the tail wag the dog, thus allowing us to become enslaved by our digital creations, trapping us inside our own minds and, therefore, isolating us from one another. Francis makes it very clear that what it means to be human and to follow in the footprints of Christ is to be in authentically human relationship, such that we mirror what God has done for us in becoming embodied and entering into our world as one like us.

The Future of Faith and Mission in a Technological Age

So where does this leave us? Haven't I simply tossed out some equivocating views that leave us without a singular approach or perspective on what it means to be Franciscan in a digital age or understand the contributions the Franciscan tradition offers spiritual seekers today? Yes and no. Yes, there is no easy, one-shot response or answer to the difficult and novel questions that arise as a result of the shifting dynamics of this technologically hegemonic era. And, no, I think there is much to consider here by way of understanding a markedly Franciscan disposition when it comes to new technology and its multiple uses. Like Aristotle's understanding of virtue as being found between two vices, so too the spiritual tradition that we inherit some eight-hundred years after Francis first began the experiment is located between two opposing and extreme views. There are those on one side that claim technology and new social media are to be avoided at all costs, that they are problematic and useless to contemporary people of faith. There are also those on the other side that claim technology should be embraced wholesale, without all that much discernment or supplemental consideration. Both sides are incorrect.

The technology to which we have access today and use in all aspects of our lives provide a wonderful opportunity for women and men of faith to engage in many different enterprises. Yet, this same technology poses a potential threat to our spiritual lives and relationships, often serving as the location of online disputes, thoughtless electronic communication, and an increasingly disembodied outlook on life. The response that Francis offers us is one rooted in the both/and approach representative of so much of the Catholic Christian tradition. Technology and new social media are *both* good *and* bad. They are inherently open to whatever ends we direct their use.

To offer a little lighthearted illustration of what this might look like, I share here an example I used in an article I wrote in 2010 titled, "*Koinonia* and the Church in the Digital Age."

> If Jesus had been born in 1980 and began his public ministry in 2010, would he have "friended" the twelve apostles on Facebook instead of visiting the Sea of Galilee?… Had Jesus "friended" the Apostles on Facebook, he would have very likely send an "e-vite" to each one for an in-person gathering shortly thereafter.[32]

It's rather difficult to imagine the Last Supper taking place over Skype or Jesus's healing the sick through text message, and rightly so, for there are things that will never have a digital equivalent. But, I cannot help but wonder whether we might find Francis on Facebook had he been born in our lifetime and not nearly a millennium ago. If he did not personally join Facebook or use Twitter or build a profile on LinkedIn, then I imagine that those friars who might find themselves compelled to reach out to others and preach the Gospel online might ask for his blessing. In return, Francis might give his approval as he did to St. Anthony of Padua when the friar asked if he could teach the other friars theology – something that seemed contrary to Francis's original "game plan" of Gospel living. Francis's response might read something like this: "I am pleased that you want to be present on Facebook and through other social media providing that, as is contained in the Rule, you 'do not extinguish the Spirit of prayer and devotion' during this activity." And with that, a new age of mission and ministry would have begun.

---

[32] Daniel Horan, "*Koinonia* and the Church in the Digital Age," *Review for Religious* 69 (2010): 230-237.

CHAPTER SIX

A NEWBORN AND
BONAVENTURE'S
TREE OF LIFE AS
INCARNATIONAL
ENCOUNTERS

It had been a long time since I last held a newborn baby. To the best of my memory, my younger brother, born thirteen years after me, may have been the last newborn I held prior to the visit of my best friends from college. Andrew and Sarah, who at the time had recently celebrated their one-year-anniversary of marriage, became the proud parents of the cutest baby on Earth (at least in my opinion). I have had the great honor of seeing the love of these two friends grow and mature over many years. First, as Andrew's four-year college roommate and Sarah's close friend, I saw the beginning of a special and life-giving relationship. Later, as they professed their vows in marriage, I, Andrew's best man, witnessed the transformation of two lives made one. Finally, holding their seven-week-old baby in my arms, I encountered a love that refused to be contained in the hearts of two people, a love that needed to be shared through the gift of co-created life.

Vincent, born on Holy Thursday 2008, is nothing less than the very expression of love shared between his parents. This perfect little human, fragile and weak, beautiful and unique, is quite possibly the greatest sign of God's love that I have seen in a long time. The power of the experience of God's love made manifest in the creation of new life has been difficult for me to put into words.

Shortly after my friends returned home, I found myself reading

Bonaventure's *The Tree of Life*.[1] This relatively unknown work of the thirteenth century Franciscan saint and theologian has helped me to both articulate the awesome nature of the experience of being present to God's love in the life of a newborn child, and reflect on that experience as an incarnational encounter. In a real and powerful way, I was able to see Christ in baby Vincent.

The aim of this chapter is to suggest two avenues to consider encountering Christ in the routine of our daily lives with a uniquely Franciscan approach. While the nature of such a reflection makes it relevant at all times, it is especially pertinent each fall and winter as we approach the celebration of the Incarnation, first with the present-waiting of Advent followed by the joyous feast of Christmas. Here, I will identify two ways that we can encounter Christ. Next, we will look at the pride of place the Incarnation held in the spirituality of Francis of Assisi and how we might draw on that aspect of prayer today. Then, I will suggest that Bonaventure's *The Tree of Life*, with particular attention given to the first third of the text, might better guide us toward an encounter with Christ. Finally, we will examine the practical application of these two approaches as components of contemporary Franciscan spirituality that all can draw upon in their spiritual journeys.

Incarnational Encounters

How do we meet Christ? If we understand our contact with the Second Person of the Trinity as a real relationship, then we can look to other relationships in our lives to identify the possible approaches for encountering Christ. The saying, "a relationship is a two-way street," has great relevance for our examination of meeting Christ. The two streets denote mutual communication, commitment, and willed effort in supporting and contributing to a relationship. I suggest that there are two ways, or streets, modeled after the above-mentioned metaphor for relationships through which we can encounter the living Christ. The first street is the encounter that is our reception of a moment uninitiated by us. While we can say that *all* encounters with God are initiated by God, some experiences of the transcendent occur unexpectedly and spontaneously

---

[1] Bonaventure, *The Tree of Life*, in *Bonaventure: The Soul's Journey Into God, The Tree of Life, The Life of St. Francis*, trans. Ewert Cousins (Mahwah, NJ: Paulist Press, 1978), 119-175. Hereafter cited as *Tree of Life*.

within the context of ordinary life. The second street is the outward search to seek Christ. This can be understood as our conscious efforts of prayer and contemplation. Bonaventure, in his more famous work, will describe this street as "The Soul's Journey into God."

As a parent can attest, those transcendent moments of the Divine conveyed through the life of a newborn child are not something sought out deliberately. Such moments are real gifts. A newborn child's complete vulnerability and dependence on us can remind us of our vulnerability and dependence on God. Such an encounter with a newborn can also reveal something of the nature of God's love, much like my encounter with baby Vincent did. It is in this sense that we might experience an incarnational encounter through the presence of a newborn.

There appear to be two levels of mediation occurring in the incarnational encounter on this first street of the uninitiated encounter. The first level is the plain awe that accompanies the wonder and power of new life. It is amazing to consider a love strong enough to generate another person. The second level is the shift or progression from the awe of new life to contemplating God Incarnate. By this I mean that experiencing the vulnerability and dependence of a newborn child could lead one to reflect on the vulnerability and dependence of the newborn Christ. This is a powerfully prayerful meditation on the true humility of God. At a particular point in history, at a particular place on Earth, God became a human being and looked, acted, felt, and responded much like any baby boy born more than two thousand years after Him. In this way we can see Christ in every child and in every person because Christ comes to us in all.

The second street is our conscious search to find God. This is an effort launched by us to actively encounter Christ. It is here that Bonaventure's meditation, *The Tree of Life*, is extraordinarily helpful. Bonaventure provides a guide for those who engage in this outward quest for a connection with God. The desire to transcend the ordinary and ascend toward the Divine is the one prerequisite for such an encounter with Christ. Bonaventure recognizes the need for spiritual assistance on the path toward relationship with our Creator. For Bonaventure, humanity, due to the weight of sin and brokenness, is bent downward and unable to see the light of God above.[2] Through the grace of God we are drawn upward to see that light, and in

---

[2] See Ilia Delio, *The Humility of God: A Franciscan Perspective* (Cincinnati: St. Anthony Messenger Press, 2005), esp. 49-68.

that light, see the Other. Because of our brokenness and human frailty we are often in need of spiritual mentorship or assistance in recognizing the gift of God's grace already given to us. Bonaventure's *The Tree of Life* serves as an example of a prayerful guide to enter more deeply into the mystery of God.

Francis and the Humility of the Incarnation

Francis of Assisi is credited with the establishment of the Christmas crèche tradition. Thomas of Celano, Francis's most famous biographer, describes that first experience of Francis organizing the celebration of Christmas in a real-life stable complete with a manger and animals. He begins his recounting of that celebration with a description of Francis's spirit. He writes, "Indeed, so thoroughly did the humility of the Incarnation and the charity of the Passion occupy his memory that he scarcely wanted to think of anything else."[3] Not only was the proceeding encounter with the living Christ foremost on his mind, but the humility of God that led to the gift of the Incarnation so enthralled the saint that he is remembered to be preoccupied by the thought.

Francis is known to have recognized God in all of creation, but it is in the most marginalized and vulnerable of his time, namely the lepers, that he identified the Incarnate Word of God. However Celano tells us that the vulnerability and dependency of an infant also provided Francis a window into the experience of Christ. In reflecting on his desire to reenact the Christmas scene, Francis is recorded to have said, "I wish to enact the memory of the babe who was born in Bethlehem: to see as much as is possible with my own bodily eyes the discomfort of his infant needs, how he lay in a manger, and how, with an ox and an ass standing by, he rested on hay."[4] Here in Francis's reflection on the Christ child, we see part of the impetus that led to the establishment of a tradition that lives on today in the re-creation of the Bethlehem manger scene.

While his personal writings contain few explicit references to the infant Jesus – in fact his writings generally avoid discussing the earthly life of Jesus – there is a strong incarnational spirituality serving as an undercurrent to the thought, prayer, and praxis of Francis. Norbert Ngyuyen-Van-Khanh, in his seminal study on the role of Jesus Christ in the thought

---

[3] Thomas of Celano, *The Life of Saint Francis*, XXX:84 in *FAED* 1:254.
[4] Celano, *The Life of Saint Francis*, XXX:84, in *FAED* 1:255.

of Francis, observes that the frequency with which Francis discusses the Incarnation "proves to us that he would rather direct his gaze toward the loving condescension of God than linger on the details of the earthly life of the incarnate Word."[5] Francis does not get caught up in the details of the "Historical Jesus" as much as he desired to focus his thought and prayer on the humility of the Word-Made-Flesh. Perhaps it is this divesting of the need to "know the details" of the earthly Jesus that allows Francis to revel in the joy of the Incarnation and daily encounter Christ in such powerful ways.

It is in this way that we can interpret our incarnational encounters. Through the lens of Christ made present to us in the life of others, particularly the poor, marginalized, and vulnerable (like a newborn child), we can identify with Francis's experience of the Word-Made-Flesh in daily life. Those moments of transcendence that engage us in the random moments of the ordinary are the privileged experiences of God in our world, or the presence of the living Christ. The experience of seeing Christ in others is the result of openness to the power of God's spirit working in and through all people. It is the reorientation of one's view from the lofty and mighty to the simple and humble, even to the most despised and neglected among us. Francis's insight or ability to see Christ in others emerged from his gratitude for God's loving will to descend from the loftiness of absolutely transcendent Divinity to share in our humble and weak humanity.[6] Francis's invitation to us is to share in his awe for God's loving humility and presence on Earth. Here, among our brothers and sisters in Christ, we are able to experience God in a unique way. Our only requirement is the openness to the gift of the incarnational encounter.

The Tree of Life as a Guided Meditation

What makes *The Tree of Life* so special? Unlike some of Bonaventure's more famous works, his *Life of Saint Francis* or *The Soul's Journey Into God* for example, this short reflection is written in an incredibly engaging and interactive style. Bonaventure tends to be philosophical in most of his writing (he did hold a Chair in Theology at the University of Paris in the 1200s), but in *The Tree of Life* Bonaventure is more pastoral and

---

[5] Norbert Nguyen-Van-Khanh, *The Teacher of His Heart: Jesus Christ in the Thought and Writings of St. Francis* (St. Bonaventure, NY: Franciscan Institute Publications, 1994), 106.

[6] Nguyen-Van-Khanh, *The Teacher of His Heart*, 106.

inviting. Whereas Francis avoided reflecting on the historical Jesus as a source of prayer, Bonaventure compliments Francis's approach with an explicit prayer-guide modeled after the life of Jesus as we have it in scripture. He invites the reader to encounter the living Christ through what we have called the second "street," or the active journey outward. As the famed Bonaventure scholar Ewert Cousins observes, *The Tree of Life* is a meditation that resembles something of an interactive imaginary experience not unlike the Spiritual Exercises of Ignatius of Loyola. Cousins suggests that "Bonaventure's *The Tree of Life* is in many respects a forerunner of Ignatian meditation in both its subject matter and its techniques."[7] In this way we can appreciate the creative work of Bonaventure as the continuation of Francis's humble incarnational spirituality, and today draw on this thirteenth-century work as a prayerful guide to encountering Christ.

Bonaventure begins this meditation with an introduction to his method. The key word, a term repeated five times in the English translation of the prologue, is imagination. Bonaventure invites the reader to leave the realm of intellectual inquiry or rational investigation to embark on a journey of imagination that will better enable one to encounter Christ in the process. The structure of *The Tree of Life*, like most Bonaventurean works, is threefold. Constructed as an imaginary tree that contains twelve branches, each bearing a particular spiritual fruit, there are four branches (each with its respective fruit) or chapters in each of three sections. Following the prologue, Bonaventure presents the first section, "On the Mystery of His Origin," a collection of meditations on the birth and life of Jesus Christ. The second section of four chapters is titled, "On the Mystery of His Passion," which focuses on Christ's betrayal, passion and death. The last section is called, "On the Mystery of His Glorification," a series of reflections on the Resurrection, Ascension, and Glorification of Christ.

The entire work is aimed at providing the reader with a guide to deeper reflection and meditation on the life, death and resurrection of the Word-Made-Flesh. For Bonaventure, the Tree of Life is Christ. Each chapter – or "branch" – suggests a spiritual fruit that the reader should pray to receive while aspiring to emulate Christ, the exemplar and source of the fruit. Such fruits include piety, humility, patience, constancy, and the

---

[7] Ewert Cousins, "Introduction," in *Bonaventure: The Soul's Journey Into God, The Tree of Life, The Life of St. Francis*, 37.

like.[8] It is the hope of Bonaventure that, in addition to recognizing and encountering Christ, the reader might become a better Christian through the adoption of these virtues or spiritual fruits. The whole work is visceral and vivid. Each chapter begins with a descriptive reflection on the theme, heavily reflective of the scriptural source, and concludes with – what we might anachronistically call – a prayerful "guided meditation." He invites the reader to place herself into the life of Christ. While the whole text provides a rich landscape within which one can enter into the mystery of the life, death, and resurrection of Christ, we will look at the first section that focuses on His life with particular attention given to the first two branches or chapters that include His birth and young life.

The first branch, titled "His Distinguished Origin," invites the reader to reflect on the preexistence of Jesus and His relationship within the Trinity. After a brief introduction to the idea of the coeternal presence of the Son with the Father, Bonaventure draws the reader into the place of Mary and to imagine the experience of the annunciation and conception. Speaking directly to the reader, Bonaventure says:

> Oh, if you could feel in some way the quality and intensity of that fire sent from heaven, the refreshing coolness that accompanied it, the consolation it imparted; if you could realize the great exaltation of the Virgin mother, the ennobling of the human race, the condescension of the divine majesty; if you could go with your Lady into the mountainous region; if you could see the sweet embrace of the Virgin and the woman who had been sterile and hear the greeting in which the tiny servant recognized his Lord, the herald his Judge and the voice his Word, then I am sure … with the tiny prophet you would exalt, rejoice and adore the marvelous virginal conception![9]

Bonaventure leaves the realm of narrative description and takes on the task of spiritual guide. As if directing a play or writing a script, the reader is made to play a role in the unfolding of the story and encounter the Incarnate Christ; first as Mary did, next as her cousin Elizabeth did, followed by the infant John the Baptist, and finally as ourselves present to the mystery and sharing in the joy of those who were present to the newly conceived infant

---

[8] Cousins, "Introduction," 35.
[9] *Tree of Life*, 127-128.

Jesus.

At the end of this section, Bonaventure closes his reflection on the conception and birth of the Word-Made-Flesh with an invitation to enter into an intimate relationship with the newborn Christ. Like parents in awe of their newborn, gently caring for their child, Bonaventure leads us into the stable to meet the Incarnate Christ. He says, "Now, then, my soul, embrace that divine manger; press your lips upon and kiss the boy's feet."[10] The tone is strikingly different from most reflections on the Birth of the Lord. Bonaventure guides our meditative prayer toward a very real experience of an intimate connection with the newborn Christ.

In the second section, we are asked to walk and worship with the magi, to rejoice and celebrate with Anna and Simeon, and to flee and hide with the Holy Family in Egypt. Two of the most inspiring invitations are found as Bonaventure guides us toward Bethlehem with the magi and to hold the infant with Simeon. We are asked to imagine journeying from the East, as Bonaventure says:

> "Do not now turn away from the brilliance of that star in the east which guides you. Become a companion of the holy kings… adore, confess and praise this humble God lying in a manger."[11]

We are not asked to consider this experience as an event from the past. Rather, the tense is always present and the invitation always new. We are reminded that our journey is always toward the humble God who is our end and our reason for being. Like the magi, we walk the challenging path in hope of encountering the Incarnate Christ.

Later, Bonaventure calls us to enter into the experience of standing in the presence of Christ like Anna and Simeon. Bonaventure directs us to,

> Rejoice, then, with that blessed old man and the aged Anna; walk forth to meet the mother and Child. Let love overcome your bashfulness; let affection dispel your fear. Receive the Infant in your arms and say with the bride: I took hold of him and would not let him go.[12]

---

[10] *Tree of Life*, 129.
[11] *Tree of Life*, 130.
[12] *Tree of Life*, 131.

We are asked to stay close to the newborn, to celebrate the joy of His arrival, and to remain near to Him always. There is a real recognition that this process is not easy, that we need to let go of our fear and bashfulness and share in the love of Christ. We need to open our arms to hold Christ today like Anna and Simeon opened their arms to hold the newborn infant.

The Tree of Life continues in similar fashion. Bonaventure traces the earthly journey of the Word-Made-Flesh and invites us into that life each step of the way. When looking for a helpful guide for direction along the second street, or approach, toward an encounter with the Incarnate Christ, Bonaventure provides a path that has aided Christians on this journey for centuries and continues to be helpful today.

An Incarnational Spirituality of the Everyday

While anecdotal evidence suggests that contemporary people are interested in developing and strengthening their relationship to Jesus, there is little to show a renewed interest in the Incarnation as a focal point of modern spirituality. Rather, films like Mel Gibson's *The Passion of The Christ* (2004) depict a theology of atonement rather than a spirituality of incarnation, which emphasizes sin and guilt instead of focusing on the Love of God. There is certainly a place for prayerful meditation and reflection on the passion and death of the Lord, but it should be complemented by a recollection of Christ's entrance into our world and the reason, namely love, that he came as one like us.[13]

As twenty-first-century Christians who are often distracted by the trappings and noise of our modern world, we are aided in our search for Christ by the two-way-street metaphor. With an appreciation for the presence of God in the lives of our sisters and brothers, we can encounter Christ in each other, seeing God in the newborn child and in other vulnerable, weak, and marginalized people of society. With a seasoned guide like St. Bonaventure, we can follow the path of our imagination to meet Christ in our search. Both approaches broaden our spiritual horizons and pave avenues toward a prayerful experience of the Incarnate Christ today. We can understand these experiences as ordinary, everyday prayers; no special training is necessary. So, the next time you pick up a newborn

---

[13] For more on the Franciscan theological contribution to the necessity of the Incarnation, see Daniel Horan, "How Original Was Scotus on the Incarnation? Reconsidering the History of the Absolute Predestination of Christ in Light of Robert Grosseteste," *The Heythrop Journal* 52 (2011): 374-391. Also see chapter nine of this book.

child or a copy of *The Tree of Life*, be open to the presence of Christ in your life and God's Spirit working in the world.

CHAPTER SEVEN

THE
WISDOM of st. FRANCIS
for ALL CHRISTIANS

Listen, little poor ones called by the Lord, who have come together from many parts and provinces. Live always in truth, that you may die in obedience. Do not look at the life without, for that of the Spirit is better. I beg you out of great love, to use with discernment the alms the Lord gives you. Those weighed down by sickness and the others wearied because of them, all of you: bear it in peace. For you will sell this fatigue at a very high price and each one will be crowned queen in heaven with the Virgin Mary. *St. Francis of Assisi*[1]

This short passage from the writings of Francis of Assisi provides an array of instructions, emotions and edifying words upon which to reflect. The text's wealth surpasses its brevity and continues to be a living resource for the prayerful examination of our Christian lives. Such investigation also supplies the contemporary sisters and brothers of Francis with that spirit of hope that comes from the authentic embrace of the *vita evangelica*. The aim of this chapter is to provide a brief introduction to and then prayerfully examine the *Canticle of Exhortation for the Ladies of San Damiano*.[2] It is my

---

[1] Francis of Assisi, "The Canticle of Exhortation for the Ladies of San Damiano" 1-6, in *FAED* 1:115. Further citations of this source, "The Canticle of Exhortation," will be noted as CtExh followed by verse number.

[2] *Cantico Audite Poverelle*. For the sake of consistency with the English critical translation (see note above), I have chosen to adopt the title "The Canticle of Exhortation for the Ladies of San

hope that this reflection on the *Canticle of Exhortation* might serve to renew interest in the text as a source for contemporary Franciscan spirituality and function as a wellspring of prayerful inspiration for all Christians.

Unlike most of Francis's work that has been passed down to us in Latin, *The Canticle of Exhortation* shares the special status with his *The Canticle of the Creatures* of being written in the Umbrian dialect of the time.[3] While there continues to be some scholarly debate over the proper dating of the text, it is generally held that is was written in 1225 shortly after, or concurrently with, Francis's writing of the *Canticle of the Creatures*. In the *Assisi Compilation*, the early friars record that Francis composed this canticle while regaining his strength at San Damiano while ill.[4] It appears that Clare and the early Franciscan sisters were distressed at the severity of Francis's illness and in response to their concern, Francis sent this canticle. Regis Armstrong suggests that part of the beauty of this text lies in the other-centeredness Francis demonstrated in his desire to console and inspire his sisters. Armstrong notes that usually when one is severely ill it is easy to become introspective and concerned about one's own needs and wishes. Francis, on the other hand, composes two canticles that express his outward gaze to find God in the whole of creation and to remind his sisters in religion to do the same.[5]

There are two ways we can look at this text. There is the historical-critical approach that allows us to recall the context of those last months of Francis's life when he composed this canticle and there is the contemporary retrieval of its significance for us today. Commentaries on the context and meaning of the text for Clare and her sisters have already been written.[6] However, its contemporary relevance remains a depth unexplored. Francis continues to speak to us as he did to his sisters at San Damiano nearly eight centuries ago. Here we will examine the text by verse to illuminate its present-day application.

Damiano."

[3] See Francis of Assisi, "The Canticle of the Creatures," in *FAED* 1:113-114.

[4] See *The Assisi Compilation*, 85, in *FAED* 2:188-189.

[5] Regis Armstrong, ed., *Clare of Assisi: The Early Documents* (New York: New City Press, 2006), 393.

[6] See Armstrong, *Clare of Assisi*, 393; Armstrong et. al., *FAED* 1:115; and Regis Armstrong and Ignatius Brady, *Francis and Clare: The Complete Works* (New York: Paulist Press, 1986), 3-10 and 40. For more on the relationship between Francis and Clare see Ingrid Peterson, "Francis's Tenacious Lady," *Church History* 13 (1994): 33-37.

"Listen, little poor ones called by the Lord, who have come together from many parts and provinces."[7]

This introduction, originally addressed to Clare and her sisters, is also addressed to us. The Franciscan family has grown from Francis and a few brothers to include women and men from every direction on earth. As contemporary *fratres minores* and *poverelle* we are the inheritors of the simplicity and humility of Francis and Clare, bearing the title "little poor ones." In an age dominated by competitive capitalism and pervasive materialism, we are called to rise above the temptation to acquire earthly riches and power in order to walk in the footprints of Christ who, Himself, came as a poor and lowly human. It is this connection to Christ through the emulation of our Franciscan founders that we can read, "called by the Lord" as the affirmation of our Christian vocation.

Like those early women who left their homes and families and came from all over Italy to live the Franciscan life modeled by Clare and inspired by Francis, the Christian community is represented all over the world and continues to grow in number. While this portion of the address at first appears geographical, it also calls us to consider the states of life from which we emerge to follow Christ in the manner of Francis. It is from many locations, many social strata, and many degrees of spiritual peace that the Franciscan family and the broader Christian community are composed. Our challenge is to recognize the varied backgrounds and statuses of our sisters and brothers and accept them as once Christ accepted all those he encountered.

"Live always in truth, that you may die in obedience."[8]

As noted earlier, when Francis could be reasonably expected to focus on his impending death, he instead offers a note of concern to the sisters and, by extension, to us. We know that earlier in his life Francis was deeply troubled by the thought of death. Even more than the simple fear of the mystery that lies before all living things, Francis was concerned about himself and others dying in sin.[9] However, toward the end of his life,

---

[7] CtExh, 1, in *FAED* 1:115.

[8] CtExh 2, in *FAED* 1:115.

[9] Francis, on at least two occasions, writes polemical and sardonic reflections on death. See "Earlier Exhortation to the Brothers and Sisters of Penance" ("The First Version of the Letter to the Faithful") II: 14-18, in *FAED* 1:43-44; and "Later Admonition and Exhortation to the Brothers and Sisters of Penance" ("Second Version of the Letter to the Faithful"), 72-85, in *FAED* 1:50-51.

Francis was able to make peace with his fears and welcome death as his sister.[10] It is in this light that we interpret this verse.

Like Francis's message to his original audience, today we, too, hear a dispatch of eschatological hope in these words. Our world has witnessed much violence and many injustices, to the degree that our social environment has been called "a culture of death."[11] Working for justice and moving toward a culture of life, we are commissioned to dwell not on the violence of death around us, but to redirect our gaze toward the life that is within and among us. As Francis was not afraid to face death at the end of his life, so, too, we are encouraged to see death as a natural part of God's creation and welcome Sister Bodily Death. We are empowered to do this through a life lived in truth and obedience to the Gospel. From the time we enter this world until the time we leave it, our shared vocation is to follow in the footprints of Christ.

"Do not look at the life without, for that of the Spirit is better."[12]

The meaning of this verse appears to be twofold. Francis is originally writing to cloistered women who lived an "interior life" of the monastery. [13] In this way Francis might have been encouraging his sisters in their religious vocation, praising their particular state of life as superior to some alternate way of living. However, the theme of following the Spirit or living the life of the Spirit emerges with force. This reading could be taken as general encouragement for all Christians to forego the distraction of the material and passing world for those things of God, in order not to accumulate earthly riches, but to store up treasure in heaven.[14] If such an

---

[10] This of course is made manifest in "The Canticle of the Creatures" v. 12, in *FAED* 1:114. We read, "Praised be You, my Lord, through our Sister Bodily Death, from whom no one living can escape."

[11] John Paul II, *Evangelium Vitae* 12 (Vatican City: Libreria Editrice Vaticana, 1995).

[12] CtExh, 3, in *FAED* 1:115.

[13] It is important to note here that recent scholarship suggests that the community of Franciscans at San Damiano may not have been exclusively composed of cloistered women. Rather, it is posited that there was something resembling a contemporary "intentional community" made up of both Franciscan women and men engaged in a joint apostolate, living a religious life in common. For more see Michael Robson, *St. Francis of Assisi: The Legend and the Life* (New York: Continuum, 1999), 199 and following; Maria Pia Alberzoni, "Clare of Assisi and Women's Franciscanism," *Greyfriars Review* 17 (2004): 5-38; and Lezlie Knox, "Audacious Nuns: Institutionalizing the Franciscan Order of Saint Clare," *Church History* 69 (March 2000): 41-63.

[14] Matt 6:19-20.

exhortation was pertinent to Clare and her sisters in 1225, how much more relevant are these words today?

Our age is marked by increased globalization and commercialization.[15] Today those things of the "life without," money, power and status for example, are even more pervasive in all parts of our globe. Francis provides us with a succinct reminder of what should be our *forma vitae*: the life of the Spirit. Our task then is to constantly recall that our life should be the Gospel of Christ and not the propaganda of the world. When distracted by the trappings of the worldly life, we need to redirect our view to the Spirit.

"I beg you out of great love, to use with discernment the alms the Lord gives you."[16]

In both talent and treasure, we are exhorted to be good stewards of all gifts. The sisters are told that these gifts are from the Lord and should be used with discernment, or prayerful reflection. At a time when the Franciscan Orders were becoming more established and stable, the message to care for that with which the sisters and brothers had been entrusted was more necessary than in the early days of the Franciscan movement. The message pertains to Francis's contemporary sisters and brothers all the more.

The notion of discerned use or good stewardship extends from that which constitutes monetary acquisition to all that we are entrusted with by God. In addition to our material assets, we are challenged to exercise discernment and good stewardship with all of creation. The earth is one such gift or form of alms from the Lord. The fraternal worldview of Francis so exhibited in *The Canticle of the Creatures* should call our attention to the ecological crises of our day. Invoking this powerful fraternal worldview, Keith Warner suggests that what is needed in our time of ecological turmoil is the move from a model of stewardship to a model of "nature as family."[17]

---

[15] For more on this theme see *Theological Studies* 69 (June 2008) [a special volume containing essays on theology, ethics, and globalization]; Manfred Steger, *Globalization: A Very Short Introduction* (New York: Oxford University Press, 2003); Joseph Ratzinger and Jurgen Habermas, *Dialectics of Secularization: On Reason and Religion* (San Francisco: Ignatius Press, 2006); Greg Ott and Harold Netland, eds., *Globalizing Theology: Belief and Practice in an Era of World Christianity* (Grand Rapids: Baker Academic, 2006); and Charles Taylor, *A Secular Age* (Boston: Belknap/Harvard University Press, 2007).

[16] CtExh, 4, in *FAED* 1:115.

[17] Keith Warner, "Out of the Birdbath: Following the Patron Saint of Ecology," *The Cord* 48 (March/April 1998): 80. Also see the next chapter in this book for more on a Franciscan approach to

This process of shifting our paradigm from caretaker to family member is the next step in our journey toward seeing the world around us with the eyes of Christ. When we view ourselves and the rest of creation as intimately linked to God our Creator, we move closer toward the Franciscan ideal of *fraternitas* that Francis strove to live.

"Those weighed down by sickness and others wearied because of them, all of you: bear it in peace."[18]

Clare and the sisters were troubled by the illness and possibility of Francis's impending death. Here he encourages them to carry the cross of concern with the same peace with which he assures them he is facing his own illness. The message is not one of surrender nor is the tone despairing; rather, Francis hopes to remind his sisters (and perhaps himself) of that which he instructed in his *Earlier Rule*. Francis instructs those who come after him, whether sick or healthy, to thank God for everything and to pray for and desire to fulfill God's will.[19] His concern is that in the weakness of illness a brother or sister might be more preoccupied with his or her body than with his or her soul.

Our reflection has to do with the way we handle misfortune and illness in our lives and the lives of others. Do we over-exaggerate the troubles we encounter in this life and slip into despair? Do we become preoccupied with our own physical, economic, or social wellbeing to the point of neglecting those around us? Do we only trust in ourselves as the sole arbiter of our health and security? Or do we trust in the Lord and bear our infirmities with peace?

As Christian women and men, we recognize a future that is not limited to our present condition. While we should work to alleviate suffering in the world and in our own lives, its eradication is impossible. In light of the Gospel and Francis's instruction, we recall that God remains with us and works through us in ways we do not completely understand. It is by trusting in the Lord that we are able to bear all in peace.[20]

---

a theology of creation.

[18] CtExh, 5, in *FAED* 1:115.

[19] Francis of Assisi, "The Earlier Rule," X:3, in *FAED* 1:71.

[20] For a good reflection on Franciscan spirituality and bearing infirmity with peace see Robert Stewart, *Making Peace with Cancer: A Franciscan Journey* (New York: Paulist Press, 2001).

"For you will sell this fatigue at a very high price and each one will be crowned queen in heaven with the Virgin Mary."[21]

The author of the Letter to the Hebrews encourages us, that, "since we are surrounded by so great a cloud of witnesses, let us rid ourselves of every burden and sin that clings to us and persevere in running the race that lies before us."[22] As a runner I know first-hand that after a long race I am duly fatigued. In concluding his remarks to Clare and her sisters, Francis chose to describe the experience of Gospel living as a tiring venture, as something like a "Christian race" that results in "runners' fatigue." The message throughout this canticle remains consistently supportive of living the *vitae evangelica* in truth, in the Spirit, and in peace. Francis notes that in the end such a life is worth "a very high price." Written as he prepares for his own death, Francis anticipates joining the cloud of witnesses described by the author of Hebrews and encourages his sisters to look forward to their own arrival in heaven someday.

The language of this final verse might at first appear off-putting to a modern reader. Rarely today do we speak of being crowned queen (or king for that matter) in heaven. However, the choice of language and its implied imagery is consistent with Francis's earlier work. First we have a clearly feminine expression of eschatological reward. Although it appears exclusive, barring male readers from appreciating or participating in the message, we must remember Francis's previous use of traditionally feminine images in a broader context.[23] Consider his *A Rule for Hermitages*, where Francis instructs,

> Let those who wish to stay in hermitages in a religious way be three brothers or, at the most, four; let two of these be "the mother" and have two "sons" or at least one. Let the two who are "mothers" keep the life of Martha and the two "sons" the life of Mary."[24]

Here he is speaking of the friars in feminine terms that convey another

---

[21] CtExh, 6, in *FAED* 1:115.
[22] Hebrews 12:1.
[23] For an overview of the subject see Jacques Dalarun, *Francis of Assisi and the Feminine* (St. Bonaventure, NY: Franciscan Institute Publications, 2006).
[24] Francis of Assisi, "A Rule for Hermitages" 1-2, in *FAED* 1:61.

dimension of our shared humanity, one not encumbered by the politics of gendered expression.[25] In this way we can understand this concluding passage to include not only the Poor Clare sisters of the thirteenth century but also all women and men.

The reward of sharing in the crown of Mary has a second implication of a more timely nature. We can understand this idea as made manifest through our bearing the Word in our lives and actions. Like Mary who became pregnant with the Word Incarnate, so too we are called to echo the *Magnificat* and answer yes to becoming "pregnant" with the word of God. While Francis understood this concept well, this perspective is perhaps best understood in the life and spirituality of Clare of Assisi. She believed that by living the Gospel we partly share in Mary's title of *theotokos* (God-bearer) through, "enfleshing [Christ] in our own lives and laboring to bring him to birth in the lives of others."[26] Like Mary, after bearing Christ in the world our reward is to be found in heaven.

The Continued Relevance of Francis's Letter

Although the collection of letters, prayers and hagiographic material is nearly eight centuries old, the written corpus of Francis of Assisi continues to inspire people from all over the world. Through the retrieval of the texts' fundamental significance, we uncover the Franciscan spirit that can serve as a foundational spirituality for contemporary Christians. The *Canticle of Exhortation* is one such text. While originally destined to comfort and exhort Clare of Assisi and her fellow Franciscan sisters, it contains wisdom relevant for our age, too. As we go about our days in a modern world filled with competing distractions, we can benefit from six brief verses from this thirteenth-century Saint. Francis reminds our generation of the need to live the life of the Spirit, to endure suffering in peace, and to face death with the hope of eternal life.

---

[25] Again Francis makes an explicit reference to the brothers as "mothers" in the *Regula non bullata*. We read, "Let each one love and care for his brother as a mother loves and cares for her son" ("The Earlier Rule," IX:. 10, in *FAED* 1:71).

[26] Marie Beha, "Clare's Trinitarian Prayer," *The Cord* 48 (1998): 177.

PART II

FRANCISCAN SPIRITUALITY, THEOLOGY, AND INTELLECTUAL TRADITION

FROM STEWARDSHIP TO KINSHIP:

A Franciscan Understanding of Creation

While introducing the doctrine of creation to my college students in an introductory course in systematic theology, I asked the thirty young adults seated before me to think about the way they might treat something entrusted to their care (something like their on-campus student apartments) and something that has been passed on to them that they now own (something like their parents' or grandparents' house). Upon reflection, the students confessed that there is indeed a distinction in their attitude toward the two objects in each situation. The evidence is not simply hypothetical, but is empirically rooted in the statistical reports that colleges and universities generate every year that account for the destruction of property on campus and the subsequent repair or replacement costs. The students, rather casually, admitted that they feel less compelled to "take care" of something that was not "theirs."

This conversation provided a segue to a discussion about language and its role in shaping the way we view something like one's obligation or responsibility to care for this or that thing. The way we talk about our connection to creation impacts the way we treat creation. Provided that one is expected to care for something, as when a student is expected to care for the university property on loan to him or her for the academic year, how does one's understanding of the thing's relationship to another relate to the way the care is described?

Traditionally, the command of the Creator for human beings to care for the rest of creation in the book of Genesis has been interpreted in one of two ways: dominion or stewardship. The dominion model is particularly problematic for it elicits any number of dysfunctional and generally abusive types of relationship. Dominion is often associated with monarchical or tyrannical structures of power that necessarily subordinate one party to another, a description of control rather than mutuality. It is this mindset — of unaccountable sovereignty in human beings dealing with creation — that has given rise to twentieth-century critiques of Christianity for its ostensible responsibility in contemporary ecological disasters. Historians like Lynn White suggest that it is precisely the "Christian" (by which he means, "dominion") view of creation that has led to human beings plundering the earth, destroying habitats, and bringing about the extinction of thousands of species of plants and animals.[1] Are Christians solely responsible for these catastrophes? Certainly not, but the challenge raised suggests that Christians, in general, have not helped prevent such events nor have they offered a satisfactory alternative to their generally appropriated model of dominion, at least for a while.

More recently, certain Christians have become attuned to the inadequacy of the dominion model of the human-creation relationship, proposing instead that the command in Genesis be understood in terms of right stewardship. Comparatively, this is indeed a grammatical improvement in terms of reshaping the collective interpretation of humanity's role in creation. Diminished is the sense of sovereignty and monarchical authority over the rest of the economy of creation (*oikos*) and, instead, there is increased sensibility of the obligation human beings have to tend to non-human creation. Willis Jenkins summarizes the emergence of a stewardship model of creation within the Christian tradition well:

> The strategy of Christian stewardship frames environmental issues around faithful response to God's invitation and command. By appropriating the biblical trope of stewardship,

---

[1] See the now-famous essay, Lynn White, "The Historical Roots of Our Ecological Crisis," *Science* 155 (1967): 1203-1207. Some theologians have responded to the critique, suggesting that White's views are based on an untheologically-sophisticated reading of scripture and Christian history. However true that may be, the challenge remains pertinent and worthy of consideration. For more see Daniel Migliore, *Faith Seeking Understanding: An Introduction to Christian Theology*, 2nd ed. (Grand Rapids: Wm. B. Eerdmans, 2006), 93-94.

this strategy organizes concern for environmental problems around obligatory service to the Creator, who entrusts to humans measured responsibilities for creation. To specify the character of this earthkeeping trust, the strategy looks to biblical accounts of how God invites humans into relationship. Stewardship thus situates the specific call to care for the earth within a general divine call to faithful relationship.[2]

This perspective does seem to introduce an improvement over that of the dominion model in terms of the relational dimension of care for creation. It suggests that God invites us to relationship with God, while at the same time inviting us to care for God's creation partly in response to God's gratuitous invitation of love.

However, like a number of today's theologians, I have serious reservations about the efficacious dimensions of the stewardship model of creation.[3] Perhaps the most telling concern is that of the "obligatory service to the creator" that Jenkins rightly notes arises from this outlook on creation and human-divine relationship. There remains a relational vacuum in terms of the connection between humanity and the rest of creation that is overlooked in the explicit advocation of stewardship arising out of the human-divine relationship. To put it another way, one could see in this model of creation vestiges of the dilemma in which my undergraduate students find themselves concerning the stewardship of campus property. If humanity's obligation to care for creation is rooted in a response to God's command to be in relationship with God and not from some intrinsic connection humanity has to creation *in se*, then what is different about the obligation of students to care for their dormitories that arises out of their relationship to the college, the school's administration, their parents' expectations, and so on?

The stewardship model, while an improvement to the previous approach, continues to bear the disjointed sense of connectivity to creation that places humanity over and against the rest of creation as if to "lord" (or, perhaps more aptly, "landlord") over it, albeit in a more subtle fashion than is found in the dominion model. Stewards tend to something to

---

[2] Willis Jenkins, *Ecologies of Grace: Environmental Ethics and Christian Theology* (New York: Oxford University Press, 2008), 79.

[3] For an excellent collection of essays on this point, see *Environmental Stewardship*: Critical Perspectives, ed. R. J. Berry (London: T & T Clark, 2006).

which they generally have no inherent connection. Stewards, in popular parlance, are those employed to care for something, a property or inventory. Likewise, humanity is seen as obliged to tend to creation because of God's command, a deontological approach that lacks the necessary recognition of the intrinsic relationship humanity has with the rest of creation by virtue of precisely *being part of creation.*

It is here that the Franciscan tradition offers us a heuristic key. At the end of his essay criticizing the Judaic and Christian models of creation that have seemingly led to ecological crises, Lynn White suggests that Francis of Assisi provides us with a Christian model of creation that is in fact more acceptable, going so far as to name him "the patron saint for ecology" (something Pope John Paul II would make a reality on November 29, 1979).[4] While White's understanding of Francis was less-than substantial, his intuition was correct in that Francis and his followers provide us with a more authentically Christian and scripturally based model of creation. While never explicitly articulated as such, I believe that we can name the Franciscan approach one of kinship in place of dominion or stewardship. This is a recent theological development that has been explored by thinkers such as Elizabeth Johnson and Denis Edwards.[5] Edwards writes:

> We cannot treat any of our fellow creatures as if they exist
> without value. In spite of all the distinctions between us, we are
> family. In my view both kinship and the call "to till and keep"
> creation (Genesis 2:15) are fundamental in locating the human
> vocation within the wider creation before God. But the heart
> of ecological conversion is the invitation to see, feel and act in
> this kinship with creation.[6]

Adopting the theological moniker of kinship and exploring it in light of the Franciscan tradition, we will be able to further develop a comprehensive and Franciscan theological grammar of creation.

This chapter is divided into two parts. First, drawing on the systematic theological insight of some contemporary theologians, we will examine the

---

[4] White, "The Historical Roots of Our Ecological Crisis," 1207.

[5] See Elizabeth Johnson, *Women, Earth, and Creator Spirit* (New York: Paulist Press, 1993); and Denis Edwards, "Foreword," in *Care For Creation: A Franciscan Spirituality of the Earth*, by Ilia Delio, Keith Douglass Warner and Pamela Wood (Cincinnati: St. Anthony Messenger Press, 2008), 1-3.

[6] Edwards, "Foreword," 1.

theological significance of adopting a grammar of "kinship" in place of stewardship. At this point, it is generally agreed that the dominion (or what Johnson calls, the *king*ship) model of creation is entirely inadequate and wholly problematic. Such a view does not sustain an authentically scriptural conceptualization — from either the perspective of the Hebrew or Christian scriptures — and will, therefore, not be considered at length in this essay.

Second, following the work of three contemporary Franciscan thinkers — the late British friar Eric Doyle, the former friar Leonardo Boff, and the American friar and environmental scientist Keith Douglass Warner — we will look at how an expressly Franciscan view of kinship might be constructed. In this way, we might better uncover a Franciscan theological grammar of creation. What should become clear is that what we say and the way we say it about creation influences how we envision, relate to, and ultimately care for creation.

From Stewardship to Kinship

The renowned German systematic theologian Wolfhart Pannenberg made a telling observation about the state of creation theology when he wrote, "theology has to reckon with the fact that right up to our own day there is no general agreement about the Christian truth claim as concerns the understanding of the world as God's creation."[7] Unlike certain dogmatic or even lesser doctrinal claims asserted by Christianity, the doctrine of creation remains one of the more malleable and tentative of the tradition. Pannenberg, for one, believes that this is in part due to the reliance on science that any legitimate theology of creation must depend. Others, however, find the divergence among scriptural and historical sources to be a stumbling block to doctrinal clarity. In any event, the truth remains: the condition of myriad articulations of creation theology presents a problem, but it also presents an opportunity. The problem is clearly seen in the lack of a singular, authoritative approach to creation. But an opportunity is also latent in this situation, for there remains a space within which we might explore and better articulate a Christian theology of creation.

Some theologians have already responded to the opportunity, seeking to clarify a sustainable theological vision of creation. One such thinker is

---

[7] Wolfhart Pannenberg, *Systematic Theology*, vol. 2, trans. Geoffrey Bromiley (Grand Rapids: William B. Eerdmans, 1994), 59.

Elizabeth Johnson who, although she is perhaps best known for her early work in feminist theology, has made some significant contributions to the theology of creation. It should come as no surprise that for Johnson the issues of ecology and creation are closely tied to justice issues of subjugated populations, namely women and the poor of the world. Drawing on her work in feminist theology, Johnson critiques the traditional dominion view of creation – which she calls the "kingship" model to emphasize the coextensive embedded patriarchy and sovereignty – and suggests that such a view is both inherently dualistic and practically unjust.[8] Johnson does not stop there. In addition to critiquing the dominion perspective, she also raises serious concerns about the inadequacies of the stewardship model.

Granting that the stewardship model of creation is an improvement on the dominion model, Johnson suggests that it still lacks the necessary sense of interdependency found among all creation. Instead, it bears the dualistic and hierarchical distinctions – albeit in more subtle ways – found in the dominion model, and appears to offer a deontological motivation for human care for creation. In other words, it is primarily for "our purposes" or plainly selfish reasons that humans are moved to tend to the rest of creation, again as one over and against the rest of the created world.[9] What results is a subcontractor-like relationship among creation, humanity, and God that places human beings in the position of "God's landlord" or "building manager" for creation. The relationship between humanity and the rest of creation is seen as defined by explicitly distinct roles with an intrinsically uneven power structure.

Pannenberg's work further highlights the problems with a stewardship-based perspective of creation. He reminds us, citing New Testament scriptural evidence, that "the goal of *all creation*, not just humanity, is to share in the life of God."[10] If that is the case, as St. Paul seems to insist time and again in his epistolary, then there is an eschatological or salvation-related reason why stewardship lacks the necessary relational character to articulate an authentically Christian view of creation. Creation is not simply the rental property of humanity in which women and men inhabit and promise to take good care of according to the lease agreement between God and Noah (talk about a long-standing rent-stabilized property!), but

---

[8] Johnson, *Women, Earth, and Creator Spirit*, 10ff.
[9] Johnson, *Women, Earth, and Creator Spirit*, 30.
[10] Pannenberg, *Systematic Theology*, vol. 2, 136.

instead creation is, in some sense, humanity's partner in salvation. Its goal is intrinsically connected to ours. Our return to God takes place along with and is dependent upon creation. One reason this is the case is because human beings *are part of* creation. We are not disembodied souls "trapped" in a Platonic world of creatureliness awaiting our salvific release apart from the material world. No, we are creation as Mary Grey so poetically writes, "It follows that the challenge is to see both men and women as bodily-enspirited organisms, interdependent with plant and animal life yet with particular responsibilities towards the sustains of this life."[11]

Humanity's relationship with creation is best described as familial rather than viewed as contractual. The interdependence Grey describes stands at the heart of the Christian eschatological vision of creation. Johnson explains, "If separation is not the ideal but connection is; if dualism is not the ideal but the relational embrace of diversity is; if hierarchy is not the ideal but mutuality is; then the kinship model more closely approximates reality."[12] Our interconnectedness is not simply poetic or sentimental, instead it is a statement of the most profound truth affirmed as it were by both science and religion.

The scientific narrative of the emergence and history of the cosmos tells of the unifying origins of both humanity and the rest of the universe. As Johnson is fond of saying, we are literally made of the same space dust that the rest of creation – the earth, the stars, and so on – is made.[13] Our interconnectedness is as biological as it is theological. The air we breathe, the iron in our blood, the calcium in our bones, all of who we are materially is part of and originated out of some other part of God's creation. From the theological perspective, we see this interconnectedness play out in a number of ways. Scripturally, we find God's creation intimately connected to the actions of human suffering, flourishing and sinfulness (e.g., Hosea 4:2-3). We also see the inchoate cosmological perspective expressed scientifically in the wisdom tradition of the Book of Job (12:7-10) where we read that God cares and sustains *all* creation including humanity. We note the Hebrew prayers of the Psalms that time and again recall the familial relationship the rest of creation shares with humanity as God's beloved creation (e.g., Psalms 65, 135, 145, 147, 148 and *passim*). Yet, the most compelling scriptural

---

[11] Mary Grey, *Sacred Longings: Ecofeminist Theology and Globalization* (London: SCM Press, 2003), 133.

[12] Johnson, *Women, Earth, and Creator Spirit*, 30.

[13] Johnson, *Women, Earth, and Creator Spirit*, 37.

articulation of this kinship model is found in St. Paul's eschatology and theology of salvation, such as it appears, for example, in Romans 8: 20-23:

> For the creation was subjected to futility, not of its own will but by the will of the one who subjected it, in hope that the creation itself will be set free from the bondage to decay and will obtain the freedom of the glory of the children of God. We know that the whole creation has been groaning in labor pains until now; and not only the creation, but we ourselves, who have the first fruits of the Spirit, groan inwardly while we wait for adoption, the redemption of our bodies.

The delineation of human and nonhuman creation as found in the stewardship model, the former as caregiver and the latter as the dependent charge, is not present in a contemporary cosmological and theological reading of the universe and the Christian tradition.

In light of the ongoing discoveries of the manifold areas of scientific inquiry and the richer exploration of our biblical and theological tradition, we are left with a mandate to shed the previously appropriated notion of stewardship and adopt a more familial model of creation. It is in this sense that the notional implications of language, expressed most clearly in the intimate signification of "kinship," plays a role in our understanding of a theology of creation. Johnson summarizes why this approach, the use of "kinship" to articulate the reality of human-nonhuman creational interdependence is essential:

> Appreciating the deep patterns of affiliation in the cosmos, the kinship model knows that we are all connected. For all our distinctiveness, human beings are modes of being of the universe. Woven into our lives is the very fire from the stars and the genes from the sea creatures, and everyone, utterly everyone, is kin in the radiant tapestry of being. This relationship is not external or extrinsic to who we are, but wells up as the defining truth from our deepest being.[14]

This theological imperative, to recognize the truth in the intrinsic kinship of all creation, is found in the Franciscan spiritual and theological tradition.

---

[14] Johnson, *Women, Earth, and Creator Spirit*, 39.

It should come as no surprise to anyone at least vaguely familiar with the Franciscan movement that such identification with creation as kinship expresses well what St. Francis and his followers understood in fraternal terms.

The Franciscan View of Kinship with Creation

Francis of Assisi's understanding of a theology of creation was in no way systematic or scholarly. Ilia Delio, building on the work of earlier thinkers like Ewert Cousins, suggests that a good way to understand Francis's experience of creation was as a "nature mystic." Delio writes:

> A nature mystic is one whose mystical experiences involve an appreciation of creation as God's handiwork; nature manifests the divine. Francis's nature mysticism included a consciousness of God with the appropriate religious attitudes of awe and gratitude ... he took spontaneous joy in the material world, singing its praises like a troubadour poet. With a disarming sense of immediacy, he felt himself part of the family of creation.[15]

While not expressed in the scholastic categories of his day, the thought of Francis of Assisi as articulated in his own writings – prayers, rules of life, and letters – and in the writings of the early Franciscans about Francis reveals a theology of creation that is easily identifiable with the kinship model.

There is perhaps no more accessible example of this characteristic of Franciscan thought than that of Francis's *The Canticle of the Creatures*.[16] Eric Doyle explains: "As a prayer of praise to God the Creator, *The Canticle* is a sublime expression of the authentic Christian attitude to creation, which is to accept and love creatures as they are."[17] What makes Francis's attitude toward creation "authentically Christian," to borrow Doyle's phrase, is precisely this innate sensitivity to the universal kinship of all creation as experienced in the mystical and fraternal worldview of the *Poverello*. The

---

[15] Ilia Delio, *A Franciscan View of Creation: Learning to Live in a Sacramental World*, Franciscan Heritage Series, vol. 2 (St. Bonaventure, NY: Franciscan Institute Publications, 2003), 7.

[16] Francis of Assisi, "The Canticle of the Creatures," in *FAED* 1:113-114.

[17] Eric Doyle, "'The Canticle of Brother Sun' and the Value of Creation," in *Franciscan Theology of the Environment: An Introductory Reader*, ed. Dawn Nothwehr (Quincy, IL: Franciscan Press, 2002), 157-158.

brilliance of the canticle is multilayered, staged as it is in overlapping strata of increasing agency within creation.[18] All dimensions of the created world (with the exception of non-human animals) – planetary bodies, weather phenomena, elemental features of the earth, vegetation, human beings and death – are included in this hymnic reflection of the interrelationship of creation. Although non-human animals are not expressly included in this canticle, Francis's reverence for all creatures shines through in the more hagiographical sources and the earliest traditions of the Franciscan movement.

Doyle continues to explain well the place of the created order for Francis as it is seen in this famous hymn of praise.

> Nature for Francis was not just a reflection of human activity and reactions, because this would have been to destroy the unique value of other creatures. They are not mirrors of us, but like us, they reflect God. He began with equality: we are all created ... we are all brethren. Francis believed the doctrine of creation with his whole heart. It told him that the entire universe – the self and the total environment to which the self belongs (microcosm and macrocosm) – is the product of the highest creative power, the creativity of Transcendent Love.[19]

How does one come to this realization or reach this degree of understanding? Doyle insists that, "the mystical experience which gave birth to *The Canticle* was a creative encounter with reality."[20] To put it another way, through prayer and a deep appreciation of God's revelation in Scripture (as St. Bonaventure will later attribute this gift), Francis became prophetic in his ability to see the world as it really is – to truly see reality. This reality, this truth in creation, is God's loving act of bringing into and sustaining all things in existence.[21] Francis of Assisi did not need to be a professor of theology at the University of Paris to come to this conclusion, his inspired

---

[18] I have written on this subject elsewhere with regard to *The Canticle's* treatment of death. See Daniel Horan, "Embracing Sister Death: The Fraternal Worldview of Francis of Assisi as a Source for Christian Eschatological Hope," *The Other Journal* 14 (January 2009). Also see chapter ten in this book.

[19] Doyle, "'The Canticle of Brother Sun' and the Value of Creation," 158-159.

[20] Doyle, "'The Canticle of Brother Sun' and the Value of Creation," 159.

[21] For more see Daniel Horan, "Light and Love: Robert Grosseteste and John Duns Scotus on the How and Why of Creation," *The Cord* 57 (2007): 243-257.

worldview, shaped as it was by his total surrender to God's grace and Gospel life, allowed him to see this truth: all of creation is one family.

Keith Warner has written on this very subject. A Franciscan friar by religious profession and an environmental scientist by training, Warner asserts that Francis did indeed have an explicitly familial sense of creation, one that we can call a "kinship model" of creation. For Warner, this means three things for a Franciscan understanding of creation: it must celebrate relationship, it promotes courtesy, and it reflects a commitment to the practice of penance.[22] Warner explains what this might mean for Franciscans and those inspired by Francis's view of creation today.

> We can imitate him by being environmental peacemakers. Just as Francis built peace in the relationship between the bishop and mayor by singing *The Canticle of the Creatures*, we can bring reconciliation to the conflicts around us by practicing and promoting respect for the existence and well-being of others. By honoring both parties in a conflictual situation we invite others to adopt a stance of respect and to acknowledge the right of others to exist. Direct confrontation of personal and corporate greed can be ineffectual. I believe that by encouraging others to acknowledge, respect and enjoy the relationships they have with others, that greed can be replaced with courtesy, and this seems fully consistent with Francis'[s] approach.[23]

Becoming "environmental peacemakers" is indeed a novel way to approach our vocational call as brothers and sisters to creation. How is it that we advocate for the "least among us," particularly when the least among us includes the earth, endangered species, rainforests, or the ocean? Following the example of Francis's fraternal worldview, his kinship theology of creation, we might help to reconcile not just the broken relationships among the world's men and women, but we might also help to reconcile the broken relationship all of humanity shares with the rest of creation.

The renowned Brazilian theologian and former Franciscan friar

---

[22] Keith Douglas Warner, "Get Him Out of the Birdbath! What Does it Mean to Have a Patron Saint of Ecology?" in *Franciscan Theology of the Environment: An Introductory Reader*, ed. Dawn Nothwehr (Quincy, IL: Franciscan Press, 2002), 370. Also see Keith Douglas Warner, "Franciscan Environmental Ethics: Imagining Creation as a Community of Care," *Journal of the Society of Christian Ethics* 31 (2011): 143-160.
[23] Warner, "Get Him Out of the Birdbath!" 371.

Leonardo Boff has also observed this creational model of kinship in the thought and practice of Francis of Assisi. Boff goes so far as to suggest that, in opposition to other models of creation, Francis was in fact "the living embodiment of another paradigm, one of a spirit that acts in kinship, one that is filled with compassion and respect before each representative of the cosmic and planetary community."[24] Unlike some of the other Franciscan theologians and environmentalists, Boff offers what appears to be a more radical interpretation of Francis's worldview. Boff suggests that what Francis innately discovered was really an intuitive sense of classical paganism. The term paganism is indeed off-putting for it conjures images of heresy, polytheism, and non-Christian religiosity. However, Boff believes that throughout Christian history, the Church has (necessarily perhaps) had to struggle to define itself against traditionally pagan cultures. In an effort to maintain something resembling orthodox Christian faith in the face of paganistic heterodoxy, anything that hinted of pre-Christian pagan religion was effectively squashed. As a result, the previously ubiquitous notion of divinity found in all aspects of the cosmos, all of creation reflecting something beyond itself, was categorized under the genus of pagan and suppressed for fear of heterodoxy.

Leonardo Boff believes that Francis was, in some way, able to transcend the limitations of the hegemonic popular worldview of Christendom to see the sacred indwelling of creation around him. Boff explains:

> St. Francis brought this whole age of purgation to an end. Eyes recovered their innocence. Now one could contemplate God and the splendor of God's grace and glory in the extensive wealth of creation, which is the great sacrament of God and Christ. Intuitively and without any previous theological training, Francis reclaimed the truth of paganism: this world is not mute, not lifeless, not empty; it speaks and is full of movement, love, purpose, and beckonings from the Divinity. It can be the place for encountering God and God's spirit, through the world itself, its energies, its profusion of sound, color, and movement.[25]

Boff goes on to note that all of the biographies of Francis written after his

---

[24] Leonardo Boff, *Cry of the Earth, Cry of the Poor*, trans. Phillip Berryman (Maryknoll, NY: Orbis Books, 1997), 203-204.

[25] Boff, *Cry of the Earth, Cry of the Poor*, 205.

death, including those works by Bonaventure and Celano as well as *The Legend of the Three Companions, The Legend of Perugia, and The Mirror of Perfection*, portray Francis as having existed in a unique relationship with all creatures and the entire creation.

Francis's way of living in the world was one of intimate relationship in which Francis lived *with* the world and not above and against it as others so commonly do. Boff explains that for Francis nothing was simply available for human possession or consumption, but instead there exists only God's magisterial creation that is related to all other parts of creation in a divine interconnectedness. Boff puts this in another, more poetic way: "Everything makes up a grand symphony – and God is the conductor."[26]

To speak of a Franciscan view of creation that resembles the dominion or even stewardship models is not possible. Such an approach is trenchantly inauthentic, for the founder of the Franciscan movement and later the patron saint of ecology lived his life in a manner expressly counter to these outlooks. The plentitude of examples to illustrate the sense of kinship associated with Francis's engagement with all aspects of creation in his own writings and those later hagiographic works about Francis is too much to rehearse here. Following Doyle, Warner and Boff, as well as Francis himself, we can say with confidence that a Franciscan view of creation is inexorably a kinship model.

Living The Prophetic Call of the Franciscan View of Creation

There is a direct relationship between what we say about creation and how we treat creation. Our theological language should not be overlooked as an area worth examination during such times of environmental crisis. Lynn White's critique, more than half a century ago, continues to echo in the halls of churches, legislative chambers, and corporate boardrooms. The way in which certain professed Christians speak of creation, such that the language of dominance and stewardship reigns supreme, is reflected in the contemporary tragedies of strip mining, off-shore drilling, wars over oil, natural gas retrieval, animal and plant extinction, and global climate change.

The Franciscan tradition has something to offer the Christian Church, which is the Body of Christ, and the global human community

---

[26] Boff, *Cry of the Earth, Cry of the Poor*, 211.

by appropriating, living, and modeling a Franciscan kinship vision of creation. To speak about the earth and all of its inhabitants – humans and nonhumans alike – as one speaks of family is to make a concerted effort to refashion the popular image of the relationship between humanity and the rest of creation. In such an image, no longer are environmental tragedies simply the consequence of human dominance over creation, but instead they become cases of ecological domestic abuse. In such an image, no longer can we step back and watch the destruction of the earth from afar, but instead we must recognize that all life is interconnected and the death of a species or the destruction of a forest is also somehow a transgression that implicates all of us and from which we all suffer. In such an image, no longer is the earth simply our rental property or dorm room to be treated as if we were its stewards, but instead we must come to see creation for what it really is: the dwelling place of the Divine in and through and among us.

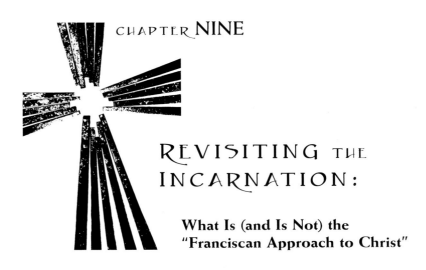

CHAPTER NINE

REVISITING THE INCARNATION:

What Is (and Is Not) the "Franciscan Approach to Christ"

Generalization and caricature are, in many ways, part and parcel of the history of theology. Because theological theses and various doctrines are difficult to grasp, in addition to being manifold, simplified versions are often drafted in order to more easily pass the faith along to subsequent generations and make complicated lines of thought more accessible. This is not to suggest that generalization and caricature are always bad. On the contrary, often times a simple glimpse is all that is needed or called for in a given context. If one is not a specialist in the particular theological field, it is doubtful that he or she would be bothered by a generalization that is more or less accurate, yet accessible. However, there is something to be said for clear *and* accurate overviews of doctrines that are at the same time accessible.

The Franciscan tradition is not exempt from the history of theological generalization and caricature. One of the most generalized themes in the Franciscan theological tradition is the so-called "Franciscan" view on the necessity of the Incarnation.[1] Given as an alternative to the standard

---

[1] Even some of the most notable writers on the Franciscan tradition have generalized the doctrine of the absolute predestination of Christ, often implying that it is a universally held position among Franciscan thinkers across many centuries. Other times, authors conflate the work of different Franciscan theologians, taking part of the thought of Bonaventure and Scotus (for example) and offering a hybrid position that is viewed as authentically "Franciscan." While each of these cases contains truths attributable to various Franciscan thinkers, the lack of nuanced clarification confuses

atonement-based model of the reason for the Incarnation, this "Franciscan Thesis" is presented as if it were (a) universally held by Franciscan thinkers, (b) finds its origin in the Franciscan intellectual tradition and/or (c) is based on the writings of Francis of Assisi. In this article I will show how these presuppositions are not completely accurate. The idea of a "Franciscan Thesis" about the necessity of the Incarnation is simply a generalization and caricature of a more nuanced and, as we shall see, not-necessarily-Franciscan argument. We will also see that there is an understandable source for the creation of this term, for major medieval Franciscan thinkers did play significant roles in the way this Christological approach has been passed down through the centuries.

The reason for this chapter is twofold. The first reason is the need to clarify a position that has been generalized by many Franciscans and non-Franciscans in recent years. While seemingly minor, if a not-so-accurate theological synthesis is passed along as such, it will eventually be taken to be accurate. The second reason is my conviction that those thinkers who have been overlooked or neglected by those positing a "Franciscan Thesis" deserve to be recognized for their contributions, originality, and role in the formation of the doctrine of the absolute predestination of Christ. In this way, it is my hope that this brief study helps the reader to better understand the history of this doctrine. The more we know about our theological tradition, the more we can appreciate the true gift such a tradition presents to the Church and the world. It is my hope that a more nuanced appreciation for the development of the doctrine of the absolute predestination of Christ to become incarnate might better inform our own theological and spiritual outlook, while also providing us with the resources to draw others into a less sin-centered perspective to embrace God's gratuitous gift of love.

This chapter is divided into five parts, each highlighting an aspect of the development of the doctrine of the absolute predestination of Christ. First we will look at what is generally held to be the standard position on the reason for the Incarnation. Next we will briefly examine what has often been referred to as the "Franciscan Thesis." In the third section we will

their respective approaches, which at times might actually be in conflict. For some recent examples of this see Kenan Osborne, *The Franciscan Intellectual Tradition: Tracing Its Origins and Identifying Its Central Components*, Franciscan Heritage Series vol. 1 (St. Bonaventure, NY: Franciscan Institute Publications, 2003), esp. 53-69; Delio, *The Humility of God*, esp. 49-65; and Ilia Delio, "Revisiting The Franciscan Doctrine of Christ," *Theological Studies* 64 (2003): 3-23.

explore the origins of this supralapsarian[2] argument in the work of Rupert of Deutz and Robert Grosseteste. In the fourth section we will briefly look at the writings of Francis to see what his views on the Incarnation were. Finally, I will close with some thoughts on how this understanding of the Incarnation, while not exclusively or originally Franciscan in the strict sense, remains both important and pastorally relevant for us today.

The Standard View on the Reason for the Incarnation

The question "Why was the Incarnation necessary?" has been around as long as Christianity has existed. It certainly dates back to the early Church and the first Christian communities in Jerusalem, Antioch, Alexandria and the missionary territories of Paul.[3] Like all dimensions of Christology, the question of the motive for the Incarnation finds its origin in soteriological concerns. In other words, all questions about Christ – including the Incarnation – are ultimately about the doctrine of salvation. The increasing need for clarification of such matters was the impetus for the earliest councils of the Church, often referred to as the Christological Councils. In fact the first seven ecumenical councils all dealt with, in some way or another, the Incarnation.[4]

The effort to clarify Christological doctrines did not stop the subsequent and ongoing exploration and elucidation of the meaning of the beliefs. For centuries (and now millennia) theologians of every age have examined the creedal statements of Christianity and have attempted to explain them in such a way that the faithful might better understand the mysteries of God.

---

[2] The theological term "supralapsarian" refers to a Christological view of the reason for the Incarnation that does not depend on the sin of Adam and Eve, representing humanity more broadly. The word originates from "supra," meaning "apart from" or "above/beyond," and "lapsarian," referring to the "Fall of Adam and Eve." The more popular, or so-called Majority Tradition, is technically called: "infralapsarian," meaning "within" or "dependent upon" the "Fall of Adam and Eve."

[3] For a good introduction to the early Christological questions of the nascent Christian communities through the first councils, see Basil Studer, *Trinity and Incarnation: The Faith of the Early Church*, trans. Matthias Westerhoff and ed. Andrew Louth (Collegeville: The Liturgical Press, 1993). With regard to the Pauline communities, see Marinus de Jounge, *Christology in Context: The Earliest Christian Responses to Jesus* (Philadelphia: Westminster John Knox Press, 1988), esp. 33-52 and 112-129; Charles Puskas, *The Letters of Paul: An Introduction* (Collegeville: The Liturgical Press, 1993); and Raymond Brown, *An Introduction to the New Testament*, The Anchor Bible Reference Library (New York: Doubleday, 1997), esp. 407-680.

[4] A new introduction to these councils has recently been published. It provides an accessible overview of each of the earliest ecumenical councils and their significance in the formation of Christological doctrine. See Stephen Need, *Truly Divine & Truly Human: The Story of Christ and the Seven Ecumenical Councils* (London: SPCK/Hendrickson Publishers, 2008).

One of the most popular doctrines to be investigated by many medieval philosophers and theologians was the necessity of the Incarnation.

Arguably, the paragon of medieval theologians who have considered the necessity of the Incarnation is Anselm of Canterbury (c. 1033 – 1109). In his text, *Cur Deus Homo*,[5] Anselm puts forward an argument for the necessity of the Incarnation based on the feudal model of satisfaction.[6] This project was grounded in his desire to produce an original justification for the doctrine that would prove the rationality of the argument to both Christians and non-Christians alike. He makes his case in two parts. The first part seeks to demonstrate that without the Incarnation human salvation is impossible. The second part contains his argument that God's intention for the human race is salvation.[7] Anselm focuses on the role of sin and the fall of humanity as the fundamental motivation for God's needing to become human. It is because of the dishonor caused to God through human sinfulness that satisfaction is needed in order to restore "the most precious piece of workmanship," that is humanity and creation, which is now completely ruined.[8] Anselm's argument concludes that neither humanity nor anything less than God – like an angel or 'superman' or anything else – is capable of restoring the honor of God diminished by human sin.[9] The ultimate conclusion drawn by Anselm is that the Incarnation is necessary inasmuch as there is no other logical way by which humanity could have been redeemed and God's honor have been restored, thereby returning creation to its rightful degree of fittingness and order.

Anselm's position has long been the standard understanding for the necessity of the Incarnation. It is this theology of the Incarnation from

---

[5] Anselm of Canterbury, "Why God Became Man [*Cur Deus Homo*]," in *Anselm of Canterbury: The Major Works*, eds. Brian Davies and G. R. Evans (New York: Oxford University Press, 1998), 260-356, hereafter cited as *Anselm of Canterbury* followed by page number.

[6] For more see Anthony Kenny, *Medieval Philosophy*, A New History of Western Philosophy, vol. 2 (Oxford: Clarendon Press, 2005), 43; and G. R. Evans, "Anselm of Canterbury," in *The Medieval Theologians: An Introduction to Theology in the Medieval Period*, ed. G. R. Evans (Oxford: Blackwell Publishing, 2001), 99.

It should be noted that while most Anselmian scholars uphold this concept of *debitum* and satisfaction, there exists a strong tradition that contests the influence of feudal society and legislation on Anselm's soteriological impulse in *Cur Deus Homo*. For more see Richard Campbell, "The Conceptual Roots of Anselm's Soteriology," in *Anselm: Aosta, Bec and Canterbury*, eds. D. E. Luscombe and G. R. Evans (London: Sheffield Academic Press, 1996), 256-263.

[7] John Galvin, "Jesus Christ," in *Systematic Theology: Roman Catholic Perspectives*, vol. 1, eds. Francis Schüssler Fiorenza and John Galvin (Minneapolis: Augsburg Fortress Press, 1991), 277.

[8] *Cur Deus Homo* bk. 1, chap. 4 (*Anselm of Canterbury* 270).

[9] Evans, "Anselm of Canterbury," 99.

which we get the famous Easter *Exsultet* line: "O happy fault, O necessary sin of Adam, which gained for us so great a Redeemer!"[10] This is also the sort of theological perspective that has saturated much of popular Christian culture and art. Perhaps the most famous case in recent years is Mel Gibson's *The Passion of the Christ*.[11] It is the approach that summarizes or represents the thought of most Christian thinkers including Augustine, Thomas Aquinas and even Bonaventure.[12] However, this is not the only theological perspective on the reason for the Incarnation, even if it has been the predominant view.

The Argument Formerly Known as "Franciscan"

Often associated with the Oxford Franciscan John Duns Scotus (c. 1266 – 1208), there is another approach to understanding the necessity of the Incarnation that has frequently been labeled the "Franciscan Thesis."[13]

---

[10] The International Commission on English in the Liturgy, *The Roman Missal* (New York: Catholic Book Publishing Company, 1985), 179.

[11] *The Passion of the Christ*, DVD, directed by Mel Gibson (New Market Films, 2004).

[12] Bonaventure adopts the Anselmian approach in his *Breviloquium* IV. I. 1-3, ed. Dominic Monti, Works of St. Bonaventure vol. IX (St. Bonaventure, NY: Franciscan Institute Publications, 2005), 131-135. "And so it was most fitting that the restorative principle of all things should be God Most High. Thus, just as God [the Father] had created all things through the Uncreated Word, so he would restore all things through the Incarnate Word" (*Breviloquium* IV. I. 2).

Zachary Hayes notes that Bonaventure's affinity to Anselm's satisfaction argument is most strongly found in his sentence commentary (III Sent. D. 18-20). See Zachary Hayes, *The Hidden Center: Spirituality and Speculative Christology in St. Bonaventure* (St. Bonaventure, NY: Franciscan Institute Publications, 1992), 152ff. See also, Christopher Cullen, *Bonaventure* (New York: Oxford University Press, 2006), 141-142; Alexander Gerken, "Bonaventuras Konvenienzgründe für die Inkarnation des Sohnes," *Wissenschaft und Weisheit* 23 (1960): 131-146; and Marilyn McCord Adams, *What Sort of Human Nature? Medieval Philosophy and the Systematics of Christology* (Milwaukee: Marquette University Press, 1999), 24-28.

Delio offers a different perspective in her "Revising the Franciscan Doctrine of Christ." I suggest that her reading of what she calls "The Franciscan doctrine" as exhibiting continuity between Bonaventure and Scotus is more accurately explained as conflation by proximity. The conclusion of her *Theological Studies* article expresses hesitancy about the authentic affinity of these two thinkers, akin to what I am suggesting. She writes: "Although it is Scotus who provided a clear and explicit articulation of the primacy of Christ, Bonaventure described a theology of primacy that underscores the mystery of the fullness of Christ" (23). Yet, in a positive way, she suggests that, read together, Bonaventure and Scotus offer an "understanding of the Incarnation that is broad, dynamic and inclusive" (23). On the first point, I do not believe Delio makes a clear enough distinction between the two thinkers' respective uses of "primacy of Christ," thereby suggesting a synonymous definition. On the second point, I could not agree more. The case of Bonaventure is complicated by passages in his work that *allude* to support of a supralapsarian argument, but in the end he remains in the anthropocentric camp.

[13] The term varies by author, but is synonymous with the moniker "Franciscan Thesis." For example, see Peter Dillard, "A Minor Matter? The Franciscan Thesis and Philosophical Theology," *The Heythrop Journal* 50 (2009): 890-900; Richard Rohr, "The Franciscan Opinion," in *Stricken by*

Generally speaking, each version of the "Franciscan Thesis" invokes the name and work of Scotus in some form to propose an alternate theological conceptualization for the necessity of the Incarnation. Scotus's approach can be summarized as follows:

> The Incarnation is the summation of Salvation History, not viewed as atonement for the grievous sin of humanity, but as the most concrete sign of God's infinite love and goodness... Scotus asserts God's unconditional love in Christ, stating that Jesus would have been born regardless of human sinfulness. Even if humanity had never sinned, the Word would still have become flesh. Scotus radically shifts the focus from us to God; from debt to gift; from sin to love.[14]

The so-called "Franciscan Thesis" of John Duns Scotus is indeed an alternative view to that of Anselm and his sin-centered colleagues. Béraud de Saint-Maurice has, in place of using a term modified by "Franciscan," described these two alternative approaches to understanding the reason for the Incarnation as the "anthropocentric" and "Christocentric" schools of thought.[15] The anthropocentric school asserts the subordination of Christ's Incarnation to the fall of humanity. Another way to understand this is that Christ enjoys only an occasional or conditional predestination that is reliant on human sinfulness. The Christocentric school holds that if Adam had remained faithful and not sinned, Christ would have still become incarnate. This Christocentric position maintains the absolute predestination of Christ to become incarnate. It has also been described as the "supralapsarian" approach.[16]

Given that Scotus was in fact a Franciscan friar and that his argument for the absolute predestination of Christ is indeed fittingly associated

---

God? Nonviolent Identification and the Victory of Christ, eds. Brad Jersak and Michael Hardin (Grand Rapids, MI: Wm. B. Eerdmans Publishing, 2007), 206-212; and Maximilian Mary Dean, *A Primer on the Absolute Primacy of Christ: Blessed John Duns Scotus and the Franciscan Thesis* (New Bedford: The Academy of the Immaculate, 2006).

[14] See John Duns Scotus, *Ordinatio* III, dist. 7, q. 3, trans. Allan Wolter, "John Duns Scotus on the Primacy and Personality of Christ," in *Franciscan Christology*, ed. Damian McElrath (St. Bonaventure, NY: Franciscan Institute Publications, 1994), 148-151.

[15] Béraud de Saint-Maurice, *John Duns Scotus: A Teacher for Our Times*, trans. Columban Duffy (St. Bonaventure, NY: Franciscan Institute Publications, 1955), 241-242.

[16] Edwin Chr. van Driel, *Incarnation Anyway: Arguments for Supralapsarian Christology* (New York: Oxford University Press, 2008).

with Saint-Maurice's Christocentric school, what is the problem with calling this the "Franciscan Thesis?" There are several problems with this term. The first is that nearly no other Franciscan thinker prior to Scotus espoused this approach.[17] As we have seen above, Bonaventure, the most significant Franciscan theologian and philosopher before Scotus, ultimately adhered to the standard Anselmian-anthropocentric model. In this respect, Bonaventure was closer to Aquinas than to Scotus, like most of the Franciscan thinkers of the time. The second problem is that Scotus is not the first to propose such an approach. In fact neither of the two theologians most famous for considering a form of the absolute predestination of Christ argument prior to Scotus were professed members of the Franciscan Order. The first to discuss the concept was Rupert of Deutz (c. 1075 – 1129/30), a monastic writer. The second was Robert Grosseteste (c. 1168 – 1253), a secular master. The final problem is the lack of conclusive evidence that Francis himself espoused this view.

Before Scotus: Rupert of Deutz and Robert Grosseteste

A. Rupert of Deutz and the Origin of the Supralapsarian Argument

Rupert of Deutz was a Benedictine monk and a contemporary of Anselm, although two decades his junior. Rupert is credited as the originator of the hypothetical query that has for so long been associated with the "Franciscan Thesis," namely, "would Christ have become incarnate if humanity had *not* fallen into sin?" In his text, *De Gloria et honore Filii hominis Super Mattheum*,[18] Rupert reconsiders the cause and necessity of Christ's Incarnation.[19] It is in the last book (XIII) of this text that Rupert develops his original insight on the theme.

This book was, most scholars believe, the product of a commission that was given to Rupert by Rudolph of St. Trond around 1127. St. Trond asked Rupert to address disputed questions on the Trinity, the proper exegesis

---

[17] The one exception to this claim is Alexander of Hales, the Parisian secular-master-turned-Franciscan. It is his unique theological starting point that allows him to consider a supralapsarian argument for the Incarnation. See Kenan Osborne, "Alexander of Hales: Precursor and Promoter of Franciscan Theology," in *The History of Franciscan Theology*, ed. Kenan Osborne (St. Bonaventure, NY: Franciscan Institute Publications, 1994), 1-38, esp. 30-32.

[18] See Rupert of Deutz, *De Gloria et honore filii hominis super Mattheum*, in Corpus Christianorum Continuatio Mediaevalis (Hereafter cited as CCCM), vol. 29.

[19] John H. Van Engen, *Rupert of Deutz* (Berkeley: University of California Press, 1983), 355.

of Genesis 49:10, and the necessity of the Incarnation.[20] In addition to the denial of the Incarnation by the Jews,[21] Rupert was motivated by two problems he saw in the previous work on the Incarnation. His first problem with earlier expositions is that many authorities believed that to demonstrate the necessity of the Incarnation one inevitably concludes that God must have willed evil.[22] The second problem is that if God did not will evil, then the Incarnation represented something of a "plan B" (*nouum concilium*), which seemingly contradicts the nature of an omnipotent and immutable God.[23]

These two concerns, while they play a prominent role in the development of his thought in *De gloria et honore*, appear to have been of interest to Rupert earlier in his career as well.[24] In *De gloria et honore* Rupert seeks to rebut these two positions. Rupert's response is that "God intended all along to have the second person of the Trinity assume a concrete, earthly role in the divine plan for His chosen people."[25] This was not an alternate plan or the result of God having willed evil, but a reflection of God's foreordained plan to "rejoice among men as their incarnate King."[26]

Rupert's position offered an alternative to the previously held views that he found so problematic. Rupert asserted that Christ's Incarnation was foreordained and necessary, but that his sacrificial atonement was not. In other words, the manner in which Christ suffered and died – or the particular manner of any other form of his earthly life – was the result of the Fall, but the Incarnation itself was not. In this sense Rupert reconfigured the question to make the Incarnation the centerpiece of God's plan. Rupert is the first to stand aside from the crowd of authorities that had for so long argued for the necessity and fittingness of the Incarnation on account of the condition of human fallenness. After Rupert, the hypothetical question and its assertive response went unnoticed until Robert Grosseteste posed a similar question.

---

[20] Van Engen, *Rupert of Deutz*, 354.

[21] Rupert enjoyed a degree of interaction with Jewish thinkers to a degree that other theologians of the time may not have. It is precisely the Jewish denial that motivates Rudolph of St. Trod and the Abbot Cuno, Rupert's two commissioners, to request Rupert's investigation into the doctrine.

[22] Van Engen, *Rupert of Deutz*, 355; and Rupert of Deutz, *De Gloria*, 13 (CCCM 29:412).

[23] Van Engen, *Rupert of Deutz*, 355.

[24] These themes appear in his *Commentary on Genesis* and his *Commentary on John* (c. 1114-1116). See Van Engen, *Rupert of Deutz*, 355.

[25] Van Engen, *Rupert of Deutz*, 356.

[26] Van Engen, *Rupert of Deutz*, 356.

B. Robert Grosseteste, Scripture, and Speculative Theology

Robert Grosseteste is perhaps best remembered as a biblical exegete.[27] As true as that characterization is, it remains insufficient and superficial since he was so much more. His interests were wide ranging and his intellectual output reflects his multifaceted mind and career. As a *magister in sacra pagina* it would be expected that the study and teaching of scripture would have occupied much of his time. Grosseteste is known for his adherence to the Bible as a teaching text in the classroom and the presence of scripture throughout his written corpus is ubiquitous.[28] It makes sense, then, that scripture would be the starting point for Grosseteste's exploration of the necessity of the Incarnation. Although Grosseteste begins with scripture, he is quickly forced to sidestep a normal exegetical path because his trajectory leads him into uncharted theological territory. Likewise, Grosseteste's investigation required that he forego the standard appeal to authoritative sources, if only because no one else – to the best of Grosseteste's knowledge – had ever explored this avenue.[29] This seems to suggest that Grosseteste was unaware of Rupert's earlier work on the matter.

Grosseteste's treatment of the necessity of the Incarnation is found prominently in three texts: *De Cessatione Legalium, Exiit Edictum* (a Christmas homily), and *Hexaëmeron*.[30] Recent scholarship has examined the Christological and Trinitarian implications of Grosseteste's *Expositio in Epistolam Sancti Pauli ad Galatas*, including the initial development of his

---

[27] See Beryl Smalley, "The Biblical Scholar," in *Robert Grosseteste: Scholar and Bishop*, ed. Daniel Callus (Oxford: Clarendon Press, 1955), 70-97 and James McEvoy, *Robert Grosseteste* (New York: Oxford University Press, 2000), 96-112.

[28] McEvoy, *Robert Grosseteste*, 96-97 and Daniel Horan, "Light and Love: Robert Grosseteste and John Duns Scotus on the How and Why of Creation," *The Cord* 57 (2007): 248-249.

[29] Robert Grosseteste, *De Cessatione Legalium*, Auctores Britannici Medii Aevi VII, eds. Richard Dales and Edward King (London: The British Academy, 1986); hereafter cited as *De Cessatione Legalium* followed by part, chapter, and paragraph number with edition pages in parenthesis. "Verumtamen, an Deus esset homo etiam si non esset lapsus homo non determinant aligui de sacris expositoribus in libris suis quos ego adhuc inspexerim, nisi fallat me memoria mea." *De Cessatione Legalium* III.1.2 (ABMA 119).

[30] These texts are first transcribed and studied in this context in Dominic Unger, "Robert Grosseteste Bishop of Lincoln (1235-1253) on the Reasons for the Incarnation," *Franciscan Studies* 16 (1956): 1-36. Subsequent critical editions of *De cessatione legalium* (for the critical edition of *De cessatione legalium* see n. 27 above) and *Hexaëmeron* have been published. See Robert Grosseteste, *Hexaëmeron*, Auctores Britannici Medii Aevi VII, eds. Richard Dales and Servus Geiben (London: The British Academy, 1982); an English translation of the *Hexaëmeron* was published by C. F. J. Martin, *Robert Grosseteste: On The Six Days of Creation* (Oxford: The British Academy, 1996), hereafter cited as *Hexaëmeron* followed by part and chapter numbers with translation edition page number in parenthesis.

understanding of the necessity of the Incarnation.[31] All four of these texts are developed within an explicitly scriptural context. The manner in which Grosseteste explores the theme of the Incarnation in these scripturally oriented works is largely exegetical in nature. He sees the theme of promised blessing, found in Genesis 12:3 and 18:17-18, as a blessing that only God is capable of fulfilling. He also believes that the prophesy calls for the best of humanity (*optimus hominum*). For Grosseteste, this seems to imply that this would necessitate the coming of the God-man.[32] Additionally, Grosseteste – like Rupert before him – considers Jacob's prophesy in Genesis 49:10. Here Grosseteste asserts that the one for whom the tribes of Israel were awaiting (*expectatio gentium*) is none other than the God-man in the Incarnation.[33] He concludes his scriptural exploration into the reason for the Incarnation with an examination of the fourth song of the suffering servant in Isaiah 52:13 – 53:12.

While Grosseteste sees Scripture as the source of his inquiry, he quickly discovers it necessary to move beyond the *Sacra Pagina* and those views that have already been established by the Fathers of the Church and other authorities. He, faithful as he is to Scripture and tradition, does not find a satisfactory answer in either. It is at this point that Grosseteste begins to engage the hypothetical question by way of reason. Having inquired as to whether or not the Incarnation would have taken place regardless of sin, and responding in the affirmative, Grosseteste presents his case to defend his affirmative hypothesis.[34]

The arguments Grosseteste lines up to support his affirmative position, that Christ would have indeed become incarnate regardless of human sinfulness, number nineteen in all.[35] In recent years scholars of Grosseteste's work have sought to organize and categorize these nineteen arguments, a process that has resulted in the presentation of five general themes. The two

---

[31] See Ian Levy, "Trinity and Christology in Robert Grosseteste's *Expositio* of Galatians," *Communio* 26 (1999): 875-891. The *Expositio* can be found in, Robert Grosseteste, *Expositio in epistolam sancti Pauli ad Galatas*, ed. James McEvoy, in *Opera Inedita Robert Grosseteste*, vol. 1 (CCCM 130).

[32] *De Cessatione Legalium* II.2.1-II.2.2 (ABMA 78-79).

[33] *De Cessatione Legalium* II.3.1-II.3.5 (ABMA 82-83). This is further emphasized in a representation of the biblical genealogy of Jesus in II.3.5-II.3.12 (ABMA 84-88).

[34] See *De Cessatione Legalium* III.1.2 and *passim* (ABMA 119ff).

[35] James McEvoy, "The Absolute Predestination of Christ in the Theology of Robert Grosseteste," in «*Sapientiae Doctrina*» *Mélanges de théologie et de littérature médiévales offerts á Dom Hildebrand Bascour* O.S.B., Recherches de Théologie ancienne et médiévale n° spécial 1(Leuven: Peeters, 1980), 213; and McEvoy, *Robert Grosseteste*, 127.

scholars who have done the most work in this respect are James McEvoy and James Ginther.[36] Each offers a slight variation from the other in their respective classifications of Grosseteste's arguments. However, I suggest that McEvoy's organizational pattern provides the most comprehensive, yet succinct, map of Grossteste's approach. What follows is taken largely from the work of McEvoy.

Grosseteste makes his first argument from the concept of God's goodness.[37] Borrowing from the ontological argument found in Anselm's Proslogion,[38] he reasserts that God is a "greater good than can even be thought." In addition to Anselm's argument, Grosseteste appears to borrow the notion of "self-diffusive goodness" as found in the work of Pseudo-Dionysius. From this combination of antecedent works on goodness and God, Grosseteste posits that God created the universe in such a way that is was capable of receiving God's goodness. Not only could creation receive God's goodness, but God also intends the perfection of creation through its participation in God's infinite power, wisdom, and goodness.[39] Therefore, God does not withhold any good the universe is capable of receiving, and communicates as much good as it has potential to receive. Grosseteste then makes the assertion that the Incarnation is the highest and primary example of creation's reception of God's goodness. What, for creation, could be a greater good than the union of the divine and human? Being that creation is obviously capable of receiving the God-man – since it already has – God must have always intended for creation's reception of the Incarnation. [40]

Moving from the concept of God's goodness and creation's ability to receive and participate in this goodness, Grosseteste asserts that a lower good could not be the cause of a higher good. What he means here is that because the Incarnation is the highest good that creation is able to receive, a lower good – or, more specifically, a privation – such as sin could not possibly be the cause for the coming of the God-man.

The next argument Grossteste makes is perhaps one of the most original. He distinguishes between the human need for redemption and

---

[36] I have previously made reference to several of McEvoy's studies. See also James Ginther, *Master of the Sacred Page: A Study of the Theology of Robert Grosseteste* (Burlington: Ashgate Publishing, 2004).

[37] *De Cessatione Legalium* III.1.3-III.1.4 (ABMA 120).

[38] See Anselm of Canterbury, "*Proslogion*," in *Anselm of Canterbury: The Major Works*, eds. Brian Davies and G. R. Evans (New York: Oxford University Press, 1998), 82-104.

[39] McEvoy, "The Absolute Predestination of Christ in the Theology of Robert Grosseteste," 214.

[40] *De Cessatione Legalium* III.1.9 (ABMA 122-123).

justification. For most medieval thinkers, the concept of justification was associated with the process of salvation. However, Grosseteste sees the process of salvation as tied up with the notion of sanctification. As such, justification has nothing to do with sin, so that Adam and Eve would have still required the Incarnation regardless of the Fall.[41] Justification would have always required the Incarnation, because humanity was always (even before sin) destined for sanctity.

Drawing on his understanding of Christ as head of the Church and the dignity of the Sacraments, Grosseteste's next argument is made from a position of the fittingness of the Incarnation. Christ as head is elaborated on in his *Hexaëmeron* where Grosseteste draws on Ephesians and cites 1 Corinthians 11:3 to highlight the revelation of this fact in scripture,[42] although his primary concern here is that of the Sacraments. Using the examples of marriage and the Eucharist, he argues that the dignity of these institutions could not rely on the Fall of humanity.[43] This is even more the case when one examines the metaphor of marriage between Christ and the Church. Grosseteste held that "God intended Christ and His Church even before the fall of Adam was in His mind. [Therefore] the absolute existence of the Church and Christ did not depend on the fall of man."[44] Considering the hypothetical implication of this position, it would be absurd to presume that the union of Christ to the Church and the establishment of the sacraments (marriage, which Grosseteste argues, existed before Adam and Eve sinned) were part of the contingent order. The only logical end to this argument is the absolute predestination of Christ to become Incarnate.

The final argument that Grosseteste puts forward comes from his understanding that creation is essentially united. For everything that is united there must be a uniting principle. Grosseteste explores whether or not the unifying principle could be anything other than the incarnate Christ. He considers, like Rupert, angels, humans, other aspects of creation only to conclude that the unifying principle could not be another creature. Grosseteste finally considers God in God's self. While God is in fact the principle of all things, God's transcendence places God beyond

---

[41] Ginther, *Master of the Sacred Page*, 133

[42] *Hexaëmeron* I.9.1 (ABMA [1996] 68).

[43] *De Cessatione Legalium* III.1.18-III.1.21 (ABMA 126-128).

[44] Unger, "Robert Grosseteste Bishop of Lincoln (1235-1253) on the Reasons for the Incarnation," 32.

participation in any species or genus directly.[45] The only thing remaining that could serve as the absolute unifying principle is the union of the God-man in the incarnate Christ.

The so-called "Franciscan Thesis" has quite the history of development before any professed member of the Franciscan Order began considering similar possibilities. It is worth noting that there are early Franciscan intersections in the history of the development of the absolute predestination of Christ. The most noticeable is found in the role Grosseteste played in the early years of the friars' history in England. Grosseteste was the first theological instructor of the newly arrived friars from across the English Channel.[46] To what extent he influenced those first British friars remains unstudied.[47] It is fair to say, though, that the first Friar Minor to seriously explore this trajectory, John Duns Scotus, does not begin his contribution to the history of this doctrine until long after the death of Grosseteste.

Francis of Assisi and the Incarnation

There is a temptation in the Franciscan world to label a multitude of things "Franciscan" without significant reflection on what Francis of Assisi actually thought, wrote or did. Not that this happens frequently, but it does happen. It seems that such might be the case with the establishment of the "Franciscan Thesis" in reference to the absolute predestination of Christ to become incarnate.

The starting point for much of Francis's reflection on the event and, by extension, the motive of the Incarnation is the dialectical paradox of the humility of God found in the contrast between the supreme glory of God alongside the birth of Jesus Christ and the Passion of Christ at the end of his earthly life. His starting point is not, as it had been for the other figures that we have examined, the reason, fittingness or necessity of the Incarnation. For Francis, the humility and gratuity of God are the foci of reflection on the Incarnate Word. What captured the imagination and prayerful devotion of Francis was, as Norbert Nguyên-Van-Khanh writes, "[Jesus's] glory and majesty on the one hand, and on the other, His free choice of a life of human poverty."[48] It is precisely the humility of God

---

[45] McEvoy, "The Absolute Predestination of Christ in the Theology of Robert Grosseteste," 216; and Ginther, *Master of the Sacred Page*, 137.

[46] For more see Horan, "Light and Love," 243-245.

[47] See Horan, "How Original Was Scotus on the Incarnation?" 374-391.

[48] Nguyên-Van-Khanh, *The Teacher of His Heart*, 104.

exhibited in the Incarnation toward which Francis turns his attention. In other words, it is the factual consideration of the Son of God's birth and death that occupy the thought of the Seraphic Saint. Thomas of Celano wrote: "Indeed, so thoroughly did the humility of the Incarnation and the charity of the Passion occupy his memory that he scarcely wanted to think of anything else."[49]

There is little to suggest that he deviated from what we have already outlined above as the "standard view on the reason for the Incarnation." Namely, that the primary motive for the Incarnation was salvific and restorative. This is emphasized in what we can discern of Francis's spiritual outlook. Nguyên-Van-Khanh summarizes this point well:

> In reality, there are not two different subjects: the incarnation and the passion. For Francis, the passion is situated along a line that leads logically from the incarnation; it is a consequence of the fact that the Son of the Father accepts the human condition to the very end. The incarnation is this movement of descent; it is not a static situation that ends in the passion and death. Therefore, in the mind of Francis, the passion is intimately linked to the birth.[50]

It is not that Francis would object to the doctrine of the absolute predestination of Christ to become incarnate. It is just that Francis never appears to have concerned himself with such an inquiry. He took what was factual or axiomatic – namely, the reality of human sinfulness and the truth of the Incarnation – and focused on those points. It is from his gaze upon these facts that Francis began to develop his rich insight into the humility of a God that would come to dwell among us. What we do not see emerging is a Christological perspective that departs from the atonement model that had been accepted by most medieval thinkers of his time.

This observation raises serious questions about terms that suggest certain historical figures espoused beliefs or perspectives that are not verifiable or, in some extreme cases, stand in contrast to the recorded views expressed by someone like Francis of Assisi. With a dedicated focus on the humility of the Incarnation and the deeply relational outlook Francis had, I believe that – had he been aware of the position of Rupert of Deutz – he

---

[49] Thomas of Celano, "The Life of Saint Francis," ch. I, v. 84, in FAED 1:254.
[50] Nguyên-Van-Khanh, *The Teacher of His Heart*, 109-110.

would have very likely adopted it himself. However, to imply that Francis would have responded to the counterfactual question, "would God have become incarnate if Adam had not sinned?" with an affirmative answer is misleading. Can something be "Franciscan" without deeply grounded roots in the life and writings of Francis? I am not sure.

Why All of This Doesn't Really Matter for Franciscans

Two words: *sine proprio*![51] Along with the rightful attribution of these theological ideas as they have developed over the centuries comes the admittance that we, as Franciscans, cannot take credit (at least exclusively) for the Christocentric argument for the absolute predestination of Christ. The development of this approach, as surveyed above, has clearly germinated close to the Franciscan intellectual tradition. Both Alexander of Hales, who should be credited with clear supralapsarian leanings in his often overlooked work, and John Duns Scotus, who history has recorded as the champion of the "Incarnation anyway" approach, have both contributed to the school of thought as we inherit it today. This should not be understated. However, the credit deserves to be spread more widely.

From this broader perspective, I suggest that the lack of exclusive attribution to the Franciscan tradition should not prevent the adoption of this theological perspective. Alexander of Hales and Scotus both adopted this position and 'made it theirs.' Like them, we too have the opportunity to adopt this Christocentric view of the Incarnation and 'make it ours.' I believe that we can do this in three particular ways.

The first way we can adopt this tradition is through our preaching and teaching. Those called to be ministers of the Word as preachers should be attentive to the way that this view of the Incarnation can inform one's homilies. Scripture read through the lens of the absolute predestination of Christ can look very different from the way it appears under the optic of the anthropocentric-atonement perspective. While we Franciscans do not have exclusive rights to this argument, we do have a natural inclination toward recognizing the gratuitous love of God in the humility God has modeled for us in the self-gift of the Incarnation. Even Francis recognized that. We have an obligation to reflect that image of God to the faithful who listen to us break open the Word and look to us for edifying catechesis.

---

[51] The phrase "*Sine Proprio*" is the actual vow professed by Franciscans to live "without anything of one's own," which is popularly referred to as "the Vow of Poverty."

The second way we might adopt this tradition is in our pastoral encounters with others. Sin-centered discourse is the last thing that should ground a pastoral conversation. I am not suggesting that this occurs often in any explicit way, although it does happen. Rather, I believe that too many of the Church's ministers operate from a place that is implicitly sin oriented. As such, the ability to reveal the compassionate face of God becomes inhibited by the need for rectification, penance, culpability, and so on. A theological foundation rooted in God's intention from all eternity to share in our earthly life by becoming incarnate offers a theological anthropology rooted in love. This is what Jesus has sent us to do after his example: "to bring good news to the poor... to proclaim release to captives and recovery of sight to the blind, to let the oppressed go free, to proclaim the year of the Lord's favor" (Luke 4:18-19). How can we fulfill this mission if our operative paradigm for Christ's coming into the world rests on our sinfulness?

A third way we might adopt this tradition is in our own prayer lives. It does not take much imagination to consider the stark contrast in spiritual outlook between a prayer life that is built on a sin-centered Christology of atonement and one centered on a Christocentric understanding of the necessity of the Incarnation. Reflecting on a God who from all eternity desires to be one with us and return all of creation back to God in glory leads one to contemplate the inherent dignity of both humanity, in which God participated fully through the Incarnation, and all of creation. Such a perspective could lead one to consider the implications for our lives based on our orientation toward a God who calls us back to God's self, with others and with all of creation. Our own worldview could begin to shift toward one that is more optimistic and communal.

So while the "Franciscan Thesis" might not actually be as Franciscan as we have previously been led to believe, it does provide Franciscans with a powerful alternative view of God, Christ, humanity, and creation than one rooted in sin. In the end, like Scotus, we might adopt this perspective, make it our own, and contribute to spreading the good news of a loving, caring, and deeply relational God.

CHAPTER TEN

EMBRACING
SISTER DEATH:

Francis of Assisi and Christian Hope

"The idea of death, the fear of it, haunts the human animal like nothing else; it is the mainspring of human activity – activity designed largely to avoid the fatality of death, to overcome it by denying in some way that it is the final destiny for man." (Ernest Becker)[1]

"Praised by You, my Lord, through our Sister Bodily Death, from whom no one living can escape." (Francis of Assisi)[2]

The subject of death is rarely, if ever, a pleasurable topic of conversation. For many it is identified as their worst fear, while others ignore its existence completely. Still others exploit death for entertainment through television, film, and news media, attracting the curious and bored, desensitizing the viewer to the reality of mortality. However, despite where one's thoughts of death fall between denial and callousness, inevitably every living thing comes to an end. Fortunately, because Christians maintain eschatological hope of life after death, death should not pose the fear and anxiety it so often evokes. To move from an unhealthy fear of death to embrace Christian hope is a lesson that each believer must grow in learning, a lifelong process of conversion and peacemaking. Such was the experience of Francis of Assisi

---

[1] Ernest Becker, *The Denial of Death* (New York: Simon & Schuster, 1973), xvii.
[2] Francis of Assisi, "The Canticle of the Creatures," 12, *FAED* 1:114.

during the thirteenth century. Early in his life, like most of us, he feared death for its threat to his continued happiness and worldly engagement, but by the end of his life he had made peace with his own mortality, going so far as to call death his "sister."[3]

Francis's understanding of the role of death within the context of God's creation was a capstone discovery that completed a lifelong process of conversion and seeking God. At the center of his ability to make peace with his own mortality is his fraternal worldview of creation.[4] Francis's most famous work, *The Canticle of the Creatures*, written near the end of his life, captures this aspect of his spirituality. Today this fraternal worldview serves as a lens through which we too can look at death and embrace its presence as a constitutive component of creation and part of God's plan. In doing so, we might find a source for Christian eschatological hope in an era often marked by pessimism, injustice, and violence.

In this chapter I will present a Franciscan vision of universal fraternity and suggest it can serve as a source of Christian eschatological hope in our world. First, drawing on some recent developments of post-enlightenment thinkers, we will look at the problem death poses within a modern/postmodern context. Second, we will examine two ways this contemporary view of death evokes a response, namely by way of avoidance and exploitation. By naming these common responses to death, we will recognize the need to find resources to move from avoidance and exploitation to a balanced embrace of death as a fundamental reality that directs us beyond our finite end. Finally, we will look at Francis's view of death. Through an examination of the way he wrote about death initially, we might situate ourselves in a similar position, recognizing our own tendencies toward avoidance and exploitation. We will study the manner in which Francis addresses death toward the end of his life and how he developed his helpful insight. Here we can glean the significance of an understanding of death as it is located within the context of a fraternal worldview and see the positive implications such an approach presents for Christian faith.

Grounding an Understanding of Death

---

[3]   See Francis of Assisi, "The Canticle of the Creatures," v. 12, in *FAED* 1:114.

[4]   It should be noted that my use of the world "fraternal" is not to the exclusion of women. Rather, it is used as the English derivative of *fraternitas*, meant in this context to refer to all of humanity from a perspective of solidarity and familial relationship shared among all women and men as children of God as understood within the Franciscan tradition. Because Francis uses *fraternitas* in his own writing, I have chosen to adopt this term. However, it may also be read as "sisterhood and brotherhood."

With Martin Heidegger's phenomenological reflection on Dasein as *Sein zum Tode* (Being-toward-death) in his masterwork *Sein und Zeit*[5] came the modern (and subsequently postmodern) quest for eschatological elucidation. Along with the existential phenomenological turn that Heidegger helped advance early in the twentieth century, his positioning of death prominently in philosophical discourse has bolstered the urgency with which philosophers and theologians have explored its meaning.[6] As a point of departure we will examine the work of some contemporary thinkers and their analysis of the condition of death.

The work of Ernest Becker provides a good overview of the contemporary concern about death. His approach, rooted primarily in the psychological and sociological methods of Marx, Freud, Kierkegaard, and Rank, examines the role of heroism in human experience. It is precisely an understanding of heroism that provides Becker with the language to describe the experience of human reflection on death. We can see this in the way we collectively ascribe the title hero to and admire those who have "the courage to face death," or the way we articulate and pass on the Christian narrative, using phrases like "Jesus Christ has 'conquered' death."[7] Closely linked to Becker's understanding of heroism is his recognition of the place of narcissism as just one human reflex to the overwhelming reality of death. Bill Polizos summarizes Becker's point well when he writes, "Each of us harbors the desire or maintains the illusion of being like a god, only to find this inclination frustrated by the natural reality that mires us in a world in which life must paradoxically be sustained by death itself."[8] However the presence of death manifests itself in our lives; its existence is undeniable.

We can say that Becker proposes that death is an existential characteristic of humanity, or, as he himself puts it, "*the* universal human problem."[9] By

---

[5] Martin Heidegger, *Sein und Zeit*, 17th ed. (Tübingen: Max Niemeyer, 1993). For the preeminent English translation, see *Being and Time*, trans. John Macquarrie and Edward Robinson (New York: Harper and Row, 1962). Further citations of this source will be noted as *Being and Time* followed by the page number. For a recent study of the interpretation of Heidegger's "Being-toward-death," see Havi Carel, "Temporal Finitude and Finitude of Possibility: The Double Meaning of Death in *Being and Time*," *International Journal of Philosophical Studies* 15 (2007): 541-556.

[6] For a helpful overview of the theological history of death, see John Hick, *Death & Eternal Life* (Louisville: Westminster John Knox Press, 1994).

[7] Becker, *The Denial of Death*, 11-12.

[8] Bill John Polizos, "Christian Orthodoxy and Existential Anxiety: The Problem of Materiality and Finitude in the Pursuit of Authentic Religious Faith" (M.A. thesis, Washington Theological Union, 1997), 15.

[9] Becker, *The Denial of Death*, 8. Original emphasis.

this, Becker does not simply refer to the mere fact that all human beings die. What he does focus his attention on is that, because of the universality of the fear of death (he often uses the word "terror"), we become consumed and overwhelmed by the notion when we think of death in categorical terms. This is the source of Becker's major critique of Sigmund Freud's analysis of human behavior. Becker believes that Freud's later development of the terror of nature and death as an "instinct," while striving to keep his sexual theory intact, weakened the thinker's argument. Becker's corrective to Freud is to suggest that one needs only to admit that human beings carry death within them unconsciously as part of their biology.[10] Paul Tillich supports this view of the biological dimension of death when he states that, "One must affirm that the moment of our conception is the moment in which we begin not only to live but also to die."[11] According to Becker, death remains the condition for the possibility of understanding the meaning of human life, because without death we would know nothing of our creaturely existence. It is also that condition for the experience of our own finitude that, while we are always somewhat unthematically aware of its facticity, remains perpetually elusive. Death is what remains the source of humanity's greatest anxiety and it is the sole element that is shared by all human beings, an element of unsolicited solidarity that unites both the Queen of England and the poorest person in Bolivia. This truth cannot be denied: everyone dies.

Allied closely to the thought of Becker, and those from whom he gleans inspiration for his work, is the twentieth century contribution toward development of a theology of death. One such pioneer in this field is Karl Rahner. With substantial articles in his *Theological Investigations*, the closing chapter on eschatology in his celebrated work *Foundations of Christian Faith*, and a small monograph on the subject, Rahner approaches the question of death with insight rooted in his transcendental theology.[12] Serving as an impetus for Rahner's reflection on death are the post-enlightenment condition of secularity, the demythologization of culture,

---

[10] Becker, *The Denial of Death*, 99.

[11] Paul Tillich, *Systematic Theology: Volume 3* (Chicago: The University of Chicago Press, 1963), 53. Tillich also engages Freud's *Todestrieb* as Becker later does (see 54-57).

[12] See Karl Rahner, "On Christian Dying," in *Theological Investigations Vol. VII*, trans. David Bourke (New York: Seabury/Crossroad, 1977), 285-293; "Ideas for a Theology of Death," in *Theological Investigations Vol. XIII*, trans. David Bourke (New York: Crossroad, 1983), 169-188; *On The Theology of Death*, trans. Charles Henkey (New York: Herder and Herder, 1961; and *Foundations of Christian Faith*, trans. William Dych (New York: Crossroad, 1978/2002), esp. 431-447.

and the privatization of eschatology.

The way secularity impacts a modern understanding of death stems from the post-enlightenment perspective that grounds all knowledge in finite reality. Here we think of Kant's critique of reason and the subsequent belief that we can know only what is before us as we substantially shape our experience of reality, thereby disregarding a human *capax infiniti*.

Demythologization of culture has led to the widespread suspicion of signifying narratives. This process, for the most part, reflects an increased focus on science and reason, which has largely taken place in the public square. Some scholars suggest that this trend serves as a foundational influence of the contemporary condition of Postmodernity in that the present culture rejects the veracity of metanarratives and is suspicious of that which is not grounded in empirical evidence.

The increased movement of eschatological reflection from the public (or community-oriented) to the private has further complicated the consideration of death. One can see a progression from widespread demythologization in the public square to privatized eschatology. As the collective body becomes increasingly hostile toward and cynical of metanarratives and the supernatural, public discourse concerning eschatological subjects is viewed as irrational, futile or, at best, naïve.

Rahner responded to these emerging tendencies of the twentieth century with an eye toward the transcendental theological project with which he was so strongly associated. His basic conviction was that where the supernatural is dismissed or forgotten, we are left with nothing more than a finitude for which there is little hope or reason. We see then where the nihilism of the later existentialists and some of the early deconstructionalist thinkers is rooted. As one becomes more and more entrenched in an operating paradigm of secularism, technology, and scientific inquiry at the cost of theological reflection, it is easy to see how meaninglessness and despair in life lead to fear and anxiety of death. This is not to suggest that science does not have a place in our world (Rahner would have been one of the first to attest to its value). Rather, it is the upholding of science and technology as the monolithic and complete response to all of our problems and concerns. However, science and technology – as much as they can answer the question "how" – cannot answer the question of "why death?" Emerging from this worldview is an understanding of death as the ultimate and inescapable end of our finite existence. Death is simply annihilation.

We can clearly anticipate the problems this worldview holds for human reflection on death.

Avoidance and Exploitation

To consider death as an existential of human *being* naturally raises questions about the manner in which we respond or react to the universality of death. I propose that faced with the awareness of death as a constitutive element of human life as conceived outside a context of theology, we most often respond to the fear and anxiety such a realization evokes in two ways. The first way is through avoidance, or what Becker would call the denial of death. The second response is the exploitation of death. While it can be argued that one's response to death might be culturally and historically conditioned, I believe that avoidance is always present in the human response to mortality, thereby transcending particularity. With regard to the cultural and historical conditions that influence or shape my second suggested response to death, I recognize the limitations associated with the concept of exploitation. It may be present in different cultures to a greater or lesser degree, but our concern here is with the current state of "American" culture and the omnipresence of death in an exploitive manner. This reflection is less concerned with universal structures of human response to death than recognizing *contemporary* and problematic reactions to that existential.

Unlikely bedfellows, the deconstructionist philosopher Jacques Derrida and the Catholic theologian Joseph Ratzinger (now Pope Benedict XVI) have both recognized the place of avoidance in the human response to death, even if they approach the subject from slightly different angles. Derrida draws on Kierkegaard's *Fear and Trembling*[13] in his reflection on death and the response of avoidance in the face of it. Picking up the theme of trembling, he notes, "Hence I tremble because I am still afraid of what already makes me afraid and which I can neither see nor foresee."[14] Here we can see the anxiety that arises in the face of death. The trembling is a response to the stark reality of the existential nature of death in life. For Ratzinger, this notion of absolute fear is seen in the repression, avoidance and denial of the truth of death. He believes that facing the reality of death

---

[13] See Søren Kierkegaard, *Fear and Trembling*, trans. Alastair Hannay (London: Penguin Books, 2005).

[14] Jacques Derrida, *The Gift of Death*, trans. David Wills (Chicago: The University of Chicago Press, 2008), 55.

necessarily requires a man or woman to reconsider the manner in which he or she lives. It challenges the ordinary quality of daily life, raising one's awareness to a plane of metaphysical and eschatological reflection.[15]

In place of conscious consideration of the reality of death, we would rather choose to avoid or deny its existence. It is precisely this response that helps one appreciate the myriad ways we seek to extend life and avoid facing our own demise. Whether it is aesthetic surgery to maintain one's exterior youthfulness or attempts to establish a sort of legacy by which to be remembered, the extraordinary lengths we take to avoid death in our culture is staggering. Derrida's observation suggests that it is because death is always before and within us that our fear of death is so strong and we will work at all costs to avoid it. Ratzinger's insight is that to stop and consider the meaning of death would call us to move beyond the banality that is often our daily existence. Neither result is immediately appealing, so we buy and sell, eat and drink, work and sleep to avoid that which is unavoidable.

The opposite approach is equally unbalanced. It is a rare day that one can turn on a television, open a newspaper or listen to the radio and not encounter an expert, pundit, or concerned parent discussing the degree of violence and death present in our contemporary American culture. Some scholars of Postmodernity have commented on the increased presence of the "spectacle" in today's society. First noted by scholars of capitalism, this observation is a reflection of the shift in consumption exhibited in manifold ways. In its most simplified form, the transformation of today's American culture into a "society of the spectacle" refers to the ongoing morphing of individuals into consumers and the manipulation of those consumers by various industries that are specifically attempting to constitute the desires and needs of the population in order to exploit them.[16] We are presented with an array of spectacles that attract us in order for others to profit, while at the same time allowing us to feel in some way satisfied regarding a desire or need. It is in this way that I suggest death has become exploited.

For as much as we avoid facing death, the desire to confront it and control it remains ever present. Subsequently, markets are created to sell and distribute a product that fulfills that desire. One of the many problems

---

[15] For more see Joseph Ratzinger, *Eschatology: Death and Eternal Life*, 2nd ed., trans. Michael Waldstein (Washington, DC: The Catholic University of America Press, 1988), 69-72.

[16] Steven Best and Douglas Kellner, *The Postmodern Turn* (New York: The Guilford Press, 1997), 83-85.

with this sort of reaction to death is the division of reality and artificiality. The consumption of grotesque films, music, literature, art, video games, and other media does not actually remedy our anxiety and fear that emerges from the intrinsic presence of death in our lives. However, the temporary cathartic quality of consumption of a spectacle eases our suffering. As Steven Best and Douglas Kellner keenly (and frankly) note, "of course, 'virtual' and 'interactive' technologies merely seduce the viewer into an even deeper tie to the spectacle, and there is no media substitute for getting off one's ass, for interactive citizenship and democracy, for actually living one's life in the real world."[17] This view helps to interpret the increasing attraction of people to horror films and violent electronic games. No matter how appealing or seducing artificial or virtual spectacles of facing death appear, exploitation ultimately leaves us dissatisfied and longing for a means to reconcile this constitutive part of our existence.[18]

The exploitation of death has yet another consequence. Ratzinger has also observed the increased effort to turn death into a commodity in today's culture. In addition to death's sale as a spectacle, its exploitive presence appears to render death mundane, as if to make its existence more palatable or matter-of-fact. Ratzinger shares, "On television, death is presented as a thrilling spectacle tailor-made for alleviating the general boredom of life. In the last analysis, of course, the covert aim of this reduction of death to the status of an object is just the same as with the bourgeois taboo on [or avoidance of] the subject."[19] The exploitation of death seems to convince us that control over death is possible. This is the objectification and the production of death in such a way as to completely dismiss its metaphysical and eschatological relationship to our lives. Like attempted avoidance of death, exploitation leaves us empty-handed. In some ways, exploitation of death is a more painful ruse, one that deceives a person in such a way that they are sold a "bill of goods." A person never faces the existential reality of death because he or she goes about thinking of it as entertainment, product, or something inconsequential.

What unites both the avoidance and exploitation of death is the hopeless interpretation of death as the finite end of our existence, which is the source of the fear and anxiety that leads to both of these reactions.

---

[17] Best and Kellner, *The Postmodern Turn*, 89.

[18] See Eric Doyle, *St. Francis and the Song of Brotherhood and Sisterhood* (St. Bonaventure, NY: Franciscan Institute Publications, 1997), 172-174.

[19] Ratzinger, *Eschatology*, 70.

While no one can deny the inevitability of death, our understanding of its meaning shapes and informs the way we respond to its constant presence in our lives. Nihilism is not the only recourse for those who choose to face death for what it is. Instead, Christianity offers us a view of this existential that provides both hope and meaning. The fraternal worldview of Francis of Assisi leaves us with a great example of an integrated and authentic approach to understanding, encountering, and reconciling our relationship to death.

Francis of Assisi and Death

From the beginning of his life until close to his death, Francis, like most people, appears to have had a response to the concept of death that was as troublesome as avoidance and exploitation. Such a response was rooted in his fear of death. We read Francis's biting admonition on death in the "Earlier Exhortation to the Brothers and Sisters of Penance." Sometime between 1209 and 1215 he wrote, "And you think that you will possess this world's vanities for a long time, but you are deceived because a day and an hour will come of which you give no thought, which you do not know, and of which you are unaware when the body becomes weak, death approaches, and it dies a bitter death."[20] Francis's view of death here is one of fear. This tone is echoed in his "Later Exhortation"[21] where he wrote, "But let everyone know that whenever and however someone dies in mortal sin without making amends when he could have [done so] and did not, the devil snatches his soul from his body with such anguish and distress that no one can know [what it is like] except the one experiencing it."[22] These are but two examples of the early thought of Francis on death. While the language is spiritualized and denotes a certain religiosity, the underlying attitude toward death is implicitly negative. There are two themes that come across strongly in these early writings of Francis. The first is the inevitability of death. As we have already seen, this is simply a matter-of-fact that all who reflect on death come to conclude and it is something that Francis realizes early on. However, the second theme, that death is both

---

[20] Francis of Assisi, "Earlier Exhortation to the Brothers and Sisters of Penance, ". II:14, in *FAED* 1:43.
[21] The dating for this text is less certain than for the Earlier Exhortation. For our purposes here, we will assume it was written near 1220.
[22] Francis of Assisi, "Later Exhortation to the Brothers and Sisters of Penance," 82, in *FAED* 1:51.

painful and to be feared, is highly problematic.

Death, as understood within the context of these early texts, is devoid of a hopeful or purposeful connection to the divine or to something beyond human finitude. Instead, Francis seems to link death to punishment for sinfulness and as a condition of human creatureliness. Additionally, Francis's focus on death during this period interprets death as the threat of annihilation, as the negation of existence.[23] While this view of death does not necessarily fit the contemporary models of avoidance and exploitation, it does indicate unease with the subject that Francis acknowledges as inevitable. If this is where his view of death had remained, he would have joined the ranks of the many that, in the face of the fear and anxiety of inescapability, never see death as anything beyond the natural end to finite existence. However, Francis's view of death does not continue on a static trajectory, but develops and matures over the course of his life.

At the end of his life, as Francis drew near to the death that he feared for so long, the tone of his expression of death changed noticeably. Along his journey of life, prayer, and ministry, Francis remained convinced of death's inevitability, but started to view its meaning and his relationship to it differently. Where once he saw death as painful and something to be feared, he now dared to call death his "sister." One way to interpret the meaning of this salutation is to examine it from within the context of the canticle where it is found. The line quoted at the beginning of this article is taken from the twelfth verse of his fourteen-verse *The Canticle of the Creatures*. It reads, "Praised be You, my Lord, through our Sister Bodily Death, from whom no one living can escape." Scholars largely believe that *The Canticle of the Creatures* was constructed in three stages, over several years. The first part (vv 1-9) is the earliest section, which highlights six natural elements from the sun and moon to wind, fire, and earth. Each of these natural elements is addressed as brother or sister. Each is named both in relation to Francis (or the reader) and as a part of God's creation. There is a fraternal and filial connection expressed that links all of creation to Francis and both creation and Francis to God. It is also through creation that Francis sees God made present, and it is likewise through creation that Francis wishes to praise God. The second section of *The Canticle of the Creatures* (vv 10 and 11) speaks to the need for reconciliation, solidarity

---

[23] Eloi Leclerc, *The Canticle of Creatures: Symbols of Union; An Analysis of St. Francis of Assisi,* trans. Matthew O'Connell (Chicago: Franciscan Herald Press, 1970), 179.

and peace. This stanza was written in response to a power struggle that was taking place in the medieval town of Assisi between the mayor and the bishop. Francis served as mediator and wrote this section of the text to prayerfully address the conflict and inspire resolution. The final section (vv 12-14), which contains the line about Sister Bodily Death and the conclusion, Francis composed on his deathbed.

The transformation from a response rooted in the fear and anxiety of death to a place where Francis – awaiting his own impeding death – could welcome death as "sister" might be made clear by looking to the threefold construction of *The Canticle of the Creatures*, which illustrates Francis process of learning to embrace death. The first section of the text in many ways summarizes the fraternal worldview of Francis of Assisi. What we find in the first nine verses is not a mere flowery poem or simple artistic expression, but an invitation to join in the hymn of praise to God rooted in our fellowship with all of creation. Human beings, like the sun, moon, and earth, are created by God and are brought into existence through God's own gift of love.[24] Franciscan scholar Ilia Delio explains this view of Francis well, "If God is the source of my life and the source of your life as well, then the fullness of my life can only be found in you and in all that is in this world, because the fullness of God is expressed in humanity and all of creation."[25] The beginning of a transformation from the avoidance and exploitation of death to a welcomed embrace starts with a realization that we are connected to all of creation in an intrinsic and holy way. Immediately, the notion of nihilism seems inadequate as the final recourse for questions of life and death. Not only does *my* life have meaning, but *all* life has meaning.

The second section of the canticle naturally builds upon the foundation laid in the first section. Reconciliation and peace can only be found where there is authentic relationship. The relationship Francis identified as shared among all of creation is sometimes referred to as kinship or fraternity.[26] It is a relationship that extends beyond dominance, control, or even stewardship. Francis's fraternal worldview situated his own life within the natural order of creation that saw the intrinsic dignity of being created by God. This dignity is present in all life, including the lives of other women and men and the life of the world. Recognizing the dignity of all life should compel

---

[24] For more see chapter twelve of this book.
[25] Delio, *Franciscan Prayer*, 171.
[26] See chapter nine of this book for more on the Franciscan approach to a theology of creation in terms of kinship.

us to see beyond our own needs and desires, our own fears and anxiety, to appreciate the connectedness that calls us to support one another and care for all creation. Peacemaking does not become an activity that one does out of kindness or sympathy, but becomes a mode of acting that is part and parcel of what it means to be a follower of Christ and a believer in a God who is love. When Francis composed the section on peacemaking for the dueling mayor and bishop, he said, "Praised be You, my Lord, through those who give pardon for Your love, and bear infirmity and tribulation. Blessed are those who endure in peace for by You, Most High, shall they be crowned."[27] He was reminding them (and us) that God is glorified when we enter into right relationship with each other, ourselves, and our world like the rest of creation does. The recognition of that right relationship challenges us to move beyond our desire to avoid or exploit those parts of our lives that frighten us. Not only do we see our rightful place among the rest of creation, but we see that our life does not end only in death.

It is through peacemaking and self-emptying that we return to our place as children of God and brothers and sisters to one another and the rest of creation. In doing so, we no longer see death as something alien and to be feared, but as another dimension of ourselves.[28] This is what is meant by the notion of facing our own death, of radically encountering that constitutive part of ourselves that cannot be avoided, or as Francis says, "[that] from whom no one living can escape." Death is always before us and always a part of us, much like we remain always connected to the rest of creation and to one another. Death maintains its fearful place as a threat to those who refuse to see themselves as intimately connected to that which is other and to that which is wholly (and Holy) Other. For Francis, it is the abandonment of the belief that we are isolated individuals – entitled to and deserving of more than others – that allows us to share in the experience of connectedness to and dependence on God. That recognition of God's presence in our lives is the beginning of the hope that arises from the fraternal worldview of Francis in the face of death.

In addition to seeing God's presence and work in the world, Francis never forgot the central truth of the Christian message that is rooted in the death and resurrection of Jesus Christ.[29] Because of the resurrection,

---

[27] Francis of Assisi, "The Canticle of the Creatures," 10-11, in *FAED* 1:114.
[28] Leclerc, *The Canticle of Creatures*, 179.
[29] Doyle, *St. Francis and the Song of Brotherhood and Sisterhood*, 177.

death is no longer conceived of as the absolute end of life. Rather, although death remains a mystery that is only fully understood through personal experience, Francis's transformative view of death becomes a source of hope. He saw, through his connectedness to creation and his relationship to God through all of creation, that death was a natural part of God's plan for humanity. Yes, death is inescapable; but it does not mark an end as much as it marks the liminal experience of a new beginning. This is the hope that transcends the worldly limits of our finite experience. "By calling death his sister, Francis is reminding us that the Christian faith has a sacred message about human death."[30] The challenge that lies before us is to embrace this vision of death and life that has been radically altered and redeemed through the resurrection.

As he approached his own earthly end, Francis, recalling the love of God made manifest in the gift of creation, looked forward with hope to his share in the resurrection of Christ. There was no longer a need to avoid or exploit death, because death was his sister, closer to him than the fear of the unknown. With arms extended, Francis did not cower from his destiny in fear and anxiety, but embraced his sister bodily death with his whole heart and left this world in peace.

From Fear of Death to Christian Hope

While death will forever remain a mystery unsolved until our earthly end, its presence in all of human life affects the way we live today. To live in light of a fraternal worldview that values the connectedness we have to all creation and one another helps to free us from the fear of death that mitigates fullness of life and influences our actions toward self-preservation and selfishness at the cost of authentic relationship. The transformation from fear to hope in the life of Francis of Assisi as he approached death provides us with a model for Christian living in an increasingly secular, violent, and pessimistic world.[31] In welcoming death as our sister, we might serve as beacons of the Christian hope of new life and live the prophetic call of the Gospel, proclaiming "that neither death, nor life, nor angels, nor rulers, nor things present, nor things to come, nor powers, nor height, nor depth, nor anything else in all creation, will be able to separate us from the

---

[30] Doyle, *St. Francis and the Song of Brotherhood and Sisterhood*, 176.

[31] For a contemporary and personal narrative of the transformation of one Franciscan in his own journey toward death, see Stewart, *Making Peace with Cancer: A Franciscan Journey*.

love of God in Christ Jesus our Lord" (Romans 8:38-39).

With an appreciation for the existential nature of death in human life, we are left with a choice. We can look at death as the end of a meaningless and limited existence that evokes fear and anxiety because it threatens us with the loss of ourselves, and so we respond to it through avoidance or exploitation. Or, we can look at death as a part of the natural order, as something that is unavoidable yet represents a truth grounded in hope, not fear.[32] We can look at death as alien and enemy. Or, we can look at death as our sister. We can see in death the ultimate problem of humanity. Or, we can see in death the hope of new life.

---

[32] Paul Ricoeur draws on this notion in his work, describing a "Fraternal tension within a unity of creation" that is understood as, "The Franciscan knowledge of necessity: I am 'with' necessity, 'among' creatures." See Ricoeur, *Freedom and Nature*, trans. Erazim Kohak (Chicago: Northwestern University Press, 1966), 481.

CHAPTER ELEVEN

LIGHT AND LOVE:

A Franciscan Look at the 'How' and 'Why' of Creation

Medieval Paris and Oxford, as most students of Franciscan history know, are considered the centers of the nascent Franciscan intellectual tradition. Thinkers like Alexander of Hales and Bonaventure are among the best known from Paris, while John Duns Scotus and William of Ockham are the most remembered from Oxford. As was the contemporary practice, each of these thinkers engaged in a scholastic form of intellectual inquiry that often covered a number of subjects related to philosophy, theology, and natural science. Frequently these subjects blended together to form a synthesis that reflected a thinker's view of the world that was not as categorized and easily distinguishable as our more specialized form of scholarship is today. This was often the case when a medieval thinker, including those within the Franciscan movement, explored the theme of creation. The practice of commenting on God's act of creation – known as *Hexaëmeron*, after the Genesis account of the six days of creation – was a common academic exercise that can be found among the major works of many scholastics alongside their commentaries on the *Sentences* of Peter Lombard.[1] Those who did not explicitly address the topic with some form of *Hexaëmeron* often breached the subject tangentially by reflecting on the

---

[1] See Philipp W. Rosemann, *Peter Lombard* (New York: Oxford University Press, 2004), for more on the *Sentences* of Peter Lombard and the impact of that work on the theological formation of medieval university masters.

act of creation and the proceeding theological implications at some point in their work.

While the popular Franciscan figures mentioned above contributed immensely to the rich Franciscan intellectual tradition, helping to plant a firm foundation for the scholars that follow, some lesser-known thinkers also have contributed to that tradition. John of La Rochelle and Odo Rigaud of Paris, and John Pecham and Matthew of Aquasparta from Oxford made significant impacts in the early years of the Franciscans at the universities, ghostwriting parts of major works, such as Alexander of Hale's acclaimed *Summa fratis Alexandri*, and developing commentaries on scripture while lecturing for their brother friars.[2] Their impact on the intellectual development of the early Franciscan movement has yet to be fully studied and widely appreciated. Another under-recognized figure is Robert Grosseteste. A scholar of the first degree, Grosseteste was the first lecturer of the friars in England. A prolific intellectual who wrote on varied topics in philosophy, theology, and science, Grosseteste helped to form what would later become the second foci of the Franciscan intellectual tradition – the Franciscan school at Oxford. Among the wide-ranging themes of his writing, one finds Grosseteste developed a cosmogony that fits well into the theological and philosophical paradigms of creation within the Franciscan movement, although never a professed friar himself. What is additionally striking about Grosseteste's cosmogony is the highly scientific and mathematical form it takes, especially considering it was authored in the early Thirteenth Century, making it extraordinarily original.

The method with which Grosseteste engages the topic of creation, highly scientific while deeply theological, provides a framework for answering the simple question of "how" creation came into existence. Presupposing God as the initiator and author of the creative act, Grosseteste methodically outlines a series of processes that begins with the first corporeal form – Light (*lux*)[3] – and ends with the created world, as understood in the Thirteenth Century. What is clearly absent from his treatise on the "how" of creation, *De Luce* (On Light), is an answer to the question "why?" While

---

[2] See *A Companion to Philosophy in the Middle Ages*, eds. Jorge J. E. Gracia and Timothy B. Noone (Oxford: Blackwell Publishing, 2003) for more on the theological contributions and biographical details of John of La Rochelle, John Pecham, and Matthew of Aquasparta.

[3] C.G. Wallis makes the point to distinguish that the Latin word for light that is used is lux in his translation "On Light" found in *Philosophy in the Middle Ages*, 2d ed., eds. Arthur Hyman and James J. Walsh, (Indianapolis: Hackett Publishing Company, 1973), 474.

he does preliminarily address this issue of "why" in his *Hexaëmeron* (On the Six Days of Creation), a fellow Oxford thinker and heir to the intellectual tradition left by Grosseteste writes more extensively on the subject of the "why" of creation. This thinker is none other than John Duns Scotus whose work has inspired so many over the centuries and whose philosophical and theological innovations had a major impact on the shaping of the growing Franciscan school at Oxford.

While this chapter is in no way intended to exhaustively draw all the connections between the work of these two great thinkers, I will show that the harmonious pairing of these two figures is not only possible, but that it lends to a unique view of creation. This Franciscan view of creation is as relevant today as it was centuries ago. The implications for our modern world torn by ecological injustices are many. Together, a relatively unknown but prolific scholar and one of the most famous Oxford thinkers provide a distinctively Franciscan perspective on creation that suggests answers to the timeless questions of "How" and "Why." Contributing each in his own way, both thinkers provide the response: light and love.

Illuminating *De Luce's* Importance

The question is simple, but the answer is nuanced. How did all of what we experience of the created world come into existence? This question has prompted the development of creation myths that are found in every human community on Earth. For thousands of years the quest to answer one of the most basic questions of existence has led to inquiry by means of imagination, theology, and science. Faced with this task in the early Thirteenth Century, Robert Grosseteste began his work to systematically address this problem in light of his Christian faith.

Grosseteste was invited by Agnellus of Pisa sometime between 1229 and early 1230 to become the first lecturer of theology to the newly arrived Franciscan brothers in England.[4] Much of Grosseteste's history prior to this invitation, including the exact date of his birth, is largely debated or altogether unknown.[5] Most scholars assert that he was born between 1168 and 1170 to a poor family,[6] he studied the Arts in Oxford and possibly

---

[4] McEvoy, *Robert Grosseteste*, 21.

[5] See McEvoy, *Robert Grosseteste*, 19-30, for more information regarding the issues surrounding the ambiguity of the early life of Robert Grosseteste.

[6] For more information regarding the divergence of theories that support the placement of Grosseteste's birth at a particular date before or after 1168, see McEvoy, *Robert Grosseteste*, xi; R.W.

Paris likely before 1186,[7] and he became the first lector of theology of the Franciscans in England holding that position until March 27, 1235 when he was elevated to the position of bishop of Lincoln.[8] Around the time he was with the friars, Grosseteste developed a rather extensive body of written work on a number of topics, crossing many disciplines. One of his major works written during this time was a treatise titled *De Luce* (On Light).

De Luce begins with God's creation of a single point of light from which the entire physical order came into existence through the expansion and extension of that one point of light.[9] It is this light created by God, which comes from nothing preexisting, that is the center of Grosseteste's cosmogony. He posits that there could be no other form of matter that so perfectly self-replicates, expanding by self-propagation in all directions while at the same time remaining one and simple.[10] To initiate the process of creation from that single point of primordial light, Grosseteste uses the image of an ever-expanding sphere of light that will diffuse in every direction instantaneously so long as no opaque matter stands in the way. Early in *De Luce* Grosseteste reflects on why light must be the first corporeal form in creation and concludes that because of its characteristics and ability to self-propagate, light must either be the first bodily form or the agent through which creation came into being.[11] But how can light, which is utterly simple and without dimension, create something – let alone everything – contained in three dimensions? To address this concern, Grosseteste relies on the mathematical model of infinity.[12]

Understanding light to replicate infinitely in all directions at an instant, Grosseteste asserts that the expanding sphere of light would eventually double back on itself, becoming increasingly denser. The light expands and retracts between the outermost points of the sphere and the center point of originating light. A simplistic analogy may be drawn to the act of churning butter. As cream is churned in on itself through the process of

---

Southern, *Robert Grosseteste: The Growth of an English Mind in Medieval Europe.* (Oxford: Clarendon Press, 1986), 64; and James McEvoy, *The Philosophy of Robert Grosseteste.* (Oxford: Clarendon Press, 1982), 4-5. It would seem appropriate to assert that, given the information at hand, McEvoy's position regarding the likelihood of Grosseteste's birth before 1170 to be most sound.

[7] There is written evidence of Grosseteste's presence as a young master signing a charter as a witness sometime between 1186 and 1190, as shown in McEvoy, *Robert Grosseteste*, 21.

[8] McEvoy, *Robert Grosseteste*, 29.

[9] McEvoy, *Robert Grosseteste*, 88.

[10] McEvoy, *Robert Grosseteste*, 88.

[11] Grosseteste, "On Light" trans. Wallis, 475.

[12] Grosseteste, "On Light" trans. Wallis, 475.

forced expansion and retraction and becomes thickened into butter, so too light "churns" itself into a denser matter establishing tri-dimensionality. Borrowing from Aristotle's *De Coelo et Mundo* Grosseteste notes that if something simple is plurified[13] an infinite number of times, it necessarily results in a finite product.[14] This finite product is the created world.

The majority of the remaining portion of his treatise is a complicated explication of his mathematical premises that support light being the first bodily form and the primary agent through which God created the world. Grosseteste closes his work with a detailed look at the created world, as he understood its makeup. Drawing on his medieval understanding of the created world that consisted of several spheres – both celestial and terrestrial in nature – he explains that God's choice to use light is the intelligent work of God, creating the perfect number of spheres, ten types in all.[15] Grosseteste, capping his explanation of creation, explains that, "Wherefore every whole and perfect thing is a ten."[16] He concludes *De Luce* by analyzing the numerals that he has identified as observable in creation and through which creation is held in balance: one, two, three and four. Mathematical to the end, Grosseteste poetically concludes his treatise with a final look at the above four numerals, "Wherefore only those five concordant ratios exist in musical measures, in dances, and in rhythmic times."[17]

Grosseteste is clearly influenced by scripture with its frequent use of light in image and metaphor.[18] One may easily see the significance scripture had in the formation of his intellectual works. Although it is often the mathematical rigor and precision of *De Luce* that is first noticed, its foundation rests in Grosseteste's understanding of God's revelation to humanity through scripture. In a time when the scholastic method of

---

[13] Wallis repeatedly uses the term *Plurification* in reference to the multiplication of light in his translation of "On Light" found in *Philosophy in the Middle Ages*, 2d ed., 475.

[14] Grosseteste, "On Light" trans. Wallis, 475.

[15] Grosseteste, "On Light" trans. Wallis, 478-80.

[16] Grosseteste, "On Light" trans. Wallis, 480.

[17] Grosseteste, "On Light" trans. Wallis, 480.

[18] Grosseteste was certainly well versed in scripture and borrows from the first chapter of Genesis: "Then God said, 'Let there be light,' and there was light" (Gen 1:3). It is likely he was also influenced by Paul who later makes reference to the light of Genesis when addressing revelation to the church in Corinth: "For God who said, 'Let light shine out of darkness,' has shone in our hearts to bring to light the knowledge of the glory of God on the face of Christ" (2 Cor 4:6). For more on Grosseteste's use of the Genesis reference to light see, C.F.J. Martin, *Robert Grosseteste: On the Six Days of Creation, a Translation of the Hexaemeron* (Oxford: Oxford University Press, 1996); and McEvoy, *Robert Grosseteste*, 89.

study was gaining prominence in the universities, John Moorman notes the impact that Grosseteste's insistent use of scripture in teaching had on his students.

> Grosseteste, who was already a mature scholar when he began his work for the friars, set the tone which Oxford scholars, both friars and seculars were to follow for many years. The special characteristics of his teaching were, first, his emphasis upon, and use of, the Bible, and 'the irrefragable authority of Scripture,' rather than the *Sentences* of Peter Lombard, as the textbook of all study.[19]

The importance of scripture as a classroom text when other scholars preferred the new scholastic text of Lombard highlights the explicit impact that the Bible had on Grosseteste's worldview. McEvoy suggests that *De Luce* be read today as a speculative interpretation of the Genesis account of creation. He also makes note of Grosseteste's use of biblically based language throughout his treatise, citing the Oxford thinker's use of "the firmament" as a deliberate attempt to emphasize that this is a theory of God's creation and not some alternate explanation of the created world.[20] For Grosseteste, God is present in and throughout the entire creative act. Fusing theology with scientific inquiry, he set a precedent at the Oxford school that had lasting impact on the Franciscan scholars to follow.

In a lecture given in 1916 on English Franciscan history, A.G. Little praises Grosseteste for the precedents he established at the school and credits him with setting the standard of scholarship that elevated the young Franciscan school to such prestige. Of great importance to Little is the work of Grosseteste in linguistics, particularly his fluency in Hebrew and Greek. This skill allowed Grosseteste, with a Christian worldview, to introduce ancient philosophers and commentators into the Oxford classroom.[21] Again, it is Grosseteste who sets the stage for the future scholars by broadening the material accessible to his students. "Robert Grosseteste, who set the standard for Franciscan study ... realized more

---

[19] John Moorman, *A History of The Franciscan Order: From Its Origins to the Year 1517* (Chicago: Franciscan Herald Press, 1988), 242-43.

[20] McEvoy, *Robert Grosseteste*, 89.

[21] A.G. Little, *Studies in English Franciscan History* (Oxford: Manchester University Press, 1917), 193-221.

and more the need for studying the books of the Bible in the languages in which they were written, for which purpose he made himself acquainted with both Greek and Hebrew."[22]

It is clear that Grosseteste had a particular fondness for the friars[23] and an often under-appreciated role in the foundation of the Franciscan intellectual tradition. As Moorman records, "Grosseteste had left Oxford by the time of Alexander of Hales's entry into the Franciscan Order, so that he must rank as among the first to lay the foundation of a Franciscan school."[24] Included among his foundational contributions can be the synthesizing of science with theology while remaining rooted in scripture. His pupils, such as Roger Bacon and those who follow, would later go on to excel in this type of scholarship. It is for this reason that Grosseteste's inquiry into the created world is so central in the early Franciscan intellectual movement. When facing the question of the "how" of creation, it is with scripture that he starts, and it is with God he remains. By isolating the first corporeal body as primordial light, Grosseteste developed an influential cosmogony that has had lasting import.

Creation as God's Free Gift of Love

About seventy years after Robert Grosseteste, John Duns Scotus, perhaps best known for his work on developing the philosophical principles that would later influence the promulgation of the doctrine of the Immaculate Conception and asserting the absolute necessity of the Incarnation, also grappled with questions regarding creation. As Grosseteste sought to articulate his understanding of how creation came to be, Scotus looked to his study of theology and his Franciscan tradition to help elucidate the "why" of creation.

Scotus studied and taught at the Franciscan school at Oxford, a beneficiary of Grosseteste's establishment of the program there. Like Grosseteste, what remains recorded of Scotus's early history leaves many questions unanswered. It is believed that he was born in Duns, Scotland

---

[22] Moorman, *A History of The Franciscan Order*, 394.

[23] Moorman notes that "Grosseteste had already seen something of the Preaching Friars (Dominicans), but it was the Franciscans who won his warmest approval, an approval which grew into an affection which at one time very nearly persuaded him to take the habit himself." (Moorman, *A History of The Franciscan Order*, 92). Additionally, Robert Grosseteste is known to have bequeathed all his books to the friars in England in 1253. (184-85).

24 Moorman, *A History of The Franciscan Order*, 243.

around 1266[25] and died on November 8, 1308 in Cologne, Germany. Scholars assert that Scotus studied in Paris after entering the Franciscan Order and doing preliminary studies in Oxford, followed by some lecturing at the university. This assignment to study in Paris indicates the caliber of thinker that Scotus was since the Minster General of the Order would appoint a select number of men to do advanced studies there. After his time in Paris, the Order would again ask him to move, this time to Cologne where he would oversee the theological studies of the Franciscan students. Scotus died three years later at the age of 42.

Although young at the time of his death, Scotus left behind a significant amount of written work, all at various stages of completion, which has contributed to the difficulty one encounters when studying his work. Like Grosseteste, other preceding thinkers and his colleagues, Scotus wrote and lectured on a great many subjects in philosophy and theology. However, creation for Scotus might be seen as the linchpin that connects his varied work. Asserting the inherit dignity of all creation, Scotus develops his thought on creation through the lens of contingency of the world and the freedom of God.[26] Ilia Delio summarizes Scotus's approach to creation: "For Scotus, *why* creation comes about is more important than *how* creation comes about... Creation is simply the work of an infinitely loving creator."[27] With the precursory and foundational work of Oxford thinkers of the Franciscan school like Grosseteste that systematically outlined the "how" of creation, Scotus picked up the issue of "why."

To understand the starting point for a thinker such as Scotus, his Franciscan experience must be viewed as his primary hermeneutic. The spirituality that defined his religious community, and therefore his own experience, is deeply rooted in the belief of Francis of Assisi that all creation is good and created by a loving God. For Scotus, God's love is the reason *par excellence* for creation. This foundational position is the springboard for his doctrine of the contingency of the world. Scotus believed that nothing was created out of necessity; nothing *had to be*. Rather, everything that is, has been, or will be is brought into intentional existence through God's divine freedom. To suggest that the world and all it contains *must*

[25] For more on the dating of Scotus's birth and early history, see Mary Beth Ingham, *Scotus for Dunces: An Introduction to the Subtle Doctor* (St. Bonaventure, NY: Franciscan Institute Publications, 2003), 13-23.
[26] Delio, *A Franciscan View of Creation*, 33.
[27] Delio, *A Franciscan View of Creation*, 33.

have been created diminishes God's freedom and detracts from the loving act of self-gift that God has so willingly granted. To believe that God's creating act is freely done says more about the Creator than it does about the creation. Mary Beth Ingham describes Scotus's perspective as, "God is the artist and creation the work of art."[28] No more than an artist *has* to create a work of art does God *have* to create the world.

If the world and all of creation are contingent, then it must have been a deliberate choice for God to create. For Scotus this is a metaphysical issue. It directs one to consider what it means for God to be God. Scotus philosophically deduces that absolutely nothing can interfere with God's ability to act freely. Every choice of God, because of its rational and free character, does not impede, limit, or narrow other possibilities vis-à-vis God's divine freedom.[29] In other words, the fact that something exists – that you or I exist – does not limit or narrow the possibility for it to have been any other way or interfere with any other choice of God. This position has extraordinary consequences in the area of creation's inherit dignity. Everything that is created is a reflection of a particular decisive act of God to bring that aspect of the created world into existence. That God has particularly chosen to create a given thing implies that thing's intrinsic value.

Scotus addresses the particular dignity of creation in his doctrine of *Haecceitas*, or "thisness."[30] While the term is at first intimidating, it is a rather simple principle. Scotus, with an appreciation for the inherent dignity of every created thing because it was individually chosen to be created by God, wished to express what makes each part of creation one thing and not another. Prior philosophical language simply stated that "this" is "not-that."[31] Scotus's perspective focused simply on the "this," establishing a positive term as opposed to a negative qualifier that defined items of creation in opposition to each other. Scotus's doctrine of *Haecceitas* is incredibly relational. Focusing on the very individuality of created beings necessarily reflects the Creator that brought the individual creation into

---

[28] Ingham, *Scotus for Dunces*, 38.

[29] Ingham, *Scotus for Dunces*, 51.

[30] "Haecceitas – From *haec* (literally *this*); the individuating principle of each being; the ultimate reality of the being." From the glossary of Ingham, *Scotus for Dunces*, 228. For more see Daniel Horan, "Thomas Merton the 'Dunce': Identity, Incarnation and the Not-so-subtle Influence of John Duns Scotus," *Cistercian Studies Quarterly* 47 (2012): esp. 157-165.

[31] Ingham, *Scotus for Dunces*, 52.

existence. Since this individuating character of each created being is a mystery known to God alone – for it is neither measurable nor empirical – *Haecceitas* refers to the ultimate reality of any being.[32] Summarizing the distinction in thought between Scotus and Aquinas, Ingham states:

> According to Scotus, the created order is not best understood as a transparent medium through which divine light shines (as Aquinas taught), but is itself endowed with an inner light that shines forth from within. The difference between these two great scholastics can be compared to the difference between a window (Aquinas) and a lamp (Scotus). Both give light, but the source of light for Scotus has already been given to the being by the creator.[33]

Scotus's vision draws on the metaphor of light, perhaps inspired by the thought of his predecessor Grosseteste. It reflects his strong position of both the sacredness of each person as individually and uniquely chosen, created and loved by God, while also acknowledging the very presence of God in all creation. Since all creation is a gift from God, God's love must be the source of that gift. Echoing John's Gospel, "For God so loved the world that He gave His only Son, so that everyone who believes in Him might not perish but might have eternal life" (Jn 3:16), Scotus develops the doctrine of the necessity of the Incarnation, strengthening his position of God's free and loving choice to create.[34] Scotus asserts that the Incarnation was always part of the overall plan of creation, not the result of human sin, as Anselm and others have speculated. As Delio puts it, "Creation was only a prelude to a much fuller manifestation of divine goodness, namely, the Incarnation."[35] As stated above, no choice resulting from God's divine freedom can limit or narrow any other choice, including human sin, as some believed was the reason for the Incarnation. For Scotus, the Incarnation was simply the quintessential expression of God's over-flowing love.

A gift is not a gift if its giving is forced. God's creation is a gift and therefore a freely chosen one, given like any other gift out of love. Scotus answers the question of the "why" of creation with the simple response:

---

[32] Ingham, *Scotus for Dunces*, 54.
[33] Ingham, *Scotus for Dunces*, 54-55.
[34] See Horan, "How Original Was Scotus on the Incarnation?"
[35] Delio, *A Franciscan View of Creation*, 34.

love. Proving that all that is created is not necessary, and that God is absolutely free to choose as God desires, Scotus makes clear the Love that is the source of all creation, exemplified by the Incarnation.

Synthesizing a Franciscan Response to Questions of Creation

Distilled to their most basic forms, the Franciscan answers to the questions of "how" and "why" creation came to be and was created are light and love. Robert Grosseteste, deeply rooted in the tradition of scripture, sought to propose a way of viewing how God might have created the world. John Duns Scotus, awed by the beauty and goodness of creation, sought to elucidate the reason for anything's existence. Together these two great Oxford Franciscan thinkers provide the world with a synthesis that calls us to recognize the inherent dignity, beauty, goodness, and presence of God in creation.

While proof of the direct influence of Grosseteste's treatise on light on Scotus may never be known with complete certitude, it is safe to assume that the "Subtle Doctor" was at least exposed to and familiar with the work. Evident is the significance of the biblical use of light featured in the work of both thinkers when addressing their respective questions on creation. The work of Grosseteste and Scotus offers us light and love as the lenses through which we can view our created world. Establishing a paradigm based on the themes articulated by these Oxford Franciscans prompts the recalling of our relational nature and reminds us of the intrinsic dignity of all of creation. Like Francis in his *The Canticle of the Creatures*[36] we are brought to awareness of the fraternal nature of our existence among and with the rest of the created world. As we strive to love our neighbors, the call to recognize the interconnectedness of creation challenges us to look beyond the human family to the entire created world.

In an age when we are faced with questions about our stewardship of our world, when we are challenged by global warming, air and water pollution, war, consumerism, over-population, deforestation, and other areas of concern, we can look to the message of the Franciscan scholastics from Oxford for grounding. Their message is a holistic, foundational view of creation upon which we can build a more sustainable vision of the future. The work of Grosseteste, far removed from the complexities

[36] Francis of Assisi, "The Canticle of the Creatures," in *FAED* 1:113.

and advances of modern scientific theory, continues to provide an allegory for our understanding of the relational nature of our existence among all creation. Reflecting on the metaphoric use of light as the primordial corporeal form through which all things come into existence, we hold a keepsake of our interconnectedness and interdependence on the rest of creation. Holding firm to that realization, we can look to Scotus to provide additional meaning to that view. With our interconnectedness and interdependence comes the truth that, along with the rest of the created world, we are individually chosen, created, and loved by God. Scotus explains that while we may come from a single source, each person and creation has an inherent dignity and value that exceeds our understanding to remain a mystery known to God alone. Looking through the lenses of light and love to better appreciate the created world and the creation act, it is marvelous to consider God's over-flowing love and divine freedom that is at the core of creation.

Our existence in the modern world demands an acute awareness of the choices we make regarding our relationship with creation. Writing on the humility of God found in the work of Francis and Bonaventure, Delio notes that the Gospel life today requires our entering into a world of global consciousness and community.[37] Following Jesus Christ in an age of increased globalization changes the way we live in the world and subsequently the way we relate to creation. Drawing on the rich Franciscan view of creation found in the work of Robert Grosseteste and John duns Scotus, we are aided in the deepening of our relationship with Jesus Christ and can, therefore, enter more deeply into our relationship with the created world. Francis's experience of relationship was not limited to human beings but extended to even the tiny creatures of creation. "As his life deepened in the life of Christ, he came to recognize that the meaning of Christ extended beyond human persons to include non-human creation."[38] Inspired by the light and love of God evident in the existence of the world around us, we are moved to embrace the call to be just stewards of creation.

Al Gore, in his acclaimed documentary on global warming, *An Inconvenient Truth*, mentions that global warming and other critical issues affecting our planet are not just political or social matters, but are ethical

---

[37] Ilia Delio, "Evangelical Life Today: Living in the Ecological Christ," *Franciscan Studies* 64 (2006): 477.

[38] Delio, "Evangelical Life Today," 489.

and moral responsibilities that impact everyone.[39] As Franciscan men and women this is not something new to us. With a tradition spanning eight centuries of viewing creation fraternally, we are entrusted with a message for the world that simply states that when creation is neglected or abused an injustice of considerable proportion is committed. Not only is such neglect or abuse a violation of the intrinsic dignity of all created things, but a turning away from the light of God that shines forth from creation, expressing God's love. To live a Franciscan life rooted in the Gospel is a way of living in the world.[40] It is a way of living that values and protects the dignity of creation with respect to our fraternal relationship. It is a love for a gift that is freely given. And it is an assurance of our commitment to pass on the gift to future generations so that they too may experience the light and love of God.

---

[39] *An Inconvenient Truth*, DVD, directed by Davis Guggenheim (Paramount Home Video, 2006).

[40] Delio, "Evangelical Life Today," 503.

CHAPTER TWELVE

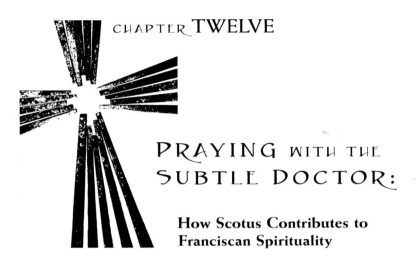

PRAYING WITH THE SUBTLE DOCTOR:

How Scotus Contributes to Franciscan Spirituality

The year 2008 marked the seven-hundredth anniversary of the death of John Duns Scotus. Much had been planned in honor of this milestone, including The Quadruple Congress, a series of conferences each exploring a particular aspect of the corpus of this renowned medieval Franciscan thinker.[1] The conference themes included his philosophical and theological works, his metaphysical and ethical system, and an historical retrospective of Scotus's influence and the development of the Scotist school through the centuries. What was not explicitly included was an examination of the spiritual component of his thought and subsequent work.

The absence of significant scholarship that explores the practical spiritual and theological implications of Scotus's work remains a disappointing reality. Few have delved into the deep-seated Franciscan spirituality that appears to have anchored the philosopher and theologian, and have neglected to produce a substantive study of Scotus's own personal experiences of prayer. One exception is Mary Beth Ingham who has, in fact, expressed a significant appreciation for that which served Scotus at his

---

[1] This first of these conferences took place at St. Bonaventure University on 18-21 October 2007 with the theme "The Opera Philosophica of John Duns Scotus." Three additional conferences followed in Oxford (21-24 July 2008), Bonn (5-9 November 2008) and Strasbourg (18-22 March 2009); with themes, "The Opera Theologica of Scotus," "The Metaphysics and Ethics of Scotus," and "Scotism through the Centuries," respectively.

spiritual core.[2] Ingham writes,

> I find that where scholars misread or misunderstand Scotus they have not taken adequate account of his spiritual vision precisely as a Franciscan... Here is a thinker who is consciously spiritual in his intellectual endeavor and consciously Christian in his understanding of the divine nature.[3]

Elsewhere, Ingham extols Franciscan scholars to be more aware of those areas of Scotistic scholarship that have gone significantly unexplored, areas such as the aesthetic-spiritual implications for matters of a moral and pastoral nature that might be beneficially informed by the work of Scotus.[4]

For many, the reading and study of Scotus's work can be burdensome. Scotus, though he died young around the age of 42, left behind a significant body of influential work that is dense and technical. People outside of academe, and even those inside the academy who do not specialize in areas related to Scotus, when faced with his philosophical and theological thought, might raise the legitimate question, "Who cares about Scotus?" This is a question rooted in concern that the medieval work of the English Franciscan bears no practical relevance today. If one is not a trained philosopher or theologian, what does Scotus have to offer? I believe the answer to that question is found in part through examination of his work, but more completely in what is not written. As Ingham acknowledges, Scotus's spiritual life should be seen as the foundation upon which all of his intellectual inquiry is built. It is here, the spiritual foundation of Scotistic thought, that we can retrieve practical relevance for today that even the most unlettered Christian might appreciate.

As a Franciscan friar, Scotus is an inheritor of and a contributor to a rich and dynamic spiritual tradition beginning with the *vita evangelica* of Francis of Assisi. So often, as Ingham reminds us, Scotus is seen as a participant and leader in the equally rich Franciscan intellectual tradition, without due regard for his role in the spiritual life of the same community. While the absence of serious consideration for the spiritual significance of

---

[2] See Mary Beth Ingham, "*Fides Quaerens Intellectum*: John Duns Scotus, Philosophy and Prayer," in *Franciscans at Prayer*, ed. Timothy Johnson (Leiden/Boston: Brill, 2007), 167-191.

[3] Ingham, *Scotus for Dunces*, 145.

[4] Mary Beth Ingham, "John Duns Scotus: Retrieving A Medieval Thinker for Contemporary Theology," in *The Franciscan Intellectual Tradition: Washington Theological Union Symposium Papers 2001*, ed. Elise Saggau (St. Bonaventure, NY: Franciscan Institute Publications, 2002), 103-104.

Scotus is jarring, he is in good company. Bonaventure, while recognized for his spiritual contribution in work like the *Itinerarium Mentis In Deum*,[5] has often been eclipsed by colossal spiritual figures like Francis and Clare. Until recently, it seems as though he was also relegated to a place among the great intellectuals of history whose scope was limited to complex philosophical and theological explication. In recent years, scholars and writers have re-engaged Bonaventure in order to retrieve his spiritual insights, thoughts, and guidance that continue to speak to us in our contemporary world.[6]

Like Bonaventure, Scotus offers contemporary Christians a great deal on which to consider and reflect, transcending the strictures of the academy to enrich the spiritual life of even the most-simple *pray-er*. While this chapter is to serve as a preliminary examination of Scotus's continued relevance in the Franciscan spiritual tradition and remains very introductory in scope, my hope is that is might animate further study of and conversation concerning Scotus's spiritual significance today.

To lift from his life and work Scotus' spiritual experiences, I propose an examination of his primary hermeneutic as a methodological starting point. Love is the foundational lens through which Scotus views his relationship to God, to others, and to creation.[7] When identifying the reason for God's creative act or exploring the reason for the Incarnation, Scotus turns to love as the existential answer. Love will serve as the thread that links the three areas of Scotistic spirituality that we will examine in this brief study. After an introduction to Scotus's view of love as the reason for God's action *par excellence*, we will look at Christ, humanity, and creation. It is in and through these particular subjects that we can better appreciate Scotus's spiritual life and his contemporary relevance.

I hope to demonstrate that his work, brilliant and complicated as it is, may also serve as a prayerful reference point in our reflection on

---

[5] See Bonaventure, *Itinerarium Mentis In Deum*, eds. Philotheus Boehner and Zachary Hayes (St. Bonaventure, NY: Franciscan Institute Publications, 2002).

[6] In the English language see Delio, *Franciscan Prayer*; Delio, *The Humility of God*; Mary Esther Stewart, *Meet Our Brother Bonaventure* (Phoenix: Tau Publishing, 2012); and Josef Raischl and Andre Cirino, *The Journey Into God: A Forty-Day Retreat with Bonaventure, Francis and Clare* (Cincinnati: St. Anthony Messenger Press, 2002). These authors engage the theological and philosophical work of Bonaventure as it relates to the foundational spiritual insight of the early Franciscan movement as articulated in the writings of Francis and Clare. All three volumes mentioned above are developed in such a way as to provide access to the everyday reader seeking a deeper appreciation for the Franciscan spiritual tradition.

[7] See Daniel Horan, "Light and Love: Robert Grosseteste and John Duns Scotus on the How and Why of Creation," *The Cord* 57 (2007): 252-253.

relationships rooted in love. Scotus speaks to us today and, through his work, articulates the reality of Divine love present in creation and in our own nature. Although the name John Duns Scotus may never stand beside those of John of the Cross, Ignatius, Francis, Clare, or even Bonaventure as spiritual masters, it is my hope that he may not be left too far behind.

All You Need Is Love

Love is an amorphous term. The confusion surrounding its meaning is complicated further by the English language's lack of specificity and our unfortunate tendency to overuse the word. When used in its proper context, love is perhaps one of the most powerful words in the English lexicon. Its authentic use connotes sacrifice, care, concern, selflessness, affection, self-gift, passion, tenderness, consideration for, loyalty, respect, attraction, fidelity, and other feelings or experiences that transcend language all together. This powerful word is at the core of Scotus's worldview. His entire system evolves from and revolves around love.

Alan Perreiah reminded scholars of a significant blind spot in Scotus scholarship. While a resurgence of interest in Scotus began in the preceding decades, little attention has been paid to emotion in the English Franciscan's theory.[8] Reflecting on the image of Scotus at that time, Perreiah confirmed the dry and serious caricature often painted of the thinker. Perreiah continues, "The idea that a human person would have an emotional life associated with each of these factors is hardly noticed by modern scholars."[9] This called the scholarly world to seriously consider the multidimensional and complex nature of the scholastic master. Beyond the intricacies of his philosophical and theological work rests a deeply spiritual and loving human person. His reflection on life, God, and his close relationships – particularly with his Franciscan brothers in community – led him to discover love as the metanarrative theme told by God and all of creation.

In a recent article Franciscan theologian Kenan Osborne proposed a reconsideration of Scotus's philosophical and theological contributions to Christian spirituality.[10] The typical view of Scotus's *Distinctio XVII of the*

---

[8] Alan Perreiah, "Scotus on Human Emotions," *Franciscan Studies* 56 (1998): 325-345.

[9] Perreiah, "Scotus on Human Emotions," 326.

[10] Kenan Osborne, "A Scotistic Foundation for Christian Spirituality," *Franciscan Studies* 64 (2006): 363-405. Osborne explores the foundation for an interpretation of the Gospel life (*vita evangelica*) through examination of *Distinctio XVII* of the *Reportatio I-A*. Osborne suggests a re-reading of *Distinctio XVII* by way of a spiritual hermeneutic in order to glean a Scotistic perspective on

Reportatio I-A is that he maintains a rejection of the position espoused by Peter Lombard, Henry of Ghent, and Godfrey of Fontaines vis-à-vis the univocal nature of *caritas* that is the Holy Spirit and caritas that is human love.[11] The position of Lombard *et al* is that "the Holy Spirit [caritas] is indeed the very love [*caritas*] by which we human beings love God and our neighbor."[12] Osborne's examination of *Distinctio XVII* is an effort to retrieve the spiritual underpinnings of Scotus's view of *caritas* in light of the Divine-human and human-human relationships strived after in Christian living.

While Osborne does not explicitly identify a uniquely Scotistic spirituality, the centrality of love in Christian living and relationship as Scotus's primary hermeneutic is certainly affirmed. Osborne's recognition that Scotus moves beyond intellectual rivalry in denouncing his intellectual predecessors' limited position in order to illuminate the primary mode of Christian response in our world, namely love freely given, helps to put Scotus's starting point in perspective. This line of inquiry suggests that Scotus's philosophical and theological work is rooted in prayerful reflection of what it means to be created in love and for love. We continually return to this omnipresent theme in the corpus of Scotus.

In his *Tractatus De Primo Principio* (Treatise On God as First Principle), Scotus begins with a prayer,

> O Lord our God, true teacher that you are, when Moses your servant asked you for your name that he might proclaim it to the children of Israel, you, knowing what the mind of mortals could grasp of you, replied: 'I am who am,' thus disclosing your blessed name. *You are truly what it means to be, you are the whole of what it means to exist.* This, if it be possible for me, I should like to know by way of demonstration. Help me then, O Lord, as I investigate how much our natural reason can learn about that true being which you are if we being with the being which you have predicated of yourself.[13]

Christian love of God and neighbor and the free will associated with making decisions to love. See also John Duns Scotus, *Ordinatio* III, suppl. Dist. 27, in *Duns Scotus on the Will and Morality*, trans. Allan Wolter (Washington: Catholic University of America Press, 1986), 422-447.

[11] For more see Osborne, "A Scotistic Foundation for Christian Spirituality," 386-399.

[12] Osborne, "A Scotistic Foundation for Christian Spirituality," 386.

[13] John Duns Scotus, *Tractatus De Primo Principio* 1.2, in *John Duns Scotus: A Treatise on God as First Principle*, trans. Allan Wolter (Chicago: Franciscan Herald Press, 1982), 2. Emphasis added.

This text presents Scotus as someone beyond simply an inquiring mind. He shows himself to be a thinker that is deeply connected to his subject – God – in a personal relationship. He connects his proceeding endeavor with the source of its origin and acknowledges that God is the definition of what it means to be and it is only with God's assistance that he might come to understand anything correctly. Allan Wolter, in his commentary on this text, informs the reader that this prayer, while repugnant to modern philosophers as being superfluous to the task at hand and even inappropriate in scholarly discourse, was extracted from the original text and presented in a condensed form in a collection of ascetical writings devoid of the philosophical argumentation.[14] At some time the prayers of Scotus were considered to be of value enough to be rewritten.[15]

More striking than the prayer itself is what follows. In his presentation of the interrelationship of ordered elements,[16] Scotus refers to God not simply as the "unmoved mover" of ancient Greek Philosophy, but as both the efficient and final cause of creation rooted in loving relationship. Scotus frequently returns to love as the central element in his metaphysical discourse. Clearly his approach, one of prayerful inquiry founded on a deep appreciation for the centrality of love, is inspired by the spirituality of Francis of Assisi. According to Ingham, Scotus's work stands on two pillars: 1) all of creation exists as a gift from God, and 2) preference is always given to love over knowledge in an effort to better enter into relationship with God.[17]

Béraud de Saint-Maurice writes of the central position that love has in the thought of Scotus when compared to intelligence,

> It is easy to perceive the primacy that love holds over intelligence, since the intellect draws its object to itself and molds it to

---

Hereafter cited as *De Primo Principio*.

[14] Allan Wolter, "Commentary on the *De Primo Principio* of Duns Scotus," in *John Duns Scotus: A Treatise on God as First Principle*, ed. Allan Wolter (Chicago: Franciscan Herald Press, 1982), 160-161.

[15] Wolter makes reference to the Berlin manuscript (Codex B) and the proximity of the condensed form of Scotus's *De Primo Principio,* minus the philosophical argumentation, to Bonaventure's *Itinerarium Mentis in Deum.* The compiler(s) of the manuscript obviously found Scotus's prayers of great spiritual value to be included alongside Bonaventure's most acclaimed spiritual work.

[16] *De Primo Principio* 2.3-2.51.

[17] Mary Beth Ingham, "John Duns Scotus: An Integrated Vision," in *The History of Franciscan Theology*, ed. Kenan Osborne (St. Bonaventure, NY: Franciscan Institute Publications, 1994), 186-187.

its own size, so to speak, whereas love goes to its object and, without restraint nor loss, attains it as it is in itself.[18]

Scotus's spirituality, found beneath and within his philosophy, makes real the dignity of humanity and creation. His focus on the individuality of the person (*haecceitas*) as created by God's infinite love reveals much about his primary hermeneutic. As we examine Scotus's approach to Christ, humanity, and creation, may we look through the lens of love to share in Scotus's worldview and, in doing so, pray with the Subtle Doctor.

Christ: Love Incarnate

The necessity of the Incarnation as argued by Scotus testifies to the great depths of his spirituality. For Scotus, the Incarnation is the summation of Salvation History, not viewed as atonement for the grievous sin of humanity, but as the most concrete sign of God's infinite love and goodness. Some before him, like Anselm of Canterbury, saw the Incarnation as what Scotus might describe as a conditional act of God's love in response to the human need for Salvation. Scotus believed such a position was intrinsically flawed for it stood against our fundamental beliefs about God and how God acts.

Scotus asserts God's unconditional love in Christ, stating that Jesus would have been born regardless of human sinfulness. Even if humanity had never sinned, the Word would still have become flesh. Scotus radically shifts the focus from us to God, from debt to gift, from sin to love. According to this hermeneutic of love, the response we have to the Incarnation is not a debt based in human sin, but a debt anchored in love.[19] Scotus summarizes this position himself:

> Neither is it likely that the highest good in the whole of creation is something that merely chanced to take place, and that only because of some lesser good. Nor is it probable that God predestined Adam to such a good before he predestined Christ. Yet all of this would follow, yes, and even something more absurd. If the predestination of Christ's soul was for the sole purpose of redeeming others, it would follow that in

---

[18] Béraud de Saint-Maurice, "The Contemporary Significance of Duns Scotus's Philosophy," in *John Duns Scotus: 1265-1965*, eds. John Ryan and Bernadine Bonansea (Washington, DC: The Catholic University of America Press, 1965), 365.

[19] Mary Beth Ingham, "Duns Scotus, Divine Delight and Franciscan Evangelical Life," *Franciscan Studies* 64 (2006): 343.

foreordaining Adam to glory, God would have had to foresee
him as having fallen into sin before he could have predestined
Christ to glory.[20]

There is no doubt that the Incarnation played a significant role in
the spirituality of Scotus. Once attuned to recognize God's love, Scotus's
prayer almost certainly involved meditation on the immense generosity and
limitless care God has for God's own creation. There is no manifestation
of this gracious gift of God's Self more explicit than in the decision to
become Incarnate. The awareness of this reality led Scotus to explore
philosophically that which he reflected upon prayerfully. It naturally
follows that the recognition of such tremendous love and humility found in
consideration of God Incarnate would lead one to a profound experience of
the transcendent. In this respect our quest for a glimpse into the spiritual
world of Scotus intersects with that of his own Franciscan tradition. Ilia
Delio's description of Franciscan Prayer reflects the Incarnational view of
Scotus:

> The simplest way to describe Franciscan prayer is that it begins
> and ends with the Incarnation. It begins with encountering the
> God of overflowing love in the person of Jesus Christ and ends
> with embodying that love in one's own life, becoming a new
> Incarnation.[21]

Connecting this insight with that of the true meaning of the Franciscan
vita evangelica, Delio reminds us that in the humility of Christ lies the
path of those wishing to follow the Gospel. It is ultimately God's love as
Trinity that remains at the center of Christ's humility; it remains our task
to constantly rediscover the love of God and our love of neighbor in our
journey to imitate Christ's humility.

We can use Scotus's Incarnational reflection as a launching point for
our own prayerful encounter with God's love. What is moving about his
adamant defense of the necessity of the Incarnation is the power of God's
forgiveness that shines through his work. Scotus's intellectual adversaries

---

20 John Duns Scotus, *Ordinatio* III, dist. 7, q. 3, trans. Allan Wolter, "John Duns Scotus on the
Primacy and Personality of Christ," in *Franciscan Christology*, ed. Damian McElrath (St. Bonaventure,
NY: Franciscan Institute Publications, 1994), 148-151.

21 Delio, *Franciscan Prayer*, 181.

were concerned about the relationship between The Fall and human Redemption gifted through the Incarnation. Scotus finds this correlation immaterial. Sin plays no major role in his understanding of God's choice to enter our world as a human being. Scotus certainly believes in sin and the problems that are associated with human brokenness. However, God's love, mercy, and goodness completely outweigh whatever sinfulness human beings encounter. Drawing again on the love of God, Scotus reminds us of the inherent dignity of humanity in God's glorification of human nature through the Incarnation.[22] Scotus makes us aware that God's love overcomes our brokenness and God's forgiveness overcomes our sin.

Scotus's prayer of the Incarnation is gratitude. Upon recognizing the tremendous gift of Jesus the *Emmanuel* (God-with-us),[23] Scotus is moved to thanks: thanks for the glorification of our human nature, thanks for the gift of redemption in spite of our brokenness, thanks for the outpouring of God's forgiveness of our sin. When we fall short of our own expectations and find it hard to see God or good in the world, Scotus points to the Incarnation as a reminder of God's imminent presence among and within us. His prayer stems from the recognition that we are not alone, but that God loves us beyond any possible conceptualization and desires to be with us. When the problems of our troubled world threaten our faith and we are unsure where to turn, Scotus's view of the Incarnation provides a starting point for prayer and sign of God's fidelity. May we share in the faith Scotus has of God's love made present in our world through the Incarnation.

Humanity: Individually Loved

Theologian Michael Himes, reflecting on the Incarnation, notes a fundamental truth that lies at the heart of our understanding of the meaning of God-becoming-human. Himes says, "[the Incarnation] is not, first and foremost, the revelation of who God is; first and foremost, it is the revelation of who we are. The Incarnation tells us what it means to be a human being."[24] This observation brings us Scotus's view of humanity.

If the Incarnation serves as the most explicit and concrete sign of God's love, while also glorifying humanity through God's physical entry into our world, then the creation of humanity must reflect the love of God

---

[22] Ingham, *Scotus for Dunces*, 77-78.
[23] Ingham, *Scotus for Dunces*, 78.
[24] Michael Himes, *The Mystery of Faith: An Introduction to Catholicism* (Cincinnati: St. Anthony Messenger Press, 2004), 20.

in tremendous ways and to unfathomable degrees. In partial response to Incarnational inquiry and additional reflection on creation, Scotus develops a concept he calls *haecceitas* (literally "this-ness").[25] As God's Divine intentionality led to the Incarnation, so too God chose to create other beings. Scotus spends a great deal of his intellectual energy on understanding and explaining what it means to be created by God, and it should come as no surprise that his foundation is again God's love.

If we look closely at the meaning of *haecceitas*, we see the inherent dignity that is ascribed to humanity – and later to all of creation – that arises from the principle that individuation is the result of God's direct creative work. In his early lecture at Oxford, *De Principio Individuationis* (The principle of individuation),[26] Scotus rejects a number of previously held theories about the nature of individuation. Ranging from the assertion of Aristotelian causes and quantity to negation and matter, Scotus found these proposals inadequate.[27] It seemed to Scotus that these views were beneath the obvious dignity of God's creative work. Instead, he insists, individuation is rooted in the very substance of a thing or person and not simply its accidents (shape, color, number, etc.).[28] Allan Wolter explains the significance of Scotus' development of the notion of *haecceity*:

> [Scotus] makes an important claim, that where rational beings are concerned it is the person rather than the nature that God primarily desired to create. His remark is in answer to an objection that individuals do not pertain to the order of the universe, for order is based on priority and posteriority, and individuals are all on par with one another. Not only do individuals pertain to the order of God's universe, Scotus retorts, but, in communicating "his goodness as something befitting his beauty, in each species" he delights in producing a multiplicity of individuals. "And in those beings which are the highest and

---

[25] Wolter summarizes the meaning of *haecceity*: "Haecceity or 'thisness' has a twofold function: (1) it makes each individual unique and incapable of duplication, even by an omnipotent God; and (2) it differentiates it radically and ultimately from each and every other individual, whether it be of the same or a specifically different type." Allan Wolter, *John Duns Scotus: Early Oxford Lecture on Individuation* (St. Bonaventure, NY: Franciscan Institute Publications, 2005), xii.

[26] The English translation is found in Allan Wolter, *John Duns Scotus: Early Oxford Lecture on Individuation* (St. Bonaventure, NY: Franciscan Institute Publications, 2005).

[27] Kenan Osborne, "Incarnation, Individuality and Diversity: How Does Christ Reveal the Unique Value of Each Person and Thing?" *The Cord* 45 (1995): 25.

[28] Osborne, "Incarnation, Individuality and Diversity," 25.

most important, it is the individual that is primarily intended by God" (*Ordinatio* II, d. 3, n. 251).[29]

This principle has dramatic implications for our lived experience of community, society, and faith. Scotus argues for the primacy of God's creative intent in the creation of every single person. Therefore, we cannot limit the reading of Genesis 1:31 to suggest that humanity in general was created "very good," but that each and every person was created very good. Wolter goes on to explain that this notion of *haecceity*, when applied to the human person, "would seem to invest each with a unique value as one singularly wanted and loved by God, quite apart from any trait that person shares with others or any contribution he or she might make to society."[30] In other words, it is not what we do, what we have, or how we act that makes us loved by God and worthy of love from others. Rather, it is *who we are* – individually created, willed and loved into being by God – that is the source of our dignity and value.

At the core of Scotus' spiritual reflection that drives this philosophical inquiry stands the Franciscan conviction of solidarity and *fraternitas*. Through this lens Scotus sees the previous theses of individuation as deficient, and he works to rectify the inadequate system of non-egalitarianism that provides the foundational subtext of bias and inequity. Even though Scotus was most likely a realist who was well aware of the historic condition of injustice in the world, I suggest the prayer of Scotus that emerges from this philosophical exercise is one for human solidarity and love of neighbor. We see in his intellectual work a window into the spirituality of someone who sincerely believes in the value of each person and who, through the same work, invited others to remember this truth.

In our world that is so ravaged by violence, hunger, marginalization, racism, terrorism, discrimination, and injustice of every kind, we can look to Scotus and remember the *haecceity* of each person. We can recall God's free and loving choice to create every person who has, who does, and who will walk the earth. We can remember that not only does God individually love us, but that every person is individually loved by God. We can, through the philosophical system of Scotus, take root in a theory that leads to a praxis of solidarity and love of neighbor. We can imitate God's love for

---

29 Wolter, *John Duns Scotus: Early Oxford Lecture on Individuation*, xxi.
30 Wolter, *John Duns Scotus: Early Oxford Lecture on Individuation*, xxi.

each member of the human family and help bring about God's Kingdom on Earth.

Creation: The Sharing in Love

As we continue our exploration of the spirituality of Scotus, we can say that there are two legs upon which his view of creation is founded: contingency and univocity. Like his belief in the inherent dignity of the human person as founded on the principle of *haecceity*, or the willing-into-being and loving by God of each individual, Scotus believes in the inherent goodness of creation rooted in divine acceptance.[31] Mary Beth Ingham explains that the existence of creation is the result of it pleasing the divine will. In other words, Scotus believes that like the loving and free choice of God to create each and every person, God likewise chose to create each and every aspect of creation. All of creation is God's gift.[32] Scotus' reflection on creation is an investigation of the "why" of God's gift, ultimately concluding that it is an act of love out of which God creates anything, and it is this love that serves as the foundation for his spirituality of relationship.

This first leg, contingency, is representative of Scotus's general preference for the primacy of love and the will over reason and the intellect. This is where he diverges from the Thomistic-scholastic school that preceded him in Paris and through which his true Franciscan colors can be seen. All that exists does so as the result of God's loving choice to create. There is no necessity associated with God's creative act in Scotus's view. Rather, God creates out of the desire (will) to be in relationship with the other (love). Because of this reasoning Scotus hails the very existence of anything at all as the direct result of God's gift of creation. Contingency, then, is the philosophical articulation of the spiritual insight that grounds the Franciscan movement in ecological *fraternitas*. What we see arise from this picture of creation is a God who does not serve simply as the "unmoved mover" at the end of a causal chain, but a God who is personal and loving, who knows each part of creation in its *haecceity*, and who chose to create it.[33] Scotus's only explanation for the beauty of creation is rooted in God's love and goodness.

The second leg of Scotus's spirituality of creation is the assertion of

---

[31] Mary Beth Ingham, *Ethics and Freedom: An Historical-Critical Investigation of Scotist Ethical Thought* (New York: University Press of America, 1989), 242.

[32] Ingham, *Scotus for Dunces*, 38.

[33] Ingham, *Scotus for Dunces*, 45.

the univocity of being. In addition to the importance of contingency in Scotus' view of God and creation is the development of his understanding of the nature of existence. Here emerges Scotus' assertion that the term "being (*ens*)" can be considered univocally. Whereas others, perhaps most notably Aquinas with his analogical discussion of being, steer clear of the position that being can be understood in an univocal way, Scotus insists that if human beings can 'know' anything at all, then we have to support this concept of the univocity of being. This fundamental epistemological question (how can we know anything?) spurs the *doctor subtilis* to understand being as that which is shared by all. Simply put, we have to 'know' being because non-being cannot be experienced. Human cognition needs to be rooted in some natural foundation in order to reflect on God, humanity or the rest of creation.[34] Therefore something can be said to be or not-be but, to know something, it must be, it must exist. Because the creative act of God is rooted in God's very nature, namely love, all of creation partakes in this divine nature to some degree. At the very core of a created thing's being stands the fact that it exists when it could otherwise not exist. Scotus, while viewed as radical by some critics who insist on negation or analogy as the way to speak about being, believes that creation does in fact share being (*ens*) with God.[35] This is how we are able to say that we "know God" or can legitimately "speak of God." If we shared nothing in common how could we possibly know God? The fact that God exists, we exist, and that tree exists, demonstrates that we share an *a priori* and intrinsic condition – namely, our being. Ultimately, we can say that there is an interconnectedness shared among all of creation that instills and supports a deep sense of dignity and value to all of creation. Like Francis before him, Scotus saw in creation the natural fraternal relationship of all that exists.[36]

Creation's contingency and Scotus's view of the univocity of being expresses some important features of Scotus's spirituality. In this sense we can say that Scotus is following in the footsteps of Francis. The final

[34] Mary Beth Ingham and Mechthild Dreyer, *The Philosophical Vision of John Duns Scotus* (Washington, DC: The Catholic University of America Press, 2004), 40.
[35] For a more detailed introduction to the five arguments Scotus proposes in defense of his theory of the univocity of being see Ingham and Dreyer, *The Philosophical Vision of John Duns Scotus*, 38-51.
[36] For an introduction to a Franciscan view of ecological theology and spirituality see Ilia Delio, Keith Warner and Pamela Wood, *Care for Creation: A Franciscan Spirituality of the Earth* (Cincinnati: St. Anthony Messenger Press, 2008).

explanation for the creation of anything in general, and the creation of this beautiful world in particular, when God could have chosen not to do so, is a sign of divine benevolence and love. That we all share our existence attests to the interconnectedness of all of creation that stems from a personal, relational God. The prayer that emerges from Scotus's view of creation is a petition for right stewardship of the earth.

As we continue to awaken to the needs of our battered and bruised earth, Scotus's perspective of creation as God's generous gift of love draws our attention to our responsibility as stewards called to live in right relationship with our world. With the threats of global warming, animal extinction, and the exhaustion of some of our natural resources looming, our prayer might echo Scotus's own appreciation for the unique and blessed gift of God's creation. We can become attuned to the cry of the suffering environment that shares its contingent existence with us. We can recognize the inherent dignity of an earth that is so perfectly designed to foster so much life. We can learn to love this world like God, the source of its existence, does.

Praying with the Subtle Doctor

It is my hope that this chapter serves as an invitation for others to join in reconsidering Scotus's place in our Franciscan spiritual tradition. There remains a great deal of work, as Ingham alludes, in shedding light on the contributions of this medieval Franciscan thinker and to present those insights in a contemporary context. As we reflect on Scotus's work, we begin to discover beneath the philosophical and theological discourse the rich spiritual and prayerful experience of a brother rooted in the Franciscan tradition.

Scotus speaks to us today. In a world of suffering and brokenness, there remains the glimmer of Christian hope that sparkles in the work of John Duns Scotus. With Scotus we can experience gratitude for God's continued presence and love. In a time of fear and terror, we can petition with Scotus to see God's love in each other and recognize our shared existence. In a world where our earth is abused and neglected, ours is a prayer with Scotus for the strength to be better stewards of God's gifts.

Scotus has much to teach us today about living in a grace-filled world. Retrieval of Scotus's spiritual insight shaped by Franciscan influence can help guide us in our contemporary world. While some will insist that the fear, greed, and violence of today has replaced the goodness in our world, Scotus's work is founded on and supported by faith and hope that transcends the challenges of the present time to recall the source of our being – God's love. As we pause to reflect and pray, may we look to Scotus's prayerful philosophical insight to find God's presence in our world, to petition and work for the wellbeing of our brothers and sisters, and to pray for the ability to serve as right stewards of creation. Our care for the earth, and the poor and marginalized within it, will help our prayer, modeled after Scotus, form us to better show the face of God in our world. Such prayer should lead us from our place of contemplation back into the world with a response of loving action.

PART III

POPE BENEDICT XVI'S ADDRESSES ON THE FRANCISCAN TRADITION

WHAT DOES ROME HAVE TO DO WITH ASSISI?

Benedict XVI's Address on the Franciscan Tradition

In the Fall of 1953 a young German priest, the very recent recipient of a doctorate in theology, set out to work on his *Habilitationsschrift* – a book-length thesis completed *after* successfully defending one's doctoral dissertation and the academic qualification that grants a scholar the eligibility to hold a professorship at a German university. Without a topic at hand, he sought the counsel of Professor Gottlieb Söhngen who advised the young scholar to consider working in the area of medieval theology, a logical choice given the recently completed doctoral research in Patristics. Söhngen, after some additional thought and in light of his advisee's previous work on the thought of Augustine, suggested Bonaventure might be a good option. More than forty years later, the now not-so-young theologian would recall, "Although I had some rudimentary knowledge of Bonaventure and had read some of his shorter writings, new worlds opened up as I made progress with my work."[1] That young priest whose research into the theological insight of the Franciscan Saint and Doctor of the Church, Bonaventure, was Joseph Ratzinger.[2] Today he goes by another

---

[1] Joseph Ratzinger, *Milestones: Memoirs 1927-1977*, trans. Erasmo Leiva-Merikakis (San Francisco: Ignatius Press, 1998), 104.

[2] The resulting text was *Die Geschichtestheologie des heiligen Bonaventura* (München: Schnell and Steiner, 1959) and recently republished in the ongoing series of the collected works of Ratzinger, fully expanded with a previously unpublished section in *Gesammelte Schriften: Offenbarungsverständnis und Geschichtstheologie Bonaventuras: Habilitationsschrift und Bonaventura-Studien*, vol. 2, (München:

name, Pope Benedict XVI.

Those unfamiliar with the scholarly work of Pope Benedict XVI, particularly his early work as a young academic, might find it surprising that the pontiff would dedicate several weeks worth of his Wednesday public audiences (designed to provide general catechesis for the universal church) this year to discussing several key figures of the Franciscan Order. However, even the briefest glimpse of the young Ratzinger's homilies, articles, and books betray a profound respect for the saint from Assisi and those men and women who would follow in his way of life. It is safe to say that Francis of Assisi is likely the most popular saint in the Church (and even beyond the church), but what is it about the beloved *Poverello* that first captured the imagination and interest of Joseph Ratzinger and continues to captivate him as Bishop of Rome? A close look at Benedict's recent addresses on themes related to Franciscan saints can help us unpack the Pope's own appreciation for and interpretation of the Franciscan tradition.

Joseph Ratzinger: A Franciscan Theologian?

In early summer 2005, just a few months after the election of Cardinal Joseph Ratzinger to succeed the late Pope John Paul II as Bishop of Rome, I began to study the writings of and interviews with the German theologian-made-pope. His elevation to the pontificate coincided with my completion of undergraduate theological studies, which is why I was already familiar with the name "Cardinal Ratzinger," or so I thought. In truth, what I – and I suspect most students and professors of theology at the time – was familiar with was the reputation of the prefect of the Congregation for the Doctrine of the Faith (CDF). Frequently portrayed as the head of the "theology" or "orthodoxy police," Joseph Ratzinger was cast in my mind as someone to be feared and whose interest was less in the development of the Roman Catholic theological tradition and more in "reigning in" scholars who did not adhere to curial standards of Catholic orthodoxy. Like most reputations, there was some truth in that characterization. However, I quickly realized that I knew little about what this person actually thought. I committed myself to spend the summer delving into his personal theological writings (as opposed to the curial promulgations and notes of the CDF) in order to find out for myself what this theologian was all about.

Herder and Herder, 2009). The English translation is *The Theology of History in St. Bonaventure*, trans. Zachary Hayes (Chicago: Franciscan Herald Press, 1971).

To my surprise, the German thinker's work was less polemic and apologetic than I had anticipated. While there have certainly been personal texts by Ratzinger that are more explicitly responsive, if not reactionary, his corpus was, by and large, not representative of a man seeking to establish narrowly conceived and hegemonic theological treatises. Instead, what I found was an intelligent theologian interested in elucidating the faith in ways that made theology more accessible. Like all scholars, he did this to a lesser and greater degree over the course of his career, but he struck me as one committed to unpacking the content of faith in timely and relevant ways.[3] This is particularly true of his earliest works, among them his most famous pre-pontifical work, *Introduction to Christianity*.[4] Additionally, I was surprised to find that there were strong "Franciscan currents" in his writing. Upon discovering his *Habilitationsschrift* in translation (*The Theology of History in St. Bonaventure*), it became clear to me that Bonaventure's contribution to theologies of prophecy, revelation, and eschatology strongly influenced the future pope in his own explorations in theology.

Though Joseph Ratzinger remained for me a controversial figure, even into his years as pope, I began to reconsider what type of theologian he might be, going so far as to posit a radical interpretation and asking whether or not he might fit more comfortably into the category "Franciscan theologian" than anyone would have previously considered. I found that raising such a possibility proved to be unpopular; nevertheless, I was not alone in considering this connection between Ratzinger and the Franciscan tradition.

On the Feast of Saint Bonaventure, July 15, 2007, the Franciscan Institute of St. Bonaventure University bestowed on Regis Armstrong, OFM Cap., the prestigious Franciscan Institute Medal, making him the twentieth recipient of that award. As is customary at such an event, Armstrong delivered an academic address as part of the festivities. The title

---

[3] For a recent article on the thought of the young Ratzinger, see John Wilkins, "Ratzinger at Vatican II: A Pope Who Can and Cannot Change," *Commonweal* CXXXVII (June 4, 2010): 12-17. It should be noted that Wilkins's assessment of the shifts in thought over the course of Ratzinger's career are without any consideration of the independent theological scholarship of the mature Ratzinger (Benedict XVI). Instead, Wilkins compares the young Ratzinger's book on the highlights of Vatican II against dicastery documents during his tenure as prefect of the CDF – no small oversight. Nevertheless, Wilkins attempts to return to the early work of Ratzinger, an admirable task.

[4] Joseph Ratzinger, *Introduction to Christianity*, trans. J.R. Foster (San Francisco: Ignatius Press, 2004).

of his talk was "Hermes and the 'Co-Incidence' of San Damiano,"[5] and soon into the address Armstrong made an observation that confirmed what I had already begun to suspect. Citing an essay on Christian spirituality and pneumatology written by Ratzinger, Armstrong remarked, "This theological insight of now Pope Benedict XVI rightfully resonates with theologians of the Augustinian and Franciscan schools. In many ways, it echoes with what both Francis and Clare maintain would have us desire above all things: 'the Spirit of the Lord and His holy activity.'"[6] Later in his address, Armstrong again visited the work of Joseph Ratzinger to illuminate the complementary relationship of Gospel living found in the life and tradition of Francis and Clare of Assisi.[7] Since delivering that address three years ago, Armstrong has returned to the thought of Benedict XVI in its more recent forms as well as in his early writings. Armstrong continues to identify parallels and Franciscan influences in the work of Benedict, drawing on these insights for contemporary engagement with the Franciscan theological tradition.[8]

The concurrent recognition by Regis Armstrong of the Franciscan influence on the thought of Benedict XVI and the contribution the pontiff's work could make to contemporary Franciscan scholarship further petitions us to consider the status of the current pope vis-à-vis the Franciscan intellectual tradition. It seems at least plausible to ascribe the moniker "Franciscan theologian" to Benedict XVI, but the true test depends on the definition of the term. Because there is no clear understanding of what makes someone a "Franciscan theologian," it is difficult to demarcate an appropriate set of characteristics by which to determine whether Benedict XVI may legitimately be included. Zachary Hayes notes that, "If we simply

---

[5] This was later published as Regis Armstrong, "Hermes and the 'Co-Incidence' of San Damiano," *Franciscan Studies* 66 (2008): 413-459.

[6] Armstrong, "Hermes and the 'Co-Incidence' of San Damiano," 420. The passage from Ratzinger was taken from the essay "The Holy Spirit as Communion," in *Pilgrim Fellowship of Faith: The Church as Communion*, ed. Stephan Otto Horn and Vinzenz Pfnür, trans. Henry Taylor (San Francisco: Ignatius Press, 2005).

[7] See Armstrong, "Hermes and the 'Co-Incidence' of San Damiano," 440-443. Later in the address, in a footnote, Armstrong writes: "I am once again most indebted to the insights of Joseph Cardinal Ratzinger's article, 'The Holy Spirit as Communion,' for what follows in these next paragraphs. They have enabled me to bring into focus many distinctions between *communitas* and *fraternitas* with which I have wrestled in the fog of my understanding of the spirituality of Francis and Clare" (452 n.119).

[8] See most recently, Regis Armstrong, "*Novellus Pazzus in Mundo*: The Call to Foolishness," *Collectanae Franciscana* 79 (2009): 469-486; and Armstrong and Peterson, *The Franciscan Tradition*.

look for a common set of themes shared by the great theologians of the past, we will probably have to conclude that there is no such thing as a Franciscan school."[9] Furthermore, to what extent must a "Franciscan theologian" be a professed member of one of the three Franciscan Orders? It is becoming increasingly more common that women and men who are not professed members of religious communities (or Secular Franciscans, for that matter) make up the academic guild that studies the Franciscan intellectual tradition. Surely religious profession cannot be such a determining mark.

Like most scholars who engage the thought of the major medieval contributors to the Franciscan intellectual tradition, Benedict XVI has a particular take on the Saint from Assisi and the movement that emerged in the wake of the *Poverello's* religious conversion in the early 13th Century. This perspective emerges from the Pope's reading of the texts and literature related to the Franciscan sources and should be considered on their own merit. While any reference to Benedict XVI as a Franciscan theologian is sure to remain contentious, study of his perspective on the Franciscan tradition – particularly in the explicit references made during his universal catechetical audiences this year – will surely contribute to contemporary Franciscan scholarship. The voice of the pope carries with it certain authority that naturally draws the attention of a broad audience. For this reason, the miniature series of addresses relating to the Franciscan tradition this year need to be examined.

Address to the Chapter of Mats (20 April 2009)

Nearly a year before the more substantial series of Wednesday general audiences delivered by Pope Benedict XVI on Franciscan themes, the pontiff greeted representatives of the Franciscan family at his residence at Castel Gandolfo. The chapter was to celebrate the eighth centenary of the approval of the nascent Franciscan rule by Pope Innocent III in 1209. Benedict XVI took this occasion to commend the friars for what a gift they are to the world, especially in the ministry of spreading the Gospel. After acknowledging the "precious gift" that the Franciscan family is for the entire Christian people, Benedict XVI spoke about the founder of the movement the Franciscan family represents today.

---

[9] Zachary Hayes, "Bonaventure of Bagnoregio: A Paradigm for Franciscan Theologians?" in *The Franciscan Intellectual Tradition: Washington Theological Union Symposium Papers 2001* (St. Bonaventure, NY: Franciscan Institute Publications, 2002), 43.

Perhaps the most striking set of comments offered by the Holy Father consisted of what we can call the "apostolic identification" of Francis. In a unique way, Benedict XVI associated Francis with St. Paul. He said, "To the *Poverello*, one can apply literally some expressions that the apostle Paul uses to refer to himself and which I like to remember in this Pauline year."[10] What followed is a veritable litany of quotations from the Pauline corpus that speak of one's kenotic embrace of poverty to live totally in Christ. Another way to describe Francis, Benedict XVI continued, is that he fully embodied the Gospel. His identity *was* the Word of God and therefore, like Paul, Francis's life says: "For me, to live is Christ" (Phil 1:21). Benedict XVI summarized this well when he said:

> [Francis] defined himself entirely in the light of the Gospel. This is his charm. This is his enduring relevance... So the *Poverello* has become a living gospel, able to attract to Christ men and women of all ages, especially young people, who prefer radical idealism to half-measures. The Bishop of Assisi, Guido, and then Pope Innocent III recognized in the proposal of Francis and his companions the authenticity of the Gospel, and knew how to encourage their commitment for the good of the Church.[11]

At this point in his address, Benedict XVI began to offer his interpretation of the contemporary value of Franciscan religious life. He identified the occasion of this meeting of the Franciscan family, the 800th anniversary of the approval of Francis's way of life by Innocent III, as a constitutive element of the Franciscan charism. In doing so, Benedict XVI made an explicitly ecclesiological[12] statement that indeed emphasized that aspect of

---

[10] Pope Benedict XVI, "Attract to Christ Men and Women of All Ages," Benedict XVI's Address to the Franciscan Family (20 April 2009). All translations of addresses by Pope Benedict XVI cited in this article have been provided by the Vatican website (Vatican.va). These texts are also available in translation in archived issues of the Vatican newspaper, *L'Osservatore Romano*.

Additionally, some of the Vatican's English translation of these texts have been made available in the following collections: Benedict XVI, *Great Teachers* (Huntington, IN: Our Sunday Visitor Press, 2011); Benedict XVI, *Doctors of the Church* (Huntington, IN: Our Sunday Visitor Press, 2011); Benedict XVI, *Holy Women* (Huntington, IN: Our Sunday Visitor Press, 2011); and Benedict XVI, *Holy Men and Women: Of the Middle Ages and Beyond* (San Francisco: Ignatius Press, 2012).

[11] Pope Benedict XVI, "Attract to Christ Men and Women of All Ages."

[12] There are several studies available on the ecclesiology of Joseph Ratzinger (Pope Benedict XVI). Perhaps the most substantial is: Maximilian Heinrich Heim, *Joseph Ratzinger: Life in the Church and Living Theology, Fundamentals of Ecclesiology with Refence to Lumen Gentium*, trans. Michael

Francis's *Regula* promising obedience to the Holy See and maintaining the Catholicity of the Order, while de-emphasizing (by way of omission) those more overt challenges Francis raised to the leadership of the Church in his day – most notably in his "ecclesiastical disobedience" with regard to the Fifth Crusade.[13]

Benedict XVI mentions the other religious movements of the age that sprung up without papal approval. He notes that Francis was not like these other groups that held a "polemical attitude towards the hierarchy." Rather, Francis "immediately thought to put his journey and that of his companions into the hands of the Bishop of Rome, the Successor of Peter. This fact reveals his true ecclesial spirit. The little 'we' that had started with his first friars he conceived from the outset inside the context of the great 'we' of the one and universal Church. And the Pope recognized and appreciated this."[14] Benedict XVI did not hesitate to remind the Franciscans of their founder's proximity to Rome. This statement, something between an admonition and exhortation, was likely formed against the backdrop of Joseph Ratzinger's personal experience. One cannot help but recall the famous and painful exchange between the former Franciscan friar and theologian Leonardo Boff and Ratzinger in his official capacity as prefect of the CDF.[15] It seems likely that beyond the vested interest any sitting pontiff would have in reminding the largest religious order in the world to stay "close to home," the Boff experience must have served as additional motivation.

Beyond the reminder to maintain ecclesiastical communion, Benedict XVI offered little by way of critique or concern. Instead, the Holy Father closed his address with words of edification that were, and indeed remain, inspirational. He said:

> As Francis and Clare of Assisi, you also commit yourselves to
> follow the same logic: to lose your lives for Jesus and the Gospel,
> to save them and make them abundantly fruitful. While you

Miller (San Francisco: Ignatius Press, 2007).

[13] For a new overview of Francis's encounter, see Moses, *The Saint and the Sultan*. For a study of the contemporary relevance of this stance, see Daniel Horan, "'Those Going among the Saracens and Other Nonbelievers': Thomas Merton and Franciscan Interreligious Dialogue," *The Merton Annual* 21 (2008): 44-66.

[14] Pope Benedict XVI, "Attract to Christ Men and Women of All Ages."

[15] For one account of the exchange, see Harvey Cox, *The Silencing of Leonardo Boff: The Vatican and the Future of World Christianity* (Oak Park, IL: Meyer Stone and Company, 1988).

> praise and thank the Lord who has called you to be part of
> such a great and beautiful family, stay attentive to what the
> Spirit says to it today, in each of its components, to continue
> to proclaim with passion the Kingdom of God, the footsteps of
> your seraphic father. Every brother and every sister should keep
> always a contemplative mood, happy and simple; always begin
> from Christ, as Francis set out from the gaze of the Crucifix of
> San Damiano and from the meeting with the leper, to see the
> face of Christ in our brothers and sisters who suffer and bring to
> all his peace. Be witnesses to the 'beauty' of God, which Francis
> was able to sing contemplating the wonders of creation, and
> that made him exclaim to the Most High: 'You are beauty!'[16]

Perhaps surprising given the speaker's personal history of engaging liberation theology, this encomium aimed at the Franciscan vocation and way of Christian living bears a certain sense of social justice that explicitly names those men and women who suffer in our world. Drawing on the tradition of Francis's own ministry to and solidarity with the poor, marginalized, and disaffected, Benedict XVI encourages Francis's sons and daughters of today to do the same.

On Francis of Assisi (27 January 2010)

Continuing the theme of renewal in the Church, something Benedict XVI illustrated in referencing the formation of the Order of Friars Minor and the Order of Preachers by Francis and Dominic respectively, the Pope highlighted the Saint from Assisi to reflect on. Beginning with a short biographical outline of the *Poverello's* starting point and conversion, Benedict XVI chose to focus on the dual symbolic foci of Francis's conversion: the call to "repair my Church in ruins" heard at San Damiano and the encounter with the leper. The Holy Father recalled that it was ultimately not a repair of manual labor that Christ was calling the Saint to, but instead the renewal of the church of Christ itself "with his radical faith and his enthusiastic love for Christ."[17] Benedict XVI directed his attention to the renewal of the Church in an effort to highlight two features of Francis's vocational activity. The first is that this renewal did not come by way of the powerful, learned or mighty, but rather through the "small

---

[16] Pope Benedict XVI, "Attract to Christ Men and Women of All Ages."
[17] Pope Benedict XVI, "Saint Francis of Assisi." (27 January 2010).

and insignificant religious" that was Francis as called by God. The second is, picking up again on the ecclesiological theme emphasized in his address a year earlier, that Francis renews the church *in communion with the Pope*. Benedict XVI said:

> It is important to note that St. Francis does not renew the Church without or against the Pope, but only in communion with him. The two realities go together: the Successor of Peter, the bishops, the Church founded on the succession of the Apostles and the new charism that the Holy Spirit created at this moment to renew the Church. True renewal grows together.[18]

Benedict XVI treats this portion of his address almost as if it were a digression, following it immediately with, "Let us return to St. Francis's life." However, in the continued recounting of Francis's experience of conversion, the current pontiff seeks yet another opportunity to connect the *vita evangelica* of Francis with ecclesiastical order: "The *Poverello* of Assisi had understood that every charism given by the Holy Spirit is placed at the service of the Body of Christ, which is the Church; hence, he always acted in full communion with the ecclesiastical authority."[19] The identification of the Church as the Body of Christ is indeed a rather unexpected surprise given the propensity Benedict XVI has for focusing his reflections on the authoritative structures of ecclesiastical governance and Church renewal. Nevertheless, the Holy Father seems at least somewhat interested in striking an ecclesiological balance between seemingly oppositional ecclesial emphases.

Following his explicit and frequent identification of Francis with the Church and its leadership, Benedict XVI addressed concerns he has with certain modern scholarly efforts to recover the "historical Francis," an endeavor not unlike the quest for the historical Jesus of recent decades. The caution issued by the Pope is one aimed at those who would like to reconstruct the person Francis of Assisi for particular political or social gains. In other words, you cannot separate Francis from the Pope and bishops, the Eucharist and full communion with the whole Church – at least that is the message that is rearticulated.

One area that Benedict XVI does not include a reference to communion

---

[18] Pope Benedict XVI, "Saint Francis of Assisi."
[19] Pope Benedict XVI, "Saint Francis of Assisi."

with the Church can be found in his praise of Francis's interreligious efforts exemplified most strikingly in the encounter with the Muslim Sultan Malek-al-Kamel in Egypt. The Pope said:

> I want to underline this episode of the life of Francis, which is very timely. At a time in which there was under way a clash between Christianity and Islam, Francis, armed deliberately only with his faith and his personal meekness, pursued with efficacy the way of dialogue. The chronicles tell us of a benevolent and cordial reception by the Muslim Sultan. It is a model that also today should inspire relations between Christians and Muslims: to promote a dialogue in truth, in reciprocal respect and in mutual understanding.[20]

This episodic recounting of Francis's experience of peacemaking and dialogue is something to be especially treasured. Benedict XVI, aware of the urgent need for tolerance, trust, peace, and dialogue in today's world, realizes the powerful example of Gospel living embodied in that heroic act of the thirteenth-century saint. What is not acknowledged in the pontiff's recollection, however, is that this paragon of interreligious dialogue and peacemaking was an action that stood in stark contrast to the official policy of both the Church and State of the day. We should not forget, nor omit, that this encounter took place during the height of the Fifth Crusade. How one reconciles the unwavering commitment of the son of the Church *par excellence* as portrayed in Benedict XVI's image of Francis and the concrete and powerfully prophetic action of the same man over and against the would-be will of the Pope is left unsolved.

After completing the brief chronology of the *Poverello's* life, Benedict XVI offers a unique reflection on Francis's evangelical life vis-à-vis scripture. What is important to know about this particular aspect of his address is that it is strongly reminsecent of Benedict XVI's early work on Bonaventure and the Seraphic Doctor's theology of prophecy and revelation. The Pope continued:

> Truly, dear friends, the saints are the best interpreters of the Bible; they, incarnating in their lives the Word of God, render it more than attractive, so that it really speaks to us. Francis's

---

[20] Pope Benedict XVI, "Saint Francis of Assisi."

witness, who loved poverty to follow Christ with dedication and total liberty, continues to be also for us an invitation to cultivate interior poverty to grow in trust of God, uniting also a sober lifestyle and detachment from material goods.[21]

For Bonaventure, and for Benedict XVI so influenced by the Seraphic Doctor, a prophet (or in this case, the saint) is one who has been imbued with the Word of God. The result of such a life, one rooted and oriented by scripture, is that such people can see the world as it really is and understand how God continues to reveal God's self to us in ever new ways. This is the freedom that comes with evangelical poverty, the surrender of one's own will for God's will, the emptying of one's self so as to be filled by the Word of God. For Benedict XVI, Francis is indeed a prophet, as he was for Bonaventure as depicted in his *Legenda Major*.

Benedict XVI concludes this address with two particularly relevant reflections. The first is a mention of Francis's expressed admiration for priests. No one familiar with the writings of Francis of Assisi could deny that the Saint had a particular respect for and deference toward ordained ministers, regardless of their individual sanctity or sinfulness. Benedict XVI ties this aspect of Francis's own spirituality and disposition to the Year for Priests (2009-2010) and directs Francis's own respect for priests toward priests themselves, admonishing those ordained to "live in a consistent way with the mystery we celebrate."[22]

The final reflection is also one of timely import. Here Benedict XVI recalls Francis's love of all people and creation that is rooted in the Saint's love of Christ. The Pope ties this recollection not only to the ecological crises of our present day, but also to his latest encyclical letter *Caritas in Veritate*. This section is worth quoting at length.

> Here is another characteristic trait of Francis's spirituality: the sense of universal fraternity and love for creation, which inspired his famous Canticle of Creatures. It is a very timely message. As I reminded in my recent encyclical *Caritas in Veritate*, the only sustainable development is one that respects creation and does not damage the environment, and in the Message for the World Day of Peace this year I underlined that also the building of a

21 Pope Benedict XVI, "Saint Francis of Assisi."
22 Pope Benedict XVI, "Saint Francis of Assisi."

solid peace is linked to respect for creation. Francis reminds us that in creation is displayed the wisdom and benevolence of the Creator. In fact, nature is understood by him as a language in which God speaks with us, in which reality becomes transparent and we can speak of God and with God.[23]

In addition to being a renewed call for ecological awareness and restoration of the integrity of creation, these comments are a powerful reflection of the Pope's own understanding of the Franciscan theological tradition. The latter part of the quote above, where Benedict XVI speaks of Francis's recognition of creation as the space within which and a medium for communication with the Divine, is a summary of Bonaventure's theology of creation.[24]

On Saint Anthony of Padua (10 February 2010)

After speaking on Francis of Assisi, Benedict XVI dedicated the following week to catechetical instruction on St. Dominic, Francis's contemporary and fellow founder of a mendicant order. In that address, Benedict XVI refers to Francis as "the luminous figure" of church renewal. The Dominican sojourn was short indeed for the following week again saw the Pope's interest in the Franciscan tradition return, this time in the figure of St. Anthony of Padua, who Benedict XVI refers to as "one of the most popular saints in the whole Catholic Church."[25] Before regaling his audience with the biographical highlights of this first-generation Friar Minor's life, the Pope said, "Anthony contributed in a significant way to the development of Franciscan spirituality, with his outstanding gifts of intelligence, balance, apostolic zeal and, mainly, mystical fervor."[26]

Recalling Anthony's almost accidental, yet providential, foray into the ministry of preaching on the occasion of an ordination Mass, Benedict XVI also recounted the lasting significance of Anthony's personal approval by Francis to teach theology.

[23] Pope Benedict XVI, "Saint Francis of Assisi."

[24] For an overview see Cullen, *Bonaventure*, 128-133; Ilia Delio, *Simply Bonaventure: An Introduction to His Life, Thought and Writings* (New York: New City Press, 2001), 54-66; and J. A. Wayne Hellmann, *Divine and Created Order in Bonaventure's Theology*, trans. J. M. Hammond (St. Bonaventure, NY: Franciscan Institute Publications, 2001).
Also see Bonaventure, *Breviloquium* II.1.1-II.12.5, ed. Dominic Monti, Bonaventure Texts in Translation Series, vol. IX (St. Bonaventure, NY: Franciscan Institute Publications, 2005), 59-98.

[25] Pope Benedict XVI, "St. Anthony of Padua," (10 February 2010).

[26] Pope Benedict XVI, "St. Anthony of Padua."

He was also among the first teachers of theology of the Friars minor, if not even the first. He began his teaching in Bologna, with Francis's blessing who, recognizing Anthony's virtues, sent him a brief letter with these words: 'I would like you to teach theology to the friars.' Anthony set the foundations of Franciscan theology that, cultivated by other famous figures and thinkers, came to its zenith with St. Bonaventure of Bagnoregio and Blessed Duns Scotus.[27]

Unlike his two earlier addresses that dealt with the person and legacy of Francis of Assisi directly, Benedict XVI does not tie Anthony in any explicit way to ecclesiastical authority. Instead, his admiration for the famous preacher, theologian and saint comes through his reflections on the more overtly spiritual and mystical nature of Anthony's legacy. Highlighting an often-overlooked dimension of Franciscan spirituality, that of eremiticism and solitude, Benedict XVI said: "Anthony reminds us that prayer needs an atmosphere of silence, which is not the same as withdrawal from external noise, but is an interior experience, which seeks to remove the distractions caused by the soul's preoccupations."[28] This reference to the place of solitude in the spiritual life evokes the recent work of Benedict XVI in his Encyclical Letter, *Caritas in Veritate* and the pontiff's concern that modern men and women learn to "disconnect" from technology in order to remember what is real and what is most profoundly human.[29]

Returning to a theme that is clearly an important one for the Holy Father, he focuses on Anthony's appropriation of "one of the specific features of Franciscan theology," that is, the primacy of divine love.[30] The association that is made between Anthony and Franciscan spirituality in general really finds a forthright articulation in the theology of Bonaventure.

---

[27] Pope Benedict XVI, "St. Anthony of Padua." Benedict XVI's paraphrase of Francis's letter to Anthony is a little off, for the original text see: Francis of Assisi, "A Letter to Brother Anthony of Padua," *FAED* 1:107. Further citations of this source will be noted as *FAED* followed by the volume and page number. For a contemporary study of Franciscan engagement in theology, see Michael Blastic, "'It Pleases Me That You Should Teach Sacred Theology': Franciscans Doing Theology," *Franciscan Studies* 55 (1998): 1-25.

[28] Pope Benedict XVI, "St. Anthony of Padua." For more on solitude in the Franciscan spiritual tradition, see Daniel Horan, "Dating God: A Young Friar's Experience of Solitude," *America* 196 (18 June 2007): 25-27; and Thomas Merton, "Franciscan Eremiticism," *The Cord* 16 (1966).

[29] For more on this insight of Benedict XVI, see Daniel Horan, "Digital Natives and Franciscan Spirituality," *Spiritual Life* 56 (Summer 2010): 73-84, esp. 78-79.

[30] Pope Benedict XVI, "St. Anthony of Padua."

It is remarkable to note the resemblance, at least in part, between the construction of the Pope's first Encyclical Letter, *Deus Caritas Est*, and the notion of Bonaventure's cosmic theology. This particular focus on the divine love present in the writings of Anthony only reemphasizes Benedict XVI's affinity for the larger Franciscan tradition.

Continuing with the theme of spirituality in the example of Anthony, Benedict XVI recalled that the Franciscan preacher always encouraged his hearers to return to prayer. Through that communication with the Creator, one is able to redirect one's focus from pride, impurity, injustice, and other forms of sinfulness to focus on "true wealth, that of the heart."[31] It is this aspect of Anthony's legacy that the Pope sees as particularly relevant given the recent economic crisis. Again drawing connections to his own work, Benedict XVI said, "Is not this perhaps, dear friends, a very important teaching also today, when the financial crisis and the serious economic imbalances impoverish not a few persons and create conditions of misery? In my encyclical *Caritas in Veritate*, I remind that: 'The economy needs ethics in order to function correctly – not any ethics whatsoever, but an ethics which is people-centered.'"[32] This ethic Benedict XVI speaks of might indeed benefit from retrieval of the wisdom of the Franciscan tradition, not just in the writings of Anthony (although that may be a good place to start), but also in the more developed ethical system of John Duns Scotus.[33]

On Saint Bonaventure (3 March 2010)

Benedict XVI begins his reflection on Bonaventure with the admission that doing so evokes for him a "certain nostalgia" because of his particular fondness for the Seraphic Doctor, whom, the Pope shares, "I particularly esteem."[34] It is immediately after this segue that he then said, "[Bonaventure's] knowledge has been of no small influence in my formation."[35] Benedict XVI goes on to describe Bonaventure as a "man

---

[31] Pope Benedict XVI, "St. Anthony of Padua."

[32] Pope Benedict XVI, "St. Anthony of Padua." Also see *Caritas in Veritate* §45.

[33] See, for example, John Duns Scotus, *Political and Economic Philosophy*, ed. Allan Wolter (St. Bonaventure, NY: Franciscan Institute Press, 2001); and Thomas Shannon, *The Ethical Theory of John Duns Scotus* (Quincy, IL: Franciscan Herald Press, 1995), esp. 71-128.

[34] Pope Benedict XVI, "St. Bonaventure I," (3 March 2010).

[35] Pope Benedict XVI, "St. Bonaventure I." For more on the role of Bonaventure's though in the theological formation of Joseph Ratzinger, see Aidan Nichols, *The Thought of Pope Benedict XVI: An Introduction to the Theology of Joseph Ratzinger*, 2nd ed. (London: Continuum, 2007), 34-44; D.

of action and of contemplation, of profound piety and of prudence in governing."[36] Indeed Bonaventure was a man of many talents and skilled in many areas. One cannot help but see yet another reason the Pope might find Bonaventure's ability to excel as a scholar and then an ecclesiastical leader, first as Minister General of the Order and later as a Cardinal-Bishop of the Church. Perhaps Benedict XVI sees in Bonaventure a model for his own life, one marked early on by theological excellence and later shaped by ecclesiastical leadership positions.

Benedict XVI keenly notes that Bonaventure's theology is richly Christocentric, and the Pope posits that it is no coincidence that the first major project of Bonaventure's, completed in order to teach theology and obtain the *licentia ubique docendi*, was the treatise *"Disputed Questions on the Knowledge of Christ."*[37] This Christocentric emphatic thrust to the wide-ranging corpus of the Seraphic Doctor contributed significantly to the development of the Franciscan intellectual tradition.

The Holy Father then recounts the internal political struggle that plagued the nascent University of Paris between the mendicant faculty (Franciscans and Dominicans) and the so-called secular masters. In doing so, he praises Bonaventure for his skillful response to the charges leveled against the mendicants by the seculars and for the ardent defense the Seraphic Doctor gives for the evangelical counsels in light of the Gospel.

> Beyond these historical circumstances, the teaching offered by Bonaventure in this work of his and in his life is always timely: The Church becomes luminous and beautiful by fidelity to the vocation of those sons and daughters of hers who not only put into practice the evangelical precepts, but who, by the grace of God, are called to observe their advice and thus give witness, with their poor, chaste and obedient lifestyle, that the Gospel is a source of joy and perfection.[38]

Vincent Twomey, *Pope Benedict XVI: The Conscience of Our Age, A Theological Portrait* (San Francisco: Ignatius Press, 2007), 50-53; and, for his own reflection, see Joseph Ratzinger, *Salt of the Earth: The Church at the End of the Millennium — An Interview with Peter Seewald*, trans. Adrian Walker (San Francisco: Ignatius Press, 1997), 61-63.

[36] Pope Benedict XVI, "St. Bonaventure I."

[37] See Bonaventure, *Disputed Questions on the Knowledge of Christ*, ed. Zachary Hayes, Bonaventure Texts in Translation Series, vol. IV (St. Bonaventure, NY: Franciscan Institute Press, 2005); and Joshua Benson, "Structure and Meaning in St. Bonaventure's *Quaestiones Disputatae de Scientia Christi*," *Franciscan Studies* 62 (2004): 67-90.

[38] Pope Benedict XVI, "St. Bonaventure I."

At a time when the number of religious vocations is noticeably declining in Europe and the Americas, a message from the Pope highlighting the evangelical contribution of those professed religious in our world is well received. That Benedict XVI ties such a contribution to Bonaventure's particular articulation of the *vita evangelica* of the mendicant orders is also edifying.

Bonaventure is then praised for his handling of the responsibility entrusted to him as the Minister General of Francis's Order. Benedict XVI notes that under Bonaventure's leadership, the Franciscan missionary zeal to spread the Gospel promoted mission journeys all over the world. Furthermore, during his tenure as Minister General Bonaventure wrote the masterpiece the *Legenda Major,* that which was to become the officially and authoritative biography of the founding saint. Here Benedict XVI offered his interpretation of Bonaventure's portrayal of Saint Francis in the *Legenda Major*:

> What is the image of St. Francis that arises from the heart and pen of his devoted son and successor, St. Bonaventure? The essential point: Francis is an *alter Christus*, a man who passionately sought Christ. In the love that drives to imitation, he was entirely conformed to Him. Bonaventure pointed out this living ideal to all of Francis's followers. This ideal, valid for every Christian, yesterday, today and always, was indicated as a program also for the Church of the Third Millennium by my predecessor, the Venerable John Paul II. This program, he wrote in the letter *Tertio Millennio Ineunte* is centered 'on Christ himself, who must be known, loved and imitated to live in Him the Trinitarian life, and, with Him, to transform history to its fulfillment in the heavenly Jerusalem.'[39]

Bonaventure, for Benedict XVI, continues to offer the world wisdom that is ever timely and ever new. This wisdom, centered on Christ, looks to the paragon of Christian living – Francis of Assisi – as the model for how all Christians should strive to live their baptismal call.

---

[39] Pope Benedict XVI, "St. Bonaventure I." Benedict XVI cites paragraph number 29 of *Tertio Millennio Ineunte.*

On Saint Bonaventure's Concept of History (10 March 2010)

Beginning this address in St. Peter's Basilica and then continuing it in the Paul VI general audience hall, Benedict XVI continued his reflection on the significance and influence of Bonaventure. The pontiff starts his catechetical reflection with the assertion that among the many merits of Bonaventure's thought, the Seraphic Doctor was primarily and authentically the interpreter of the figure St. Francis of Assisi. He understood the *Poverello* in a faithful and insightful manner and it was by this grace that Bonaventure was able to put forth an image of Francis that was at once legitimate and prophetic.

The context for Benedict XVI's address on Bonaventure's concept of history centers on the problematic movement of a small group of Franciscans in Bonaventure's day that sought to interpret the founding of the Order and the emergence of Francis of Assisi as a prophetic figure in a way that aligned snugly with Joachim of Fiore's view of history. Bonaventure, familiar with the Calabrian Abbot's work and an appreciator of at least certain features of Joachim's thought, developed a theological response in the form of both his *Legenda Major* as well as his *Collationes in Hexaëmeron*. It is in these two texts, but especially the *Hexaëmeron*, that Bonaventure outlines his theology of history.[40] The *Hexaëmeron* is the text that captured the lifelong interest of Joseph Ratzinger, beginning during his research for the *Habilitationsschrift* and continuing even through his pontificate. In his address, Benedict XVI summarized the setting and structure of Bonaventure's *Hexaëmeron*:

> St. Bonaventure addressed the problem [of errant theologies of history] in fact in his last work, a collection of conferences to [friars][41] of the Paris studio, which remained unfinished and which was completed with the transcriptions of the hearers. It was titled "*Hexaëmeron*," that is, an allegorical explanation of the six days of creation. The Fathers of the Church considered the six or seven days of the account of creation as a prophecy of the

---

[40] The *Collationes in Hexaëmeron* are found in volume V of *Doctoris Seraphici S. Bonaventurae Opera Omnia*, eds. PP. Collegii S. Bonaventurae, 10 vols. (Quaracchi: Collegium S. Bonaventurae, 1882-1902). The English translation of the *Hexaëmeron* is *Bonaventure, Collations on the Six Days*, trans. José de Vinck, Works of Bonaventure vol. V (Paterson, NJ: St. Anthony Guild Press, 1970).

[41] The Pope mistakenly uses the term "monks" in reference to the Friars minor that gathered to hear the *collationes* of Bonaventure.

history of the world, of humanity. The seven days represented for them seven periods of history, later interpreted also as seven millennia. With Christ we would have entered the last, namely, the sixth period of history, which would then be followed by the great Sabbath of God. St. Bonaventure accounts for this historical interpretation of the relation of the days of creation, but in a very free and innovative way.[42]

What follows is a very brief recapitulation of the pontiff's *Habilitationsschrift* given in the form of a commentary on Bonaventure's development of a theology of history in light of the twofold challenge that faced the Seraphic Doctor in his time; namely, (a) dealing with the unique figure of Francis and his Order as a liminal experience of ecclesiastical history and (b) safely navigating the complicated insights of Joachim of Fiore that were gaining particular attention at that time. Bonaventure's response was to illustrate how Francis's Order was not something apart from the hierarchic Church community. Instead, Francis – while remaining a unique figure of historical and spiritual significance – always remained in communion with the rest of the Church. This was a direct response to some Joachite factions of the day that were leaning toward more anarchic manifestations of Franciscan life.

In four points, Benedict XVI traces the development of Bonaventure's theology of history (and, therefore, restates his own scholarly work). The first two points are refutations of errant, or at least unorthodox, Joachite positions. Bonaventure rejects the Joachite Trinitarian view of history, insisting that God is one and therefore history is one – not divided into three divinities associated with a threefold rhythm of history. Additionally, Bonaventure insists that Jesus Christ is the "last word of God" and that "there is not another higher Gospel, there is not another Church to await."[43]

The third point occupies the largest portion of Benedict XVI's address on the subject. This feature of Bonaventure's theology of history is that of its progressive nature. According to the Pope, this is a novel introduction to the concept of history original to Bonaventure. This view rests on the Christocentric foundations for Bonaventure's theology. Unlike the view of many in the Patristic era, Bonaventure does not see Christ as the end of history, but Christ is instead the center of history. With Christ a new period in history begins. In other words, Bonaventure allows for the possibility

---

[42] Pope Benedict XVI, "St. Bonaventure II," (10 March 2010).

[43] Pope Benedict XVI, "St. Bonaventure II."

of *the new*. This is how he connects the emergence of the person Francis of Assisi and his *new* movement. Francis confirms that the richness of the word of Christ "is inexhaustible and that also new lights can appear in the new generations. The Uniqueness of Christ also guarantees novelties and renewal in all the periods of history."[44]

This third point, concerning the progressive quality of history, is especially important to the Pope who draws on this insight to speak about the Second Vatican Council. Benedict XVI has occasionally discussed the concept of both novelty and continuity in the promulgations of the Council Fathers. The Second Vatican Council did not do something entirely "different," but instead features into the ongoing progress of history in revelation.

The final point has to do with the way in which Benedict XVI sees Bonaventure's theology of history play a significant role in the pastoral and praxiological dimensions of the Seraphic Doctor's governance of the Order and leadership roles in the broader Christian community. Benedict XVI explained:

> Thus we see that for St. Bonaventure, to govern was not simply a task but was above all to think and to pray. At the base of his government we always find prayer and thought; all his decisions resulted from reflection, from thought illumined by prayer. His profound contact with Christ always accompanied his work as minister-general and that is why he composed a series of theological-mystical writings, which express the spirit of his government and manifest the intention of guiding the order interiorly, of governing, that is, not only through commands and structures, but through guiding and enlightening souls, orienting them to Christ.[45]

This reflection offers powerful insights upon which the Holy Father would do well to reflect, as would any person in pastoral leadership – lay, religious, or ordained – today. In the wake of ongoing discovery of misjudgment, abuse, and negligence on the part of so many entrusted with Church governance, this model of ecclesiastical leadership – one absolutely rooted in reflective thought and prayer – is a welcomed reminder of what the

---

[44] Pope Benedict XVI, "St. Bonaventure II."
[45] Pope Benedict XVI, "St. Bonaventure II."

vocation to servant leadership in the Church is truly about. It is only through one's own "profound contact with Christ" that Church leaders of our day might serve the Lord and the Church effectively by orienting the faithful to Christ. There is perhaps no more timely a reflection that the Pope could have offered.

On Theology According to Thomas and Bonaventure (17 March 2010)

This address marks the third and final reflection on St. Bonaventure. The Pope begins his catechesis with a summary of the manifold ways Bonaventure and Thomas Aquinas are alike. Such similarities include their membership in newly established mendicant orders, their respective academic work in Paris and the fact that they both died in the year 1274. However, it is not the likenesses that Benedict XVI desired to illustrate, but the differences.

The heading under which the two Church Doctors' differences are presented is the nature of theology. For Thomas, Benedict XVI notes, theology serves a twofold function that allows us to better know God (the theoretical quality of theology) and to live in a right and just way (the practical quality of theology). Both of these dimensions contribute to the interpretation of Thomas's approach as being rooted in the primacy of knowledge. Bonaventure, on the other hand, moves beyond the twofold function of theology (theoretical and practical) offered by Thomas to include a third (sapiential) feature that serves as the launching point for his own articulation of the ultimate destiny of men and women, which, of course, is the subject matter of theology.[46] Bonaventure maintains a primacy of love. Benedict XVI explained: "For St. Bonaventure, [humanity's] ultimate destiny is instead to love God, the encounter and the union of his love and our own. This is for [Bonaventure] the most adequate definition of our happiness."[47]

Taking this distinction between the primacy of knowledge and the primacy of love for Thomas and Bonaventure respectively, Benedict XVI

---

[46] For more on this theme see Gregory LaNave, "God, Creation, and the Possibility of Philosophical Wisdom: Perspectives of Bonaventure and Aquinas," *Theological Studies* 69 (2008): 812-833; Gregory LaNave, *Through Holiness to Wisdom: The Nature of Theology According to St. Bonaventure* (Rome: Istituto Storico Dei Cappuccini, 2005); and Charles Carpenter, *Theology as the Road to Holiness in St. Bonaventure* (New York: Paulist Press, 1999).

[47] Pope Benedict XVI, "St. Bonaventure III," (17 March 2010).

then explains that each medieval thinker posits a different highest category: For Thomas it is truth, while for Bonaventure it is the good. The Pope sees a reciprocal and complementary relationship between these two categories, for in God the good is true and truth is the good. In this way Benedict XVI asserts that Franciscans and Dominicans actually hold a shared vision if each accents that vision differently.

At this point in his address, Benedict XVI abandoned any further reflection on St. Thomas to instead focus again on Bonaventure in an exclusive way. The Holy Father is particularly interested in exploring the sources for Bonaventure's primacy of love. It might be safe to presume that the nearly hegemonic presence of Thomas's theology since Pope Leo XIII's encyclical letter *Aeternis Patris*, which established Thomas Aquinas as the paradigmatic theologian for the Roman Catholic Church, inspired Benedict XVI to emphasize the less-known work of Bonaventure. It is also certainly true that Bonaventure's primacy of love has and continues to shape Benedict XVI's own theological and spiritual outlook (recall again his first encyclical letter, *Deus Caritas Est*).

Benedict XVI identifies the source of this primacy of love in two places: the very foundational charism of Francis of Assisi and the theological treatises of the so-called Pseudo-Dionysius.[48] The Pope sees in the example of Francis's whole life a *vita evangelica* consumed with love. It was the very model of Francis's life that naturally compelled Bonaventure, at least in part, to prioritize love over knowledge as the highest category. Additionally, the ninth-century thinker, Pseudo-Dionysius, provided much of the language and theological organization that contributed to Bonaventure's articulation of the primacy of love. When Bonaventure synthesizes Francis's charism and Pseudo-Dionysius's theological insight, the result is a profound theological system rooted in love. Benedict XVI, drawing again from his own scholarly work and preempting criticism of Bonaventure's primacy of love when compared to Thomas's approach, emphatically rejected the notion that Bonaventure is "anti-intellectual" or "anti-rational." Benedict XVI suggested that Bonaventure's approach "implies the way of reason, but transcends it in the love of the crucified Christ."[49] It is the Cross that serves as the centerpiece of Bonaventure's marriage of Francis and Pseudo-

---

[48] While these two sources are incontestably antecedent influences for the development of Bonaventure's primacy of love, I would also include both the Augustinian corpus and the Victorine school, most especially Richard of St. Victor.

[49] Pope Benedict XVI, "St. Bonaventure III."

Dionysius.

Concluding his address with a short reflection on the connection between the Cross and the primacy of love in Bonaventure's theology, Benedict XVI briefly remarked on the Christocentric cosmology in the Seraphic Doctor's work that additionally links him with Francis:

> This theology of the cross, born of the encounter between the theology of Pseudo-Dionysius and Franciscan spirituality, must not make us forget that St. Bonaventure also shares with St. Francis of Assisi's love of creation, the joy of the beauty of God's creation. I quote on this point a phrase of the first chapter of the *Itinerarium*: 'He who does not see the innumerable splendors of creatures, is blind; he who is not awakened by so many voices, is deaf; he who for all these wonders does not praise God, is dumb; he who from so many signs does not rise to the first principle, is foolish.' The whole of creation speaks in a loud voice of God, of the good and beautiful God; of his love.[50]

Perhaps more than in the previous addresses, we see in these concluding remarks Benedict XVI's admiration for the Seraphic Doctor and the Franciscan tradition of which he was so much a part and contributor. In an age marked by global ecological crises and concerns for the health and safety of our planet, the focus on the Christocentric cosmological view of Bonaventure provides a refreshing endorsement of the possibility of a Franciscan contribution to ecotheological efforts that are so significant today.

On Blessed John Duns Scotus (7 July 2010)

Beginning his catechetical reflection on Blessed John Duns Scotus with an historical overview that skillfully surveys the known and surmised chronological markers of the medieval Franciscan's life, Benedict XVI presents a surprisingly laudatory account of Scotus's influence and importance in the universal life of the Church. The general structure of this reflection is guided more by the theological themes of his legacy, including the requisite subject of Scotus's proto-influence on the creation of the dogma of the Immaculate Conception.

The language that the Pope uses is particularly striking for its sensibility of the Franciscan charism. For example, in naming the Order of Friars

---

[50] Pope Benedict XVI, "St. Bonaventure III."

Minor as the community that Scotus joins as a young man, Benedict XVI describes it as "the Family of the Friars Minor,"[51] a remarkably touching way to capture the Franciscan spirit that drew the young Scotus to this way of life. Noting each of his major works, including the frequently overlooked *Quaestiones quolibetales* – too often passed over by students and scholars who are drawn to the more popular *Ordinatio, Lectura, Reportata Parisiensia or Tractatus de primo principio* – Benedict XVI concludes his introductory biographical remarks with a recollection of the political trouble in which Scotus found himself when siding with Pope Boniface VIII over French King Philip IV the Fair, which resulted in his temporary exile from France. Predictably, the Pope offers this historical encounter as an exemplary instance of a Christian's "love for the See of Peter." Benedict XVI explains during his digression:

> Dear brothers and sisters, this event invites us to remember how often in the history of the Church believers have met with hostility and even suffered persecution for their fidelity and devotion to Christ, to the Church and to the Pope. We all look with admiration at these Christians who teach us to treasure as a precious good faith in Christ and communion with the Successor of Peter, hence with the universal Church.[52]

While there is certainly much to admire in the stalwart stance of Scotus in the face of potential persecution, exile, and the revocation of his academic position for the sake of his political and ecclesiastical loyalty to Boniface VIII, it is unclear whether Scotus would recognize Benedict XVI's equating of "communion with the Successor of Peter" with communion "with the universal Church." There is certainly no doubt that Scotus had a deep appreciation for the office of the papacy, but to what extent the political scuffle between the friars in Paris and the King of France really reflected a sense of undying loyalty to the See of Peter is unclear. Here it would seem that Benedict XVI is offering more commentary than fact.

Rather than beginning with Scotus's contribution to the formation of the dogma of the Immaculate Conception, Benedict XVI, ever the systematic theologian at heart, notes perhaps one of Scotus's more overlooked contributions to Christology, namely, his supralapsarian position on the

---

[51] Pope Benedict XVI, "John Duns Scotus," (7 July 2010).
[52] Pope Benedict XVI, "John Duns Scotus."

reason for the Incarnation.[53]

> First of all he meditated on the Mystery of the Incarnation and, unlike many Christian thinkers of the time, held that the Son of God would have been made man even if humanity had not sinned. He says in his *"Reportatio Parisiensis"*: "To think that God would have given up such a task had Adam not sinned would be quite unreasonable! I say, therefore, that the fall was not the cause of Christ's predestination and that if no one had fallen, neither the angel nor man in this hypothesis Christ would still have been predestined in the same way" (in *III Sent.*, d. 7, 4). This perhaps somewhat surprising thought crystallized because, in the opinion of Duns Scotus the Incarnation of the Son of God, planned from all eternity by God the Father at the level of love is the fulfillment of creation and enables every creature, in Christ and through Christ, to be filled with grace and to praise and glorify God in eternity. Although Duns Scotus was aware that in fact, because of original sin, Christ redeemed us with his Passion, Death and Resurrection, he reaffirmed that the Incarnation is the greatest and most beautiful work of the entire history of salvation, that it is not conditioned by any contingent fact but is God's original idea of ultimately uniting with himself the whole of creation, in the Person and Flesh of the Son.[54]

There are two things worth noting here. The first is the fact that the Pope begins his thematic introduction of Scotus with a highlighting of Scotus's seemingly unique Christological position. While it is true that Scotus stood in a minority line of thinkers on the reason for the Incarnation, his view wasn't entirely original; then again Benedict XVI does not make that claim. The second is the fact that Benedict XVI draws on the *Reportatio* to highlight the view of Scotus. Most scholars draw attention to the earlier versions of Scotus's Sentences commentary in the forms of the *Lectura* or *Ordinatio*, yet the Pope considers instead the later version from Paris. This is not of any particular significance beyond raising the question of why he might do this. One answer to the question could rest with the Pope's lack of awareness of the secondary literature on the subject. Certainly, he is

---

[53] For more on this subject, see chapter 10 of this book.
[54] Pope Benedict XVI, "John Duns Scotus."

not expected to be a Scotus expert, which in any event he most certainly is not. Nevertheless, the general presentation of Scotus's life and thought throughout this address is rather well researched.

Continuing on the Christological theme, Benedict XVI correctly explains that Scotus was well aware of the place of sin and redemption in salvation history vis-à-vis the Incarnation, but adjudicates glorification from redemption. Closing the Christology section of his address, Benedict XVI offers the following summation: "Dear brothers and sisters, this strongly 'Christocentric' theological vision opens us to contemplation, wonder and gratitude: Christ is the centre of history and of the cosmos, it is he who gives meaning, dignity and value to our lives!"[55]

He moves then from Christ to Mary, presenting that for which Scotus is perhaps best known: his contribution to the formation of what would eventually become the dogma of the Immaculate Conception. Described as an argument for "preventive Redemption," Benedict XVI spends little time recapitulating Scotus's rather dense logical arguments for his view on what would eventually be deemed the Immaculate Conception. What is worth noting here is that the Pope avoids the popular Latin phrase: "*potuit, decuit, ergo fecit.*" This is perhaps a wise move, selecting instead to focus more on Scotus's contribution than seeking to cleverly summarize his argument. One should also note that Benedict XVI does not cite any primary source in his presentation of Scotus's view on the Immaculate Conception. Why he goes to great lengths elsewhere in his address to provide some material references, yet neglects such citation here is unclear.

Within the section ostensibly dedicated to Scotus on the Immaculate Conception, Benedict XVI offers a slight digression on the *sensus fidei*. At first an odd intrusion into a reflection on a medieval Franciscan's thought, the Pope's comments are very revealing and hopeful for hearers in a time of increased theological uncertainty and ideological polarization. Benedict XVI uses the fact that Scotus, as philosopher and theologian, was striving to understand the faith expressed by the populous, average believers, as an example of what it means to talk about the Holy Spirit working through the People of God long before official ecclesiastical bodies of governance or professional theologians might express the technical details of a particular doctrine. Benedict XVI writes: "The People of God therefore precede theologians and this is all thanks to that supernatural *sensus fidei*, namely,

---

[55] Pope Benedict XVI, "John Duns Scotus."

that capacity infused by the Holy Spirit that qualifies us to embrace the reality of the faith with humility of heart and mind. In this sense, the People of God is the 'teacher that goes first' and must then be more deeply examined and intellectually accepted by theology."[56] It is not always evident from the official actions and promulgations of Church leaders, including dicasteries like the Congregation for the Doctrine of the Faith, which the Pope used to head, that the *sensus fidei* as the "teacher that goes first" has been appreciated or respected. More often than not, it might appear, the relationship between the formal teaching offices of the Church and the *sensus fidei* comes across as antagonistic.[57] Yet, here we have, buried in the comments of the Pope on John Duns Scotus in a largely run-of-the-mill general audience, a wise and insightful allusion to the important role the faithful have in the exploration and expression of the faith.

The final portion of Benedict XVI's catechetical address is a succinct presentation of Socuts on freedom and its relationship as a faculty of either (or both) the will and intellect. The details of this philosophical debate, about which Scotus and Thomas Aquinas, for example, take different sides, are not important here. What is significant for us is to observe the way in which the Pope demarcates Scotus's view from those who will, in later decades and centuries after the Subtle Doctor's death, develop Scotus's thought into what is popularly known as "voluntarism." Those most familiar with Scotus's work have long insisted that there has been an historical conflation between the original source material of Scotus and what will become the voluntarist school in the proceeding centuries. Benedict XVI correctly notes a difference, although cautions his hearers to be wary of voluntarism. The one questionable instance of interpretation in the Pope's comments on freedom, will, intellect, and voluntarism is the final line of this section in which Benedict XVI claims that, if for Scotus there is a "primacy of the will… he argues this precisely because the will always follows the intellect."[58] Again, unaware of the secondary literature, the Pope seems to be making a personal interpretation or, rather, a personal eisegetical move in an effort to conform Scotus's thought *post facto* to that of his contemporaries or predecessors such as Thomas Aquinas and others.

---

[56] Pope Benedict XVI, "John Duns Scotus."

[57] For an insightful study of the *sensus fidei* and related issues, see Ormond Rush, *The Eyes of Faith: The Sense of the Faithful & the Church's Reception of Revelation* (Washington, DC: The Catholic University of America Press, 2009).

[58] Pope Benedict XVI, "John Duns Scotus."

This is not unlike what Benedict XVI has been known to do with the thought of Bonaventure when it appears to suit the pontiff.

Overall, the address on Scotus is well done and a particularly joyful occasion for the Franciscan family. Rarely these days does the Subtle Doctor garner such positive attention as in the way that Benedict XVI offers us in his address.[59] While there are many other contributions to philosophy and theology that Scotus has made through his life and work, these three thematic foci of the Pope are certainly welcome. Moreover, the way in which Benedict XVI closes his address, praising the saintly model of Scotus for all believers, is really quite moving: "Bl. Duns Scotus teaches us that in our life the essential is to believe that God is close to us and loves us in Jesus Christ, and therefore to cultivate a deep love for him and for his Church. We on earth are witnesses of this love."[60]

On Saint Clare of Assisi (15 September 2010)

The reflection on St. Clare of Assisi is insightful on many levels. Benedict XVI does more than offer a simple biographical summary of Clare's life, he weaves together instances of her faithfulness to Christianity and religious life at each stage of her earthly journey and connects those experiences to a broader picture of Christian living for all believers.

Interestingly, Benedict XVI begins his address on Clare with an acknowledgement of the sources available to modern scholars concerning her life and works. Throughout his reflection he returns to some of these sources, the letters of Clare to Agnes of Prague, the Proceedings of her Cause for Canonization, the early biographies, and the secondary witness of contemporary ecclesiastical historians and leaders such as the bishop Jacques de Vitry.

While Benedict XVI paints a picture of Clare as an excellent model for Christian living that is largely accurate by all historical standards, there is a tendency in his address to rely on outdated modes of medieval sanctity when it comes to women religious. There is little doubt that the Pope anticipates this criticism, perhaps he even senses the matter in his own writing, because half-way through the address he makes a comment about women in the medieval church. After highlighting the uniqueness of Clare's way of life

---

[59] One thinks here of the recent work of those associated with the so-called "Radical Orthodoxy" school, inaugurated by thinkers like John Milbank and Catherine Pickstock.
[60] Pope Benedict XVI, "John Duns Scotus."

modeled on the *vita evangelica* of Francis of Assisi, Benedict XVI says:

> This was a truly extraordinary exception in comparison with
> the canon law then in force but the ecclesiastical authorities
> of that time permitted it, appreciating the fruits of evangelical
> holiness that they recognized in the way of life of Clare and
> her sisters. This shows that even in the centuries of the Middle
> Ages the role of women was not secondary but on the contrary
> considerable.[61]

What exactly Benedict XVI means by "considerable" or "not secondary"
remains unknown. Surely this is an effort on the pontiff's part to
acknowledge the real concern that people have about the way women were
(and, consequently, *are*) treated in the Roman Catholic Church. There is a
tension between the exemplary holiness Clare models for all Christians and
the subjugation and limited autonomy she experienced at the hands of the
ecclesiastical authorities of her day.

Benedict XVI does not necessarily sugarcoat the resistance that Clare
experienced as she spent her whole life petitioning to live evangelical
poverty after the model of Francis, but he also goes to great lengths to avoid
highlighting the conflicts that continually arose. Many a pope fought with
Clare as she adamantly and tenaciously defended her right to live the Gospel
in terms of poverty and ministry. Predictably, this is not quite championed
in the Pope's reflection.[62]

What Benedict XVI does emphasize is the friendship that Clare and
Francis shared. Likened to some other famous and saintly friendships
like that between St. Francis de Sales and St. Jane Frances de Chantal,
the relationship Clare and Francis enjoyed is hailed as a "beautiful and
important" dimension of their stories. The Pope explains: "Indeed, when
two pure souls on fire with the same love for God meet, they find in their
friendship with each other a powerful incentive to advance on the path
of perfection."[63] This is not simply a pious reflection on the relationship
between two saints, but, as Benedict XVI alludes, this is what we are all

---

[61] Pope Benedict XVI, "Saint Clare of Assisi," (15 September 2010).

[62] For an excellent counter-example of a study of Clare's charismatic influence in her Rule and
in the life of the Franciscan Second Order that ensued, from Clare's time to today, see Diana Papa, *The
Poor Sisters of Saint Clare: Their Form of Life and Identity*, trans. Frances Teresa Downing (Phoenix,
AZ: Tau Publishing, 2010).

[63] Pope Benedict XVI, "Saint Clare of Assisi."

invited to share and live as friends of God and brothers and sisters of one another. "Friendship is one of the noblest and loftiest human sentiments which divine Grace purifies and transfigures," he continues.[64] Far too often, whether in the medium of film such as *Brother Sun, Sister Moon* or in recent biographies of the first Franciscans, there is a romanticizing of Clare and Francis's relationship that is wholly untrue. Benedict XVI, perhaps even unaware of these contemporary instances, shines a light on the significance of Clare and Francis's authentic friendship. While still human and, yes, probably attracted to others as all balanced human beings inevitably are (whether they were at all romantically attracted to each other is not at all knowable), their friendship was, as the Pope keenly observes, always rooted in God as the object. It was their mutual and shared love of Christ that drew them together, allowed their relationship to glow with the radiance of fire, and that which attracted so many other women and men to follow their examples.

On Blessed Angela of Foligno (13 October 2010)

Undoubtedly one of the more interesting figures of the Thirteenth Century, Angela of Foligno was a laywoman who followed what we would today call the rule or way of life of the Secular Franciscans. It also goes without saying that Angela is perhaps one of the least-known figures of this time and the attention that Benedict XVI pays her in such a public and laudatory way is certainly a blessing to those who have learned about her through this general audience.

The Pope begins his reflection on Angela with a passing admittance that those who are familiar with the name Blessed Angela of Foligno are likely aware of her history of mystical experiences and, although the pontiff doesn't make this point so explicitly, her rather bizarre life story and actions. Instead of dwelling on the penitential practice of serving the lepers of Foligno by washing their wounds only then to drink the wash-water or the hysterical screaming fit she had in the Basilica of St. Francis in Assisi that led to her ouster from the church, Benedict XVI makes the point that most people tend to focus on the "end" of Angela's spiritual journey. They are most "fascinated" with the "consummate experience of union with God that she reached."[65] There is little doubt that this is true, which is one

---

64 Pope Benedict XVI, "Saint Clare of Assisi."
65 Pope Benedict XVI, "Blessed Angela of Foligno," (13 October 2010).

of the reasons why she was so sought-after in her own time for spiritual direction and why those who are aware of her are drawn to her writings today, but it is also interesting to delve into her more eccentric spiritual and penitential practices. We won't examine those instances here because the Pope does not do so in his address.[66] Instead, we begin as Benedict XVI does, with the beginning of her story.

Born into a rather comfortable medieval Italian lifestyle, Angela was married by the age of 20 and had several children. Benedict XVI notes that during her early adult years her community was besieged with a number of traumatic incidents including a violent earthquake, a hurricane, and a long-standing war with a neighboring Italian town. It is believed that around 1285 Angela came to what would later be called "the starting point" of her spiritual conversion, marked as it was by her prayer to St. Francis of Assisi (Foligno is located not far from Assisi in the Umbrian region of Italy). Her prayers led her to seek the Sacrament of Penance and within a few years things took a rather dramatic turn.

The Pope uses a rather curious turn of phrase to describe one of the more surreal series of events in Angela's story. He says that Angela "was released from any emotional ties" about three years after her prayer to Francis and her general confession. The instance he is talking about here is the death of *everyone* in her family: her mother, her husband, and *all* her children. Needless to say, "released from any emotional ties" might strike some as odd, but perhaps Benedict XVI is drawing this language from Angela herself who, in retrospect, viewed the deaths of all her loved ones as a hidden blessing. At that point she sold all her possessions and entered the Third Order of St. Francis, popularly known today as the Secular Franciscans.

From this point until her death, Angela's life is a fascinating one. She was deeply prayerful, spending long hours in contemplation and making several pilgrimages, including the famous visit to the Basilica of St. Francis. She was frequently sought out for spiritual direction and was known to be a sagacious figure of faith. She was close to the local friars and one of them became her confessor and scribe, recording what would come to be known as her two major works: the *Memorial* and the *Instructions*.[67] These

---

[66] If you are interested in her writings and life, see the excellent study and English translation of her texts: Paul Lachance, ed., *Angela of Foligno: The Complete Works* (New York: Paulist Press, 1993).

[67] See Lachance, ed., *Angela of Foligno: The Complete Works*, 47-120.

texts, Benedict XVI recounts, "[tell] the story of [Angela's] conversion and points out the necessary means: penance, humility and tribulation; and it recounts the steps, Angela's successive experiences which began in 1285."[68] The beginning of Angela's conversion represents, for Benedict XVI, the most transformative and significant dimension of her story. He returns to it several times in his address, praising Angela for her "great fear of hell." Odd as it sounds, the Pope sees this constant concern Angela had about eternal punishment as the major impetus for her lifelong commitment to evangelical poverty, living a life of prayer, and the eventual mystical union she experienced with God.

In surveying but a few of Angela's spiritual "steps," Benedict XVI returns to the fear of hell as his primary focal point. He explains: "This 'dread' of hell corresponds to the type of faith that Angela had at the time of her 'conversion'; it was a faith still poor in charity, that is, in love of God. Repentance, the fear of hell and penance unfolded to Angela the prospect of the sorrowful 'Way of the Cross,' which from the eighth to the 15th stages was to lead her to the 'way of love.'"[69]

What we come to see in Benedict XVI's admiration of Angela's starting point and lifelong spiritual journey is not a sadist's appreciation for the continual fear one experiences in dread of hell, but instead the deeply integrated and complex reality of the spiritual life that came to be seen in Angela's experience of the Divine. For her, as is true throughout the Franciscan spiritual tradition, love and suffering are intertwined realities of the spiritual life. Angela recognized the "suffering love" (to use Benedict XVI's term) of Christ and, in surrendering herself to the will of God, came to recognize the closeness of Christ to her. The relationship between love and suffering is a complex dance that weaves the two threads of spiritual experience into a cloth of faith. Out of her initial fear of hell, Angela came to see the love God has for her, she became overwhelmed by her inability to repay that love, which, in a sense, is a real form of suffering.

> This was the precarious balance between love and suffering that she felt throughout her arduous journey towards perfection. For this very reason she preferred to contemplate Christ Crucified, because in this vision she saw the perfect balance brought about.

---

[68] Benedict XVI, "Blessed Angela of Foligno."
[69] Benedict XVI, "Blessed Angela of Foligno."

On the Cross was the man-God, in a supreme act of suffering which was a supreme act of love.[70]

It is only in meditating on the suffering of Christ — a sign of His most sincere and ultimate expression of love — that Angela came to understand what it means to be a Christian, a disciple of the Crucified Christ. It was a transforming experience, she explains, and it is this transformation that Benedict XVI invites all believers to pursue.

> Blessed Angela's life began with a worldly existence, rather remote from God. Yet her meeting with the figure of St Francis and, finally, her meeting with Christ Crucified reawakened her soul to the presence of God, for the reason that with God alone life becomes true life, because, in sorrow for sin, it becomes love and joy. And this is how Blessed Angela speaks to us. Today we all risk living as though God did not exist; he seems so distant from daily life. However, God has thousands of ways of his own for each one, to make himself present in the soul, to show that he exists and knows and loves me. And Blessed Angela wishes to make us attentive to these signs with which the Lord touches our soul, attentive to God's presence, so as to learn the way with God and towards God, in communion with Christ Crucified. Let us pray the Lord that he makes us attentive to the signs of his presence and that he teaches us truly to live.[71]

Benedict XVI's admiration for Blessed Angela of Foligno is easily seen. His appreciation for the details of her life that have often been overshadowed by the more sensational details of her spiritual journey reflect a keen awareness and attentiveness on his part of the potential for inspiration she offers modern Christians. It is no easy task, but to present someone like Angela to the modern world offers a glimpse at the ever diverse and creative composition of the Body of Christ and the Communion of Saints. There remains much that we can learn from Angela.

On Saint Elizabeth of Hungary (20 October 2010)
Elizabeth of Hungary holds a very special place within the history

---

[70] Benedict XVI, "Blessed Angela of Foligno."
[71] Benedict XVI, "Blessed Angela of Foligno."

and legacy of the Franciscan tradition. Her importance is most noted by the Third Order of St. Francis – the Secular Franciscans – who venerate the Saint as a patroness of their Order. Like her first cousin, St. Agnes of Prague, the Second-Order nun and famed correspondent of St. Clare of Assisi, Elizabeth was reared in a privileged setting as a member of a royal family. The daughter of King Andrew II of Hungary, Elizabeth was destined to become a significant player in the thirteenth-century monarchical political landscape. And so she was betrothed to Ludwig of Thuringia in central Germany by her father and was sent there to marry her future husband. Despite the arranged marriage, so typical of the age, Benedict XVI highlights the fact that what Elizabeth and Ludwig shared was a happy marriage. They came, rather quickly it would seem, to love one another with the affection one would wish for all spouses.

Benedict XVI, in his telling of Elizabeth's story, speaks highly of the royal relationship, but emphasizes the respective roles of wife and husband in a way that seems oddly antiquated. Granted, the dynamics of marital life in the Middle Ages differs in many ways from the experience of spousal love and responsibility today, but the Pope seems to uphold this medieval notion of relationship as a model for the contemporary setting. In describing the happiness of their marriage, Benedict XVI says: "[Elizabeth] helped her husband to raise his human qualities to a supernatural level and he, in exchange, stood up for his wife's generosity to the poor and for her religious practices."[72] It would appear that this emphasis might lead modern readers to interpret the Pope's reflection as praising Elizabeth for excelling at her spousal role of primarily aiding and bolstering her husband without acknowledgement of her own life, vocation, or work. What she is most noted for in the case of her marriage, according to Benedict XVI's rendering, is the way in which her support enabled Ludwig's "human qualities" (whatever this might include) to be raised to "a supernatural level" (whatever this might mean). In turn Ludwig patronized his wife by "allowing" or "permitting" her to engage in her extracurricular pious activities of charity and prayer. It is not entirely clear that this is what Benedict XVI intends in his description of Elizabeth's marriage and the relationship between her and her husband, but the exceptional amount of time he spends talking about her marriage inevitably draws our attention to this description, and, vague as it is, such an overview necessarily needs

---

[72] Pope Benedict XVI, "Saint Elizabeth of Hungary," (20 October 2010).

interpretation.

There are other dimensions of Benedict XVI's survey of Elizabeth's early life and marriage that are exceptionally praiseworthy and relevant today. Take, for instance, the early act of charity and humility found in Elizabeth and Ludwig's wedding celebrations. Benedict XVI explains: "Hence their marriage celebrations were far from sumptuous and a part of the funds destined for the banquet was donated to the poor."[73] Such charitable acts reflect the early disposition Elizabeth exhibited in caring for the poor. The way she treated her subjects in Germany was also a point highlighted by the Pope, and a point well worth noting. According to Benedict XVI, there were times when Elizabeth, in flagrant and overt ways, disregarded the courtly protocol of royal behavior to care for the poor, show respect and devotion to God, and meet those she encountered where they were and not as inferior subjects unworthy of her attention.

Elizabeth was, Benedict XVI keenly observes, a great model for leadership. "She is a true example for all who have roles of leadership: the exercise of authority, at every level, must be lived as a service to justice and charity, in the constant search for the common good."[74] This characterization of Elizabeth's continued relevance today is an exemplary point. While today there exist few true monarchies as were common in Elizabeth's time, those who hold public office or any sort of authority over others would do well to look to Elizabeth for insight on how to serve God by serving those that have been entrusted to them for care: politically and *ecclesially*. Bishops, including the Pope himself, would be well served to follow Benedict XVI's advice and look to Elizabeth for guidance in their own exercise of power. The Saint's deliberate embrace of a preferential option for the poor and marginalized, the shirking of formal royal procedures for basic human encounters, and the lifelong embrace of humility are all characteristics that would certainly serve the Church, which is the Body of Christ, well today.

Elizabeth's encounter with the Franciscan movement occurred when, in 1222, she and Ludwig began seeing a Franciscan friar for spiritual direction. The friars were moving into Germany and other parts of Europe from Italy at this time and happened, as it were, to be in the right place at the right time for Elizabeth's spiritual journey. Hearing the story of Francis

---

[73] Benedict XVI, "Saint Elizabeth of Hungary."
[74] Benedict XVI, "Saint Elizabeth of Hungary."

of Assisi, who was of course still living at this time, inspired Elizabeth and surely resonated with her own experience and desire to serve the poor, live the Gospel humbly, and follow Christ more closely.

After her husband's death on the way to Emperor Frederick II's crusade, Elizabeth experienced the difficulty of being ostracized by her husband's family as her brother-in-law seized power in the kingdom, claiming his right to rule. Elizabeth, with her three children and two servant-friends, wandered from village to village in exile. For her, it would seem, this was not the burden that might have befallen other royals. Elizabeth had, according to the friar Conrad of Marburg, professed to follow the way of St. Francis on Good Friday in 1228. As she and her family traveled about the countryside, she willingly and enthusiastically served where she could, aiding in hospitals and other sites of charitable work. She even founded a hospital where she would spend the last three years of her life ministering and caring for the needy. She died in November 1231 and, because the testimonies of her holiness were so widespread, she was canonized just four years later.

Benedict XVI's closing remarks about Elizabeth of Hungary provide us with much to consider in striving to follow in the footprints of Christ in the example of Francis of Assisi.

> In St. Elizabeth we see how faith and friendship with Christ create a sense of justice, of equality of all, of the rights of others and how they create love, charity. And from this charity is born hope too, the certainty that we are loved by Christ and that the love of Christ awaits us thereby rendering us capable of imitating Christ and of seeing Christ in others. St. Elizabeth invites us to rediscover Christ, to love him and to have faith; and thereby to find true justice and love, as well as the joy that one day we shall be immersed in divine love, in the joy of eternity with God.[75]

The recognition that Elizabeth of Hungary's life presents us with a Christian model for living in the world is an important contribution on the part of Benedict XVI in his ministry as pope and shepherd of the universal Church. This is a particularly joyful recognition for Secular Franciscans today, because in highlighting the sanctity and praising the good works of Elizabeth, the commitments and actions of the members of the Third

---

[75] Benedict XVI, "Saint Elizabeth of Hungary."

Order of St. Francis throughout the centuries continue to garner the praise and support they deserve. That Benedict XVI incudes two lay Franciscan women among the list of those about whom he comments in his reflections is also a laudatory point that might otherwise be overlooked.

On Saint Veronica Giuliani (15 December 2010)

The admiration Benedict XVI has for St. Veronica Giuliani is easy to see in his address. Following a number of catechetical reflections on mystics from the Middle Ages, the Pope makes a chronological jump to the seventeenth century, noting that December 27, 2010, less than two weeks after his address, marks the 350th anniversary of Veronica's birth in 1660. She entered the Capuchin Poor Clare monastery in Città di Castello, the result of a young lifetime of interest in pursuing a religious vocation to the cloistered life. Noting the importance of her religious name, Veronica, Benedict XVI explains: "She received the name of 'Veronica,' which means 'true image' and she was in fact to become a true image of the Crucified Christ."[76]

As with Clare of Assisi and Angela of Foligno, Benedict XVI holds Veronica as an exemplar of Christian living. While at first it might appear difficult to see how the life of a cloistered Poor Clare nun from the seventeenth century might provide a reasonable model for Christian living today, the Pope points to her prolific writings – a source of inspiration about which few are aware – as a modern guide. Following in the Franciscan tradition into which she became a faithful member for fifty years until her death in 1727, Veronica recognized the importance and primacy of love in God's relationship to humanity and all of creation. Benedict XVI quotes her as saying on her deathbed: "I have found Love, Love has let himself be seen! This is the cause of my suffering. Tell everyone about it, tell everyone!"[77]

This sense of God as Love, seen most immediately in her experience of the Crucified and Risen Christ, stands at the core of Veronica's appropriation of and contribution to the Franciscan spiritual tradition. There is a sense in which Benedict XVI presents Veronica's spiritual contributions almost exclusively within the realm of what would be expected of women in her time. Yet, alongside the more overt spousal imagery, there is a great appreciation on the pontiff's part for what this holy cloistered woman was

---

[76] Pope Benedict XVI, "Saint Veronica Giuliani," (15 December 2010).
[77] Pope Benedict XVI, "Saint Veronica Giuliani."

able to accomplish in her vernacular theological reflections.

> St Veronica has a markedly Christological and spousal spirituality: She experienced being loved by Christ, her faithful and sincere Bridegroom, to whom she wished to respond with an ever more involved and passionate love. She interpreted everything in the key of love and this imbued her with deep serenity. She lived everything in union with Christ, for love of him, and with the joy of being able to demonstrate to him all the love of which a creature is capable.[78]

This is one of the lengthier reflections on a Franciscan (apart from Bonaventure) that Benedict XVI offers. Perhaps it is a more extended address because of the anniversary that soon followed, but it is nevertheless interesting to consider his efforts to introduce Veronica to the modern Christian community. Time and again in his considerations of Veronica's life and model, Benedict XVI returns to the penitential example she provides the Church, especially, the Pope notes, in the search to "participate in the suffering love of Jesus Crucified." He explains at the conclusion of his address:

> St Veronica Giuliani invites us to develop, in our Christian life, our union with the Lord in living for others, abandoning ourselves to his will with complete and total trust, and the union with the Church, the Bride of Christ. She invites us to participate in the suffering love of Jesus Crucified for the salvation of all sinners; she invites us to fix our gaze on Heaven, the destination of our earthly journey, where we shall live together with so many brothers and sisters the joy of full communion with God; she invites us to nourish ourselves daily with the Word of God, to warm our hearts and give our life direction. The Saint's last words can be considered the synthesis of her passionate mystical experience: "*I have found Love, Love has let himself be seen!*"[79]

What a fine opportunity, as with the reflections on Angela of Foligno, to consider some of the lesser-known Franciscan spiritual masters. It is

---

[78] Pope Benedict XVI, "Saint Veronica Giuliani."
[79] Pope Benedict XVI, "Saint Veronica Giuliani."

especially heartening to see the Pope set aside a good amount of time to highlight some of the contributions made by Franciscan women such as Veronica. While there are certainly Franciscan men that are frequently overlooked, the dearth of serious reflection and discussion about the contributions and example offered to us by so many Franciscan women over the years is a lacuna in great need of filling. Perhaps Benedict XVI's simple efforts to publicly discuss these women and the Franciscan spiritual tradition will encourage others to delve more deeply into the abundant resources that go largely unexplored.

On Saint Lawrence of Brindisi (23 March 2011)

The Capuchin friar Lawrence of Brindisi is the last of Benedict XVI's Franciscan addresses in this series. From the outset Benedict XVI fondly recalls his visit to Brindisi in 2008 and notes his appreciation for the creative and intelligent thinker that Lawrence was. As a fellow theologian and polyglot, it is no surprise that the Pope speaks so highly of Lawrence, particularly as it concerns the saint's ability to be so productive and influential despite the many pastoral and leadership responsibilities he held throughout his life as a Friar Minor. One could easily see how Lawrence might provide an inspirational model for Benedict XVI in a very personal sense given his own history as theology professor, as bishop, as prefect of the Congregation for the Doctrine of Faith, and finally as Pope. Benedict XVI has been, like Lawrence, impressively productive in terms of writing and academic work despite the major pastoral and leadership responsibilities he has had – Benedict XVI and Lawrence are certainly kindred spirits in some ways.

One of the dimensions of Lawrence's theological thought that Benedict XVI highlights as an important thing for consideration today is the centrality of Sacred Scripture in ecumenical dialogue. In an age that long predated any formal endorsement of ecumenical and interreligious dialogue, Lawrence was held in esteem by those inside and outside of the Catholic Church. Benedict XVI explains:

> Thanks to his mastery of so many languages, Lawrence was able to carry out a busy apostolate among the different categories of people. As an effective preacher, his knowledge, not only of the Bible but also of the rabbinic literature was so profound that even the Rabbis, impressed and full of admiration, treated him

with esteem and respect.[80]

While on the one hand Benedict XVI praises Lawrence's ecumenical and interreligious acumen, lauding at the same time the sixteenth-century friar's language skills and knowledge of Scripture, the Pope interestingly enough also speaks highly of Lawrence's apologetic efforts to respond to the Lutheran criticisms of his day.

> As a theologian steeped in Sacred Scripture and in the Fathers of the Church, he was also able to illustrate Catholic doctrine in an exemplary manner to Christians who, especially in Germany, had adhered to the Reformation. With his calm, clear exposition he demonstrated the biblical and patristic foundation of all the articles of faith disputed by Martin Luther. These included the primacy of St Peter and of his Successors, the divine origin of the Episcopate, justification as an inner transformation of man, and the need to do good works for salvation.[81]

One cannot help but wonder, as with his earlier address on Blessed John Duns Scotus, whether or not this tying together of Lawrence's theological skill and apologetics with the primacy of the papacy at the head of the thematic line is more Benedict XVI's *post facto* interpretation, a form of historical eisegesis rather than an authentic rendering of Lawrence's personal ecclesiastical commitments. This is in no way to suggest that Lawrence had anything but respect for and a commitment to the Church's leaders, but one is hard pressed to find objective source material to make as strong a claim about such dispositions as Benedict XVI would seem to prefer.

In addition to his academic reputation and contributions in terms of the Franciscan tradition, Lawrence was, according to Benedict XVI, a peacemaker in the model of Francis of Assisi.

> Another trait that characterizes the opus of this son of St Frances is his action for peace. Time and again both Supreme Pontiffs and Catholic Princes entrusted him with important diplomatic missions, to settle controversies and to encourage harmony among the European States, threatened in those days

---

[80] Pope Benedict XVI, "Saint Lawrence of Brindisi," (23 March 2011).
[81] Pope Benedict XVI, "Saint Lawrence of Brindisi."

by the Ottoman Empire. The moral authority he enjoyed made him a counselor both sought after and listened to. Today, as in the times of St Lawrence, the world is in great need of peace, it needs peaceful and peacemaking men and women. All who believe in God must always be sources and artisans of peace.[82]

Benedict XVI makes a keen observation that we are greatly in need of peacemakers today. In a move that would surely have made Bonaventure, one of the Pope's own scholarly inspirations, proud, Benedict XVI concludes his reflection on Lawrence by uniting the two major thematic points of his address: that Lawrence was both a man of Scripture and a man of peace. We can only be peacemakers and followers of Christ if we imbue ourselves with the Word of God through a love of scripture, the Pope says. "This is the source from which to draw so that our Christian witness may be luminous and able to lead people of our time to God."[83]

Between Rome and Assisi:
Interpretation and Ecclesiology

The title of this chapter, "What Does Rome have to do with Assisi?" is a play on the famous Tertullian quote from around 197 C.E. that was aimed at critiquing the increasing appropriation of Hellenistic philosophy by the early Church. Following Tertullian, I pose a similar question that is aimed at highlighting the relationship between Pope Benedict XVI and the Franciscan intellectual tradition, geographically identified as Rome and Assisi respectively. There is no question that the theologian-turned-pope has a certain affinity for Francis of Assisi and subsequent intellectual and spiritual tradition that counts among its contributors luminaries the likes of Anthony of Padua, Bonaventure and Veronica Guiliani. The question that can and should be raised has to do with the type of interpretation results from Benedict XVI's engagement with the Franciscan tradition or what sort of "Franciscan hermeneutic" informs the pontiff's reading of the sources. A complete account of Benedict XVI's "Franciscanism" is beyond the scope of this current chapter, but some observations can be made in light of the Pope's recent addresses on Franciscan themes. Perhaps the most noticeable theme that emerges from these addresses is Benedict XVI's view

---

[82] Pope Benedict XVI, "Saint Lawrence of Brindisi."
[83] Pope Benedict XVI, "Saint Lawrence of Brindisi."

of the relationship between the Franciscan Order(s) and the Church, the relationship between Assisi and Rome.

In the two earliest addresses, those offering reflections on the foundation of the nascent Franciscan Order and on the figure of Francis himself, Benedict XVI dedicates a significant portion of his talks to highlighting what he perceived as Francis's loyalty to those in positions of ecclesiastical authority. Noting that Francis, unlike several of his fellow charismatic contemporaries, sought official recognition from Rome for his newly established religious movement early on, Benedict XVI offers obedience to the same ecclesiastical authorities as a constitutive element of the Franciscan charism. This is something that was articulated with particular emphasis in his address to the Franciscan family at the 2009 Chapter of Mats. While, indeed, obedience to Honorious III and his legitimate successors is in fact an early component of the Francis's way of life, it should not be overemphasized to a point that elevates perceptible allegiance (which, in Robert Bellarmine-like terms, is really what is being advocated here) at the expense of what is outlined in the proceeding chapters of the *Regula*. The way of living in the world, the particularly prophetic stance demanded by authentic embrace of Francis's *vita evangelica*, will inevitably at times speak a challenging word to the same ecclesiastical authorities, albeit in a respectful manner. To strongly identify Franciscan living with Roman governance is to impose strictures that are in fact artificial and circumscriptive. While already evoked above, the action of peace offered by Francis during the Fifth Crusade is perhaps the most powerful and perennial example to consider. It would seem that Benedict XVI's emphasis on a particular and identifiable communion with Rome reveals, more than anything, his interpretation of what constitutes "Franciscan ecclesiology."[84] In response to the Tertullian-like question, for Benedict XVI, Rome has *a lot* to do with Assisi.

With the remaining addresses, but particularly with the three on Bonaventure, we see something of a different engagement with the Franciscan tradition. Moving from what Benedict XVI seems to consider a structural or corporate contribution to the Church (the Orders of Francis), for which the pontiff is primarily concerned about continued communion, the Pope reveals more of a pastoral reflection that is significantly rooted

---

[84] For an alternative view of a constructive and contemporary "Franciscan ecclesiology," see Kenan Osborne, *A Theology of the Church for the Third Millennium: A Franciscan Approach* (Leiden: Brill Publishing, 2009).

in the theology of those sons and daughters of Francis that so shaped the theological milieu of the thirteenth century. If Benedict XVI's initial addresses where focused on what Rome has to do with Assisi, then his latter reflections had more to do with what Assisi has to do with Rome. This is perhaps most acutely perceptible in his reflection on Bonaventure's view of history at which point the Pope discusses the insights of Bonaventure's theologically grounded approach for governance. Rooted in prayer and reflective thought, Bonaventure lays before ecclesiastical authorities a *modus operandi* that prioritizes discernment of the Spirit and openness to God's will over other would-be priorities of leadership. Buttressed by a theological foundation rooted in the primacy of love, Bonaventure's example is one of timely application and worthy of serious examination today. Furthermore, Assisi presents to Rome a rich tradition of spirituality exemplified in the writings of Francis, Anthony, and Bonaventure. Benedict XVI sees the Franciscan spiritual tradition as contributing to the ongoing renewal of the Church, while at one-and-the-same time not breaking the continuity of apostolic tradition.

Pope Benedict XVI offers us a unique interpretation on the relationship between the Franciscan tradition and the wider Christian community.[85] Shaded by his own scholarly engagement with and admiration for figures like Francis, Anthony, Bonaventure, Clare, Angela, Veronica and Lawrence, Benedict XVI sees the continued value of the Franciscan tradition for contemporary appropriation by the whole Church. These wisdom figures provide insight that has not been emphasized to the degree that they could be and therefore often remain largely unexamined beyond superficial portrayal in birdbaths and among lilies. Although the conversation remains ongoing

---

[85] Coincidentally, the young Joseph Ratzinger himself, many years earlier, identified the problem of reader-projected identities of St. Francis of Assisi. In his 1959 study on Bonaventure, Ratzinger (now Benedict XVI) draws an analogous comparison between the so-called "quest for the historical Jesus" and that of scholarly interest in Francis and the Franciscan tradition. One of the outcomes of the quest(s) is, as biblical scholar Albert Schweitzer famously noted, the creation of a Jesus more in the image and likeness of the respective scholar than of some objective historical figure. Zachary Hayes, the former student of Ratzinger, explains: "Joseph Cardinal Ratzinger, in a study of Bonaventure written in 1959, made a comparison between this situation and that of St. Francis. Referring to the problem of the various biographies of Francis, he spoke of a 'Francis of history' and a 'Francis of faith.' As there have been different understandings of the meaning and purpose of the Franciscan Order, so there have been different images of St. Francis developed to support those views." Zachary Hayes, *Bonaventure: Mystical Writings* (Phoenix: Tau Publishing, 2011), 24. It would appear that Benedict XVI, for better or worse, has also fallen into the pitfall he previously identified, for he has also presented a unique and individual image of Francis and the Franciscan Order.

concerning Benedict XVI's status as a "Franciscan theologian," it is fair to say that the current pontiff has a deep appreciation for the broad Franciscan tradition that transcends that of many other Church leaders. What sort of "Franciscan theologian" Benedict XVI might be also remains to be seen. For now, at least we can say that he sees an important relationship between Rome and Assisi. Time will tell whether those that constitute "Rome" and "Assisi" will each see that relationship as he does.

CONCLUSION

Living according to the Gospel of Jesus Christ is the centerpiece of the Franciscan life for every woman and man who embraces one of the rules inspired by the model of Christian living proposed by Francis of Assisi. In a sense, this is not an exclusive or original concept, but rather the baptismal call that each person receives at the start of her or his Christian journey. So what makes Francis of Assisi and the subsequent Franciscan spiritual and theological tradition so unique? Perhaps more intriguing is the question, what makes the Franciscan tradition so attractive and for such an extended period of time?

My initial and likely inadequate response to these questions is to point toward what has been implicitly portrayed in the previous thirteen chapters of this book. One dimension of the uniqueness of the Franciscan tradition rests in the microcosmic reflection it offers of Christianity, more generally in terms of its ability to maintain unity amid diversity. There are hundreds of independent religious communities of women and men that trace their spiritual lineage back to Francis and Clare of Assisi. These communities span a wide spectrum of diversity according to popular markers, yet are still united in the same Franciscan family. The radical inclusivity and fraternal spirit that distinguishes the *Poverello* of Assisi lives on in the manifold way the Franciscan tradition speaks to the various ideological, political, ecclesiastical, and other distinguishing characteristics that typically divide people rather than bring them together. Regardless of one's nationality, native language, sexual orientation, gender, religious denomination, race, or social location, there's a good chance that some aspect of the spiritual legacy of Francis of Assisi and those who followed him will appeal to you. Perhaps there is more we can learn about dialogue from the ways in which the Franciscan tradition can at one and the same time be the identity of two ideologically opposed institutions or groups. Even centuries after his death, Francis continues to bring people together, at least in spirit.

This diversity, seen in the lives of those Christian women and men of our own day who are still drawn to the Franciscan way of life, is also found in the theological and spiritual inheritance we are so blessed to receive. As I explained in the introduction, one of the principle aims of this book is to highlight the richness of the diversity found in the tradition that counts among its leading contributors Francis, Clare, Bonaventure, Anthony of Padua, John Duns Scotus, Angela of Foligno, and so many others. Whereas there is a lifetime of inspiration and spiritual wisdom to glean from the writings and life example of Francis himself, the beauty of what we have examined in this book (albeit in a rather nascent or preliminary way) is that we are not limited to just Francis for material or insight. Over the centuries there have been – and continue to be – theologians and philosophers, women and men, laity and clergy, all of whom offer a particular contribution and insightful reading of the Gospel life Francis calls us to follow.

This richness is a gift, a blessing to a world that is filled with spiritual seekers who are hungering for the nourishing wisdom of the Good News of Jesus Christ. The spiritual and theological tradition that Francis fortuitously, if inadvertently, inaugurated provides a profound resource for the women and men of our age and for generations to come. Whether they are members of the Millennial Generation who are striving to understand themselves, the world in which they live, and God better or they are members of an older generation that see the abuse of the planet and long for a theological worldview that could empower them to express the deep feelings of kinship with creation, the Franciscan spiritual and theological tradition has something to say.

This is another dimension of what makes the Franciscan tradition unique in the history of Christianity. For a movement that is more than eight-hundred-years old, it remains ever new and perennially relevant. Part of the aim of this collection of essays is to help introduce readers to some of the ways in which the Franciscan spiritual and theological tradition continues to speak to women and men today and, I hope, will continue to speak in a constructive, inspirational and relevant way for the years to come. In this sense, the ongoing appeal of Francis of Assisi's way of life and its associated spirituality and theological spirit can set the tone for Christians striving to follow the Gospel and to live out their baptismal vocation long into the future. Hopefully this book helps to illuminate some of the many ways the Franciscan tradition might provide a pathway to the future of faith.

BIBLIOGRAPHY

Primary Medieval Sources

Angela of Foligno, *Angela of Foligno: The Complete Works*, edited and translated by Paul Lachance. New York: Paulist Press, 1993.

Anselm of Canterbury. *Cur Deus Homo, in Anselm of Canterbury: The Major Works*, edited by Brian Davies and G. R. Evans. New York: Oxford University Press, 1998.

———. *Prosologion, in Anselm of Canterbury: The Major Works*, edited by Brian Davies and G. R. Evans. New York: Oxford University Press, 1998.

Bonaventure. *Breviloquium*, edited by Dominic Monti. Bonaventure Texts in Translation Series, volume IX. St. Bonaventure, NY: Franciscan Institute Publications, 2005.

———. *Collations on the Six Days*, translated by José de Vinck. Works of Bonaventure, volume V. Paterson, NJ: St. Anthony Guild Press, 1970.

———. *Disputed Questions on Evangelical Perfection*, edited by Thomas Reist and Robert Karris. Bonaventure Texts in Translation Series, volume XIII. St. Bonaventure, NY: Franciscan Institute Publications, 2008.

———. *Disputed Questions on the Knowledge of Christ*, edited by Zachary Hayes. Bonaventure Texts in Translation Series, volume IV. St. Bonaventure, NY: Franciscan Institute Publications, 2005.

———. *Doctoris Seraphici S. Bonaventurae Opera Omnia*, eds. PP. Collegii S. Bonaventurae, 10 vols. (Quaracchi: Collegium S. Bonaventurae, 1882-1902).

———. *Itinerarium Mentis in Deum*, edited by Philotheus Boehner and Zachary Hayes. Bonaventure Texts in Translation Series, volume II. St. Bonaventure, NY: Franciscan Institute Publications, 2002.

———. *Bonaventure: The Soul's Journey Into God, The Tree of Life, The Life of St. Francis*, translated by Ewert Cousins. New York: Paulist Press, 1978.

Clare of Assisi. *Clare of Assisi: The Early Documents*, edited by Regis Armstrong. New York: New City Press, 2006.

Duns Scotus, John. *Tractatus de Primo Principio*, in *John Duns Scotus: A Treatise on God as First Principle*, translated by Allan Wolter. Chicago: Franciscan Herald Press, 1982.

———. *Opera Omnia: Studio et Cura Commissionis Scotisticae ad fidem codicum edita*. 21 volumes, edited by Carlo Balíc et al. Vatican City: Typis Polyglottis Vaticanis, 1950 – .

———. *Opera Omnia*. 26 volumes, edited by L. Vivés. Paris: 1891-1895. (Revised Luke Wadding edition).

_____. *Opera Philosophica*. 5 volumes, edited by Girard Etzkorn, Romuald Green and Timothy Noone. St. Bonaventure, NY: Franciscan Institute Press, 1997-2006.

_____. *Philosophical Writings*, edited and translated by Allan Wolter. Indianapolis: Hackett Publishers, 1987.

_____. *Reportatio IA*. 2 volumes, edited and translated by Allan Wolter and Oleg Bychkov. St. Bonaventure, NY: Franciscan Institute Press, 2005-2008.

_____. *Quaestiones Quodlibetales*, edited and translated by Allan Wolter and Felix Alluntis. Princeton, NJ: Princeton University Press, 1975.

Francis of Assisi. *Die Opuscula des Hl. Franzikus von Assisi: Neue textkritische Edition*. Spicilegium Bonaventurianum XIII. Grottaferrata: Collegio San Bonaventura, 1976.

———. *Francis of Assisi: Early Documents*, edited by Regis Armstrong, J. A. Wayne Hellmann, and William Short. 3 Volumes. New York: New City Press, 1999-2001.

———. *Francis and Clare: The Complete Works*, edited by Regis Armstrong and Ignatius Brady. New York: Paulist Press, 1986.

———. *Francisci Assisiensis Scripta*, edited by Carlo Paolazzi. Spicilegium Bonaventurianum XXXVI. Rome: Collegio San Bonaventura, 2009.

Grosseteste, Robert. *De Cessatione Legalium*, edited by Richard Dales and Edward King. Auctores Britannici Medii Aevi VII. London: The British Academy, 1986.

————. *Expositio in epistolam sancti Pauli ad Galatas*, in *Opera Inedita Robert Grosseteste*, volume 1, edited by James McEvoy. *Corpus Christianorum Continuatio Mediaevalis*, volume 130. Turnhout: Brepols Press, 1995.

————. *Hexaëmeron*, edited by Richard Dales and Servus Geiben. Auctores Britannici Medii Aevi VII. London: The British Academy, 1982.

————. *On Light*, translated by C. G. Wallis, in *Philosophy in the Middle Ages*, 2nd edition, edited by Arthur Hyman and James Walsh. Indianapolis, IN: Hackett Publishing Company, 1973.

————. *On The Six Days of Creation*, edited by C. F. J. Martin. London: The British Academy, 1996.

Rupert of Deutz. *De Gloria et honore filii hominis super Matthaeum*, in *Corpus Christianorum Continuatio Mediaevalis*, volume 29, edited by Rhaban Haacke. Turnhout: Brepols Press, 1979.

Secondary Sources

Adams, Marilyn McCord. *What Sort of Human Nature? Medieval Philosophy and the Systematics of Christology*. Milwaukee, WI: Marquette University Press, 1999.

Alberzoni, Maria Pia. "Clare of Assisi and Women's Francsicanism." *Greyfriars Review* 17 (2004): 5-38.

Armstrong, Regis. "Hermes and the 'Co-Incidence' of San Damiano." *Franciscan Studies* 66 (2008): 413-459.

————. *"Novellus Pazzus in Mundo*: The Call to Foolishness." *Collectanae Franciscana* 79 (2009): 469-486.

Armstrong, Regis and Ingrid Peterson. *The Franciscan Tradition*. Collegeville, MN: The Liturgical Press, 2010.

Becker, Ernest. *The Denial of Death*. New York: Simon & Schuster, 1973.

Beha, Marie. "Clare's Trinitarian Prayer." *The Cord* 48 (1998): 11-20.

Bennett, W. Lance, ed. *Civic Life Online: Learning How Digital Media can Engage Youth*. Cambridge, MA: MIT Press, 2008.

Benson, Joshua. "Structure and Meaning in St. Bonaventure's *Quaestiones Disputatae de Scientia Christi*." *Franciscan Studies* 62 (2004): 67-90.

Berry, R. J., ed. *Environmental Stewardship: Critical Perspectives*. London: T & T Clark, 2006.

Best, Steven and Douglas Kellner. *The Postmodern Turn*. New York: Guilford Press, 1997.

Blastic, Michael. *A Study of the Rule of 1223: History, Exegesis and Reflection*. New York: Holy Name Province, 2008.

———. "Contemplation and Compassion: A Franciscan Ministerial Spirituality," *Spirit and Life, Volume Seven*, edited by Anthony Carrozzo, Vincent Cushing, and Kenneth Himes. St. Bonaventure, NY: Franciscan Institute Publications, 1997.

———. "'It Pleases Me That You Should Teach Sacred Theology': Franciscans Doing Theology." *Franciscan Studies* 55 (1998): 1-25.

Boff, Leonardo. *Cry of the Earth, Cry of the Poor*, translated by Phillip Berryman. Maryknoll, NY: Orbis Books, 1997.

———. *Francis of Assisi: A Model for Human Liberation*, translated by John Diercksmeier. Maryknoll, NY: Orbis Books, 2006.

Brown, Raymond. *An Introduction to the New Testament*. New York: Doubleday, 1997.

Buckingham, David, ed. *Youth, Identity and Digital Media*. Cambridge, MA: MIT Press, 2008.

Campbell, Richard. "The Conceptual Roots of Anselm's Soteriology," in *Anselm: Aosta, Bec and Canterbury*, edited by D. E. Luscombe and G. R. Evans. London: Sheffield Academic Press, 1996.

Carel, Havi. "Temporal Finitude and Finitude of Possibility: The Double Meaning of Death in *Being and Time*." *International Journal of Philosophical Studies* 15 (2007): 541-556.

Carpenter, Charles. *Theology as the Road to Holiness in St. Bonaventure*. New York: Paulist Press, 1999.

Chinnici, Joseph. "Penitential Humanism: Rereading the Sources to Develop a Franciscan Urban Spirituality." In *Franciscans in Urban Ministry*, edited by Roberta McKelvie. St. Bonaventure, NY: Franciscan Institute Publications, 2002.

Cox, Harvey. *The Silencing of Leonardo Boff: The Vatican and the Future of World Christianity*. Oak Park, IL: Meyer Stone and Company, 1988.

Cullen, Christopher. *Bonaventure*. New York: Oxford University Press, 2006.

Dalarun, Jacques. *Francis of Assisi and the Feminine*, translated by Anne Bartol. St. Bonaventure, NY: Franciscan Institute Publications, 2006.

———. *Francis of Assisi and Power*, translated by Anne Bartol. St. Bonaventure, NY: Franciscan Institute Publications, 2007.

D'Antonio, William, James Davidson, Dean Hoge, and Mary Gautier. *American Catholics Today: New Realities of Their Faith and Their Church*. Lanham, MD: Rowman & Littlefield Publishers, 2007.

Dardess, George and Marvin Krier. *In the Spirit of St. Francis and the Sultan: Catholics and Muslims Working for the Common Good.* Maryknoll, NY: Orbis Books, 2011.

Dean, Maximilian Mary. *A Primer on the Absolute Primacy of Christ: Blessed John Duns Scotus and the Franciscan Thesis.* New Bedford, CN: The Academy of the Immaculate, 2006.

De Jounge, Marinus. *Christology in Context: The Earliest Christian Responses to Jesus.* Philadelphia, PA: Westminster John Knox Press, 1988.

Delio, Ilia. A *Franciscan View of Creation: Learning to Live in a Sacramental World.* St. Bonaventure, NY: Franciscan Institute Publications, 2003.

———. *Compassion: Living in the Spirit of St. Francis.* Cincinnati, OH: St. Anthony Messenger Press, 2011.

———. "Evangelical Life Today: Living in the Ecological Christ." *Franciscan Studies* 64 (2006): 475-506.

———. *Franciscan Prayer.* Cincinnati, OH: St. Anthony Messenger Press, 2004.

———. *The Humility of God: A Franciscan Perspective.* Cincinnati, OH: St. Anthony Messenger Press, 2005.

———. "Revisiting the Franciscan Doctrine of Christ." *Theological Studies* 64 (2003): 3-23.

———. *Simply Bonaventure: An Introduction to His Life, Thought and Writings.* New York: New City Press, 2001.

Derrida, Jacques. *The Gift of Death,* translated by David Wills. Chicago: University of Chicago Press, 2008.

De Saint-Maurice, Béraud. *John Duns Scotus: Teacher for Our Times*, translated by Columban Duffy. St. Bonaventure, NY: Franciscan Institute Publications, 1955.

———. "The Contemporary Significance of Duns Scotus's Philosophy," in *John Duns Scotus, 1265-1965*, edited by John Ryan and Bernadine Bonansea. Washington, DC: The Catholic University of America Press, 1965.

Dillard, Peter. "A Minor Matter? The Franciscan Thesis and Philosophical Theology. *The Heythrop Journal* 50 (2009): 890-900.

Doyle, Eric. *St. Francis and the Song of Brotherhood and Sisterhood*. St. Bonaventure, NY: Franciscan Institute Publications, 1997.

———. "'The Canticle of Brother Sun' and the Value of Creation," in *Franciscan Theology of the Environment: An Introductory Reader*, edited by Dawn Nothwehr. Quincy, IL: Franciscan Press, 2002.

Dowd, Maureen. "Killing Evil Doesn't Make Us Evil." *The New York Times* (May 8, 2011).

Edwards, Denis. "Foreword," in Ilia Delio, Keith Douglass Warner, and Pamela Wood. *Care for Creation: A Franciscan Spirituality of the Earth*. Cincinnati, OH: St. Anthony Messenger Press, 2008.

Evans, G. R. "Anselm of Canterbury," in *The Medieval Theologians: An Introduction to Theology in the Medieval Period*, edited by G. R. Evans. Oxford: Blackwell Publishing, 2001.

Galvin, John. "Jesus Christ," in *Systematic Theology: Roman Catholic Perspectives*, volume 1, edited by Francis Schüssler Fiorenza and John Glavin. Minneapolis, MN: Fortress Press, 1991.

Gerkin, Anthony. "Bonaventuras Konvenienzagründe für die Inkarnation des Sohnes." *Wissenshaft und Weisheit* 23 (1960): 131-146.

Ginther, James. *Master of the Sacred Page: A Study of the Theology of Robert Grosseteste*. Burlington, VT: Ashgate Publishing, 2004.

Gracia, Jorge and Timothy Noone, eds. *A Companion to Philosophy in the Middle Ages*. Oxford: Blackwell Publishing, 2003.

Greenberg, Eric and Karl Weber. *Generation We: How Millennial Youth Are Taking Over America and Changing Our World Forever*. Emeryville, CA: Pachatusan Press, 2009.

Grey, Mary. *Sacred Longings: Ecofeminist Theology and Globalization*. London: SCM Press, 2003.

Hayes, Mike. *Googling God: The Religious Landscape of People in Their 20s and 30s*. New York: Paulist Press, 2007.

Hayes, Zachary. "Bonaventure of Bagnoregio: A Paradigm for Franciscan Theologians?" in *The Franciscan Intellectual Tradition: Washington Theological Union Symposium Papers 2001*. St. Bonaventure, NY: Franciscan Institute Publications, 2002.

———. *Bonaventure: Mystical Writings*. Phoenix: Tau Publishing, 2011.

———. *The Hidden Center: Spirituality and Speculative Christology in St. Bonaventure*. St. Bonaventure, NY: Franciscan Institute Publications, 1992.

Heidegger, Martin. *Sein und Zeit*, 17th edition. Tübingen: Max Niemeyer, 1993.

Heim, Maximilian Heinrich. *Joseph Ratzinger: Life in the Church and Living Theology, Fundamentals of Ecclesiology with Reference to Lumen Gentium*, translated by Michael Miller. San Francisco: Ignatius Press, 2007.

Hellmann, J. A. Wayne. *Divine and Created Order in Bonaventure's Theology*, translated by Jay Hammond. St. Bonaventure, NY: Franciscan Institute Publications, 2001.

Herzog, Ronald. "Social Media: Friend or Foe, Google or Hornswoggle?" Unpublished address delivered at the USCCB Fall 2010 annual meeting (November 15, 2010).

Hick, John. *Death & Eternal Life*. Louisville, KY: Westminster John Knox Press, 1994.

Himes, Michael. *The Mystery of Faith: An Introduction to Catholicism*. Cincinnati, OH: St. Anthony Messenger Press, 2004.

Horan, Daniel. "Dating God: A Young Friar's Experience of Solitude." *America* 196 (18 June 2007): 25-27.

———. *Dating God: Live and Love in the Way of St. Francis*. Cincinnati, OH: St. Anthony Messenger Press, 2012.

———. "How Original Was Scotus on the Incarnation? Reconsidering the History of the Absolute Predestination of Christ in Light of Robert Grosseteste." *The Heythrop Journal* 52 (2011): 374-391.

———. "*Koinonia* and the Church in the Digital Age." *Review for Religious* 69 (2010): 230-237.

———. "The Grammar of the Kingdom in a World of Violence: The (Im) possible Poetics of John D. Caputo," in *Violence, Transformation and the Sacred: They Shall Be Called Children of God*, edited by Margaret Pfeil and Tobias Winwright. Maryknoll, NY: Orbis Books, 2012.

———. "Thomas Merton the 'Dunce': Identity, Incarnation and the Not-so-subtle Influence of John Duns Scotus." *Cistercian Studies Quarterly* 47 (2012): 149-175.

———. "'Those Going Among the Saracens and Other Nonbelievers': Thomas Merton and Franciscan Interreligious Dialogue." *The Merton Annual* 21 (2008): 44-66.

Howe, Neil and William Strauss. *Millennials Rising: The Next Great Generation*. New York: Vintage Books, 2000.

Ingham, Mary Beth. "Duns Scotus, Divine Delight and Franciscan Evangelical Life." *Franciscan Studies* 64 (2006): 337-362.

———. *Ethics and Freedom: An Historical-Critical Investigation of Scotist Ethical Thought*. New York: University Press of America, 1989.

———. "John Duns Scotus: An Integrated Vision," in *The History of Franciscan Theology*, edited by Kenan Osborne. St. Bonaventure, NY: Franciscan Institute Publications, 1994.

———. "John Duns Scotus: Retrieving a Medieval Thinker for Contemporary Theology," in *The Franciscan Intellectual Tradition: Washington Theological Union Symposium Papers 2001*, edited by Elise Saggau. St. Bonaventure, NY: Franciscan Institute Publications, 2002.

———. "*Fides Quarens Intellectum*: John Duns Scotus, Philosophy and Prayer," in Franciscans at Prayer, edited by Timothy Johnson. Leiden: Brill, 2007.

———. *Scotus for Dunces: An Introduction to the Subtle Doctor*. St. Bonaventure, NY: Franciscan Institute Publications, 2003.

Ingham, Mary Beth and Mechthild Dreyer. *The Philosophical Vision of John Duns Scotus*. Washington, DC: The Catholic University of America Press, 2004.

International Commission on English in the Liturgy (ICEL), *The Roman Missal*, 2nd edition. New York: Catholic Book Publishing Company, 1985.

Jenkins, Willis. *Ecologies of Grace: Environmental Ethics and Christian Theology.* New York: Oxford University Press, 2008.

Johnson, Elizabeth. *Women, Earth, and Creator Spirit.* New York: Paulist Press, 1993.

Kenny, Anthony. *Medieval Philosophy*, volume 2. Oxford: Clarendon Press, 2005.

Kierkegaard, Søren. *Fear and Trembling*, translated by Alastair Hannay. London: Penguin Books, 2005.

Knox, Lezlie. "Audacious Nuns: Institutionalizing the Franciscan Order of Saint Clare." *Church History* 69 (2000): 41-63.

————. *Creating Clare of Assisi: Female Franciscan Identities in Later Medieval Italy.* Leiden: Brill, 2008.

Leclerc, Eloi. *The Canticle of Creatures: Symbols of Union; An Analysis of St. Francis of Assisi*, translated by Matthew O'Connell. Chicago: Franciscan Herald Press, 1970.

LeNave, Gregory. "God, Creation, and the Possibility of Philosophical Wisdom: Perspectives of Bonaventure and Aquinas." *Theological Studies* 69 (2008): 812-833.

————. *Through Holiness to Wisdom: The Nature of Theology According to St. Bonaventure.* Rome: Istituto Storico Dei Cappuccini, 2005.

Levy, Ian. "Trinity and Christology in Robert Grosseteste's Expositio of Galations." *Communio* 26 (1999): 875-891.

Little, A. G. *Studies in English Franciscan History.* Oxford: Manchester University Press, 1917.

Matura, Thaddée. "Francis of Assisi and His Posterity Today." In *Gospel Living: Francis of Assisi Yesterday and Today*, edited by Elise Saggau. St. Bonaventure, NY: Franciscan Institute Publications, 1994.

———. *Francis of Assisi: The Message in His Writings*, translated by Paul Barrett. St. Bonaventure, NY: Franciscan Institute Publications, 1997.

Mayer, Suzanne. "Merton and the Millennials." *Spiritual Life* 50 (2004): 229-239.

McEvoy, James. *Robert Grosseteste*. New York: Oxford University Press, 2000.

———. "The Absolute Predestination of Christ in the Theology of Robert Grosseteste," in *«Sapientiae Doctrina» Mélanges de théologie et de litérature médiévales offerts á Dom Hildebrand Bascour O.S.B.*, Recherches de Théologie ancienne et médiévale n° spécial 1(Leuven: Peeters, 1980).

———. *The Philosophy of Robert Grosseteste*. Oxford: Clarendon Press, 1986.

McPherson, Tara, ed. *Digital Youth, Innovation, and the Unexpected*. Cambridge, MA: MIT Press, 2008.

Merton, Thomas. "Franciscan Eremiticism." *The Cord* 16 (1966).

Migliore, Daniel. *Faith Seeking Understanding: An Introduction to Christian Theology*. 2nd edition. Grand Rapids, MI: Wm. B. Eerdmans, 2006.

Monti, Dominic. *Francis and His Brothers: A Popular History of the Franciscan Friars*. Cincinnati, OH: St. Anthony Messenger Press, 2008.

Moorman, John. *A History of the Franciscan Order: From its Origins to the Year 1517.* Chicago: Franciscan Herald Press, 1988.

Moses, Paul. *The Saint and Sultan: The Crusades, Islam and Francis of Assisi's Mission of Peace.* New York: Doubleday, 2009.

Need, Stephen. *Truly Divine & Truly Human: The Story of Christ and the Seven Ecumenical Councils.* London: SPCK/Hendrickson Publishers, 2008.

Nichols, Aidan. *The Thought of Pope Benedict XVI: An Introduction to the Theology of Joseph Ratzinger,* 2nd edition. London: Continuum, 2007.

Nguyen-Van-Khanh, Norbert. *The Teacher of His Heart: Jesus Christ in the Thought and Writings of St. Francis.* St. Bonaventure, NY: Franciscan Institute Publications, 1994.

Ortved, John. "Is Digital Killing the Luxury Brand?" *Ad Week* 52 (September 12, 2011).

Osborne, Kenan. "A Scotistic Foundation for Christian Spirituality." *Franciscan Studies* 64 (2006): 363-405.

———. *A Theology of the Church for the Third Millennium: A Franciscan Approach.* Leiden: Brill, 2009.

———. "Alexander of Hales: Precursor and Promoter of Franciscan Theology," in *The History of Franciscan Theology,* edited by Kenan Osborne. St. Bonaventure, NY: Franciscan Institute Publications, 1994.

———. "Incarnation, Individuality and Diversity: How Does Christ Reveal the Unique Value of Each Person and Thing?" *The Cord* 45 (1995).

———. *The Franciscan Intellectual Tradition: Tracing Its Origins and Identifying Its Central Components.* St. Bonaventure, NY: Franciscan Institute Publications, 2003.

Ott, Greg and Harold Netland, eds. *Globalizing Theology: Belief and Practice in an Era of World Christianity.* Grand Rapids, MI: Baker Academic, 2006.

Palfrey, John and Urs Gasser. *Born Digital: Understanding the First Generation of Digital Natives.* New York: Basic Books, 2008.

Pannenberg, Wolfhart. *Systematic Theology*, volume 2, translated by Geoffrey Bromiley. Grand Rapids, MI: Wm. B. Eerdmans, 1994.

Papa, Diana. *The Poor Sisters of Saint Clare: Their Form of Life and Identity*, translated by Frances Teresa Downing. Phoenix, AZ: Tau Publishing, 2010.

Perreiah, Alan. "Scotus on Human Emotions." *Franciscan Studies* 56 (1998): 325-245.

Peterson, Ingrid. "Francis's Tenacious Lady." *Church History* 13 (1994): 33-37.

Polizos, Bill John. "Christian Orthodoxy and Existential Anxiety: The Problem of Materiality and Finitude in the Pursuit of Authentic Religious Faith. Master's Thesis: Washington Theological Union, 1997.

Pope Benedict XVI. "Attract to Christ Men and Women of All Ages." Vatican English translation (20 April 2009).

———. *Caritas in Veritate.* Vatican City: Libreria Editrice Vaticana, 2009.

———. "Different Accents in an Essentially Shared Vision." Vatican English translation (17 March 2010).

———. "One of the Most Popular Saints in the Whole Catholic Church." Vatican English translation (10 February 2010).

———. "Proposing This Theme I feel a Certain Nostalgia." Vatican English translation (3 March 2010).

———. "The Priest and Pastoral Ministry in a Digital World: New Media at the Service of the Word." Vatican English translation (16 May 2010).

———. "The Secret of True Happiness: To Become Saints." Vatican English translation (27 January 2010).

Pope John Paul II. *Evangelium Vitae.* Vatican City: Libreria Editrice Vaticana, 1995.

Preston, Jennifer. "Facebook Page for Jesus, with Highly Active Fans." *The New York Times* (September 4, 2011).

Puskas, Charles. *The Letters of Paul: An Introduction.* Collegeville, MN: The Liturgical Press, 1993.

Raischl, Josef and André Cirino. *The Journey Into God: A Forty-Day Retreat with Bonaventure, Francis and Clare.* Cincinnati, OH: St. Anthony Messenger Press, 2002.

Rahner, Karl. *Foundations of Christian Faith*, translated by William Dych. New York: Crossroad, 2002.

———. "Ideas for a Theology of Death," in *Theological Investigations*, volume XIII, translated by David Bourke. New York: Crossroad, 1983.

———. "On Christian Dying," in *Theological Investigations*, volume VII, translated by David Bourke. New York: Crossroad, 1977.

————. *On The Theology of Death*, translated by Charles Henkey. New York: Herder and Herder, 1961.

Ratzinger, Joseph. *Die Geschichtestheologie des heiligen Bonaventura.* München: Schnell and Steiner, 1959.

————. *Eschatology: Death and Eternal Life*, 2nd edition, translated by Michael Waldstein. Washington, DC: The Catholic University of America Press, 1988.

————. *Introduction to Christianity*, translated by J. R. Foster. San Francisco: Ignatius Press, 2004.

————. *Milestones: Memoirs* 1927-1977, translated by Erasmo Leiva-Merikakis. San Francisco: Ignatius Press, 1998.

————. *Salt of the Earth: The Church at the End of the Millennium – an Interview with Peter Seewald*, translated by Adrian Walker. San Francisco: Ignatius Press, 1997.

————. "The Holy Spirit as Communion," in Pilgrim Fellowship of Faith: Church as Communion, edited by Stephan Otto Horn and Vinzenz Pfnür, translated by Henry Taylor. San Francisco: Ignatius Press, 2005.

————. *The Theology of History in St. Bonaventure*, translated by Zachary Hayes. Chicago: Franciscan Herald Press, 1971.

Ratzinger, Joseph and Jürgen Habermas. *Dialectics of Secularization: On Reason and Religion.* San Francisco: Ignatius Press, 2006.

Ricoeur, Paul. *Freedom and Nature*, translated by Erazim Kohak. Chicago: Northwestern University Press, 1966.

Robson, Michael. *St. Francis of Assisi: The Legend and the Life.* New York: Continuum, 1999.

Robson, Michael, ed. *The Cambridge Companion to Francis of Assisi*. New York: Cambridge University Press, 2012.

Rohr, Richard. "The Franciscan Option," in *Stricken by God? Nonviolent Indentification and the Victory of Christ*, edited by Brad Jersak and Michael Hardin. Grand Rapids, MI: Wm. B. Eerdmans, 2007.

Rosemann, Philipp. *Peter Lombard*. New York: Oxford University Press, 2004.

Rush, Ormond. *The Eyes of Faith: The Sense of the Faithful & the Church's Reception of Revelation*. Washington, DC: The Catholic University of America Press, 2009.

Shannon, Thomas. *The Ethical Theory of John Duns Scotus*. Quincy, IL: Franciscan Herald Press, 1995.

Smalley, Beryl. "The Biblical Scholar," in *Robert Grosseteste: Scholar and Bishop*, edited by Daniel Callus. Oxford: Clarendon Press, 1955.

Southern, R.W. *Robert Grosseteste: The Growth of an English Mind in Medieval Europe*. Oxford: Clarendon Press, 1986.

Spyker, Stephen. *Technology and Spirituality: How the Information Revolution Affects Our Spiritual Lives*. Woodstock, NY: SkyLight Paths Publishing, 2007.

Steger, Manfred. *Globalization: A Very Short Introduction*. New York: Oxford University Press, 2003.

Stewart, Robert. *Making Peace with Cancer: A Franciscan Journey*. New York: Paulist Press, 2001.

Studer, Basil. *Trinity and Incarnation: The Faith of the Early Church*, translated by Matthias Westerhoff and edited by Andrew Louth. Collegeville, MN: The Liturgical Press, 1993.

Tapscott, Don. *Grown Up Digital: How the Net Generation is Changing Your World*. New York: McGraw-Hill, 2009.

Taylor, Charles. *A Secular Age*. Boston: Belknap/Harvard University Press, 2007.

Tillich, Paul. *Systematic Theology: Volume 3*. Chicago: University of Chicago Press, 1963.

Twenge, Jean. *Generation Me*. New York: Free Press, 2006.

Twomey, Vincent. *Pope Benedict XVI: The Conscience of Our Age, A Theological Portrait*. San Francisco: Ignatius Press, 2007).

Unger, Dominic. "Robert Grosseteste Bishop of Lincoln (1235-1253) on the Reasons for the Incarnation." *Franciscan Studies* 16 (1956): 18-23.

Van Driel, Edwin Chr. *Incarnation Anyway: Arguments for Supralapsarian Christology*. New York: Oxford University Press, 2008.

Van Engen, John. *Rupert of Deutz*. Berkeley, CA: University of California Press, 1983.

Warner, Keith. "Franciscan Environmental Ethics: Imagining Creation as a Community of Care." *Journal of the Society of Christian Ethics* 31 (2011): 143-160.

———. "Out of the Birdbath: Following the Patron Saint of Ecology." *The Cord* 48(1998): 74-85.

Wilkins, John. "Ratzinger at Vatican II: A Pope Who Can and Cannot Change." *Commonweal* CXXXVII (June 4, 2010): 12-17.

Winfield, Nicole. "Pope Benedict XVI Weighs in on Social Media." *The Associated Press* (January 24, 2011).

White, Lynn. "The Historical Roots of Our Ecological Crisis." *Science* 155 (1967): 1203-1207.

Wolter, Allan. "John Duns Scotus on the Primacy and Personality of Christ," in *Franciscan Christology*, edited by Damian McElrath. St. Bonaventure, NY: Franciscan Institute Publications, 1994.

—————. *John Duns Scotus: Early Oxford Lecture on Individuation.* St. Bonaventure, NY: Franciscan Institute Publications, 2005.

—————. *John Duns Scotus: Political and Economic Philosophy.* St. Bonaventure, NY: Franciscan Institute Publications, 2001.

Wuthnow, Robert. *After the Baby Boomers: How Twenty-and Thirty-Somethings are Shaping the Future of American Religion.* Princeton, NJ: Princeton University Press, 2007.

Earlier Versions of Essays Contained in this Book

Horan, Daniel. "A Franciscan Approach to Ministry." *Review for Religious* 68 (2009): 132-143.

—————. "A Franciscan Millennial and the Memory of 9/11" in *Franciscan Voices on 9/11*, edited by Jennifer Scroggins and John Feister. Cincinnati, OH: St. Anthony Messenger Press, 2011.

—————. "A Franciscan Theological Grammar of Creation." *The Cord* 61 (2011): 5-20.

—————. "A Newborn and St. Bonaventure's *The Tree of Life* as Incarnational Encounters." *Spiritual Life* 54 (2008): 199-209.

—————. "Digital Natives and Franciscan Spirituality." *Spiritual Life* 56 (2010): 73-84.

———. "Embracing Sister Death: The Fraternal Worldview of Francis of Assisi as a Source for Christian Eschatological Hope." *The Other Journal* 14 (2009).

———. "Finding Francis on Facebook: Franciscan Spirituality and Mission in the Digital Age." *The Cord* 62 (2012): 243-267.

———. "Light and Love: Robert Grosseteste and John Duns Scotus on the How and Why of Creation." *The Cord* 57 (2007): 243-257.

———. "Praying with the Subtle Doctor: Toward a Contemporary Scotistic Spirituality." *The Cord* 58 (2008): 225-242.

———. "Revisiting the Incarnation: Why the 'Franciscan Thesis' Is Not So Franciscan and Why It Does Not Really Matter." *The Cord* 59 (2009): 132-143.

———. "St. Francis and the Millennials: Kindred Spirits." *St. Anthony Messenger Magazine* 118 (October 2010): 30-34.

———. "The Contemporary Relevance of *The Canticle of Exhortation for the Ladies of San Damiano* for all Christians." *Spirtu U Hajja* 86 (2008): 6-10.

———. "What Does Rome Have to Do with Assisi? Benedict XVI's Recent Addresses on the Franciscan Tradition." *The Cord* 60 (2010): 289-319.

ABOUT THE AUTHOR

Daniel P. Horan, OFM is a Franciscan friar of Holy Name Province in New York and is completing a Ph.D. in systematic theology at Boston College. He previously taught in the Department of Religious Studies at Siena College near Albany, New York, and currently serves on the Board of Directors of the International Thomas Merton Society, in addition to several other boards and committees. The author of dozens of scholarly and popular articles and book chapters, he is also the author of the book *Dating God: Live and Love in the Way of St. Francis* (St. Anthony Messenger Press, 2012) and the recipient of a 2011 Catholic Press Association Award for spiritual writing. He lectures frequently around the United States and Europe on topics including the Franciscan tradition, Thomas Merton, and contemporary themes in systematic theology. To learn more about his work and other publications visit his website **www.DanHoran.com** or his blog **www.DatingGod.org**.